ANGELS BY MY SIDE

Inspirational Stories of the Invisible Made Visible

By

Jayne Howard Feldman

ISBN: 1-4140-1195-4 (e-book)
ISBN: 1-4140-1194-6 (Paperback)
ISBN: 1-4140-1193-8 (Dust Jacket)

Library of Congress Control Number: 2003097674

This book is printed on acid free paper.

Printed in the United States of America
Bloomington, IN

1stBooks - rev. 02/05/04

DEDICATION

This book is dedicated to my loving husband,
Charles,
Who truly is an angel by my side.

Table of Contents

FORWARD

In 1994 my friend, Joey Brenneman, wrote lyrics which I then set to music and sang at the Annual Candlelight Winter Solstice Celebration that I do every December. Joey's lyrics perfectly summarize Jayne Howard Feldman's message in this book.

The Gift of Flight
by Joey Brenneman

I know you're an angel
I can see it in your eyes
so please can you tell me
can you teach me how to fly?

I wander through my journey
too often looking down
yet I know down deep inside me
there are gifts all around

Sometimes I can't see them
I seem to lose my way
and forget that I'm surrounded
by wings everyday

A small child's laughter
A stranger's sparkling eyes
The sun in all its glory
They're all angels in disguise

The homeless on the corner
The man who shines my shoes
They're all here to teach us
and bring us the news

That we're all angels
searching for our wings
often losing sight
of the simple things

Yes, we're all angels
with the gift of flight
heaven's companions
in our own special light

Dear angels, please help me
help me spread my wings
and open my eyes
to the simple things

Help us see each other,
the possibility of flight
in every human being
in every guiding light

'Cause we're all angels
searching for our wings
often losing sight
of the simple things

Yes, we're all angels
with the gift of flight
heaven's companions
in our own special light!

In this tender and beautiful book, Jayne Howard Feldman helps us to know that there are so many ways in which we are supported in this life, and that the powerful, loving, protective, inspirational presence of angels in our every moment is one of them. In every experience of every day, the angels are present. Jayne says, "The angels are by our sides reminding us that each of us began as a God-thought."

The first of the Hermetic Laws of the Universe is the Law of Mentalism, which says that everything exists within the mind of God or Spirit, and the mind of God or Spirit exists within everything. To use Jayne's words, we are each "God-thoughts," and this Law helps us to understand that we are also each God thinking! When we bring that understanding home to our daily experience, it means that every single person we encounter is a human manifestation of an aspect of God. The angels are ever present to help us remember that—to show us, guide us, teach us, support us in that remembering.

In this book, Jayne shares many stories of the presence of angels—usually a presence that you have to really "pay attention to" in order to even notice. Angels are usually "unseen" to the unaware eye. They seek no notice or adulation, rarely calling attention to themselves. They are simply present and serving. Angels serve the Light in ways that we will never know about. The gift of *Angels By My Side* is helping us realize what is going on behind the scenes.

We all live within an infinite, multi-dimensional web of life. It stretches out in every direction, breaking through all bounds of time and space, and links us to all that is, all that ever has been, and all that ever will be. In the angelic realm, there is no time and space. Angels come to join us in our linear time dimension and bring us blessing, guidance, protection, and the wisdom or all-knowingness of a being that is pure Light energy and dwells in a realm where all is indeed one. The second of the Hermetic Laws, the Law of Correspondence, says, "As above, so below; as below, so above." This law helps us understand many metaphysical sciences, including astrology and numerology, but it also helps us grasp the concept of the presence of angels in our lives. Whatever exists in one dimension of reality exists, in some form, in all.

We, too, exist in all dimensions of reality, but our limited human awareness holds us within this physical dimension. As much as we may feel trapped by this human experience, the "box" of the human dimension is actually a great gift. By being able to reflect on the past and learn from it, and make choices in the present, we get to create our future. We experience the gift of only a few things happening in our lives at any one time. Imagine if we lived in a realm of simultaneous time and space, the realm of the angels, and had to process all of our lessons and experiences at the same time! That would be incredibly overwhelming! The Creator in whose wisdom we are held and whose wisdom we carry and can learn to access, gave us this incredible gift of linear time and space, without which our lives would be challenging beyond imagination.

I have been blessed to know Jayne for many years now, first as a student in spiritual conferences and in later years as fellow faculty members. Jayne has been an angel in my life in a number of ways, but perhaps the most significant is that she was the first to introduce me to the concept of life coaching and suggest that it was a path I might consider. Today I work with clients from around the world, have written two books, lead workshops and retreats throughout North America, and have been a guest presenter for the annual International Coach Federation conference. Jayne Howard Feldman was the angel who planted the seed for this incredible unfolding of my life's work, and I will be forever grateful.

To read this book is to know Jayne, for she writes just as she speaks. Her energy jumps off the page, and I can hear the sweetness, energy, excitement, joy, and compassion within her in these words. Take your time with this book. Drink in the many stories. Check out the many resources that Jayne shares for further knowledge and information on the ways angels make their presence known. But most of all, as you read these words, breathe into the angel that is you, the "God-thought" that you are. Know your divine essence and shine your Light. For you are an angel to many!

Alan Seale author of Soul Mission * Life Vision and Intuitive Living: A Sacred Path

INTRODUCTION

At the age of eleven, I had an experience that I can describe as a slight variation of the words in a Steven Spielberg classic movie title. My experience was a "close encounter of the angelic kind." I was officially introduced to my guardian angel and with that encounter, my life changed.

There are things that occur in our lives where "turning back" to a consciousness in which we existed one second before is no longer an option. You change. Your world changes. What was once important to us and what is important to us now changes. I awakened to a reality that there are worlds existing within our world, that is, the world of the angels shares space with us. I came to recognize that there are angels standing by us. Every beat of our heart, every breath that we take, we have angels by our side. I remember years ago hearing Rev. Thomas Keller of Virginia Beach preach. He said, "When God looks down he sees two of you walking side by side, you and your guardian angel."

There any many ways that God supports, guides, loves and protects us. The angels are one of those ways. The angels are standing with us because God has placed them there. This truth is reflected to us by the words of Psalm 91, "For He shall give His angels charge over you, To keep you in all your ways," God has placed the angels as our guardians to keep us on the path known as 'God's will" for our lives. Our Father does know best, and yet loves us so much that He gives us the gift of free will. The angels are there when our free will guides us right into a brick wall, or causes us to stumble over our own ego and pride. The angels are faithfully with us to help us. They brush our knees off whenever we've fallen and encourage us to choose more wisely in our future use of free will. Someone once confided in me that she felt her angel must be pretty disgusted with her, because this individual kept making the same dumb mistakes in choosing male partners. I replied, "Not at all. The angels simply encourage us to choose again, and this time choose more wisely using the wisdom we have gained from our past mistakes."

Sometimes the distractions and negativities around us cause us to turn our eyes away from God and the many gifts He gives to us in our lives. I hope as you read this book you are comforted in knowing the angels are always with you.

I like to imagine that when God created us He called upon the angels and asked them to get out their angel cameras and take a divine baby picture of us. Those of you who are parents have probably received a "first photo" of your newborn from the hospital where the baby was born. Perhaps God says to the angels, "It's your job to support my children in remembering to see themselves as I saw them when I first created them. To see themselves with light sight, to see themselves through my eyes." And so the angels are by our sides whispering to us, "Remember. Remember God's vision of you." I adore Albert Einstein's words, "I want to know God's thoughts. Everything else is details." The angels are by our sides reminding us that each of us began as a God-thought.

For myself, I have felt the presence of the angels when I sat by my Dad's bedside as he was dying; I know many of you, too, have had similar experiences with those you love dearly. When someone is dying, it's "standing room only" when it comes to the presence of angels. There were angels by Dad's side, helping him close his eyes to earth and open them to heaven. They came to carry Dad to the waiting arms of Jesus. There were angels by my side to help me embrace God's peace in the midst of this great loss in my life.

The angels have radiated God's healing and love through the fuzzy wonders here on earth known as "teddy bears". When teddy bears are placed in the arms of children and adults who are in need of "bear hugs", when their lives have been impacted by tragedy or sickness, the angels are right there standing by their side.

The angels are with us to inspire us to get to know the saints, who also are universal messengers of the love of God. We are one big family of God. Just as my first book encouraged readers to Commune with the Angels, in this book you will find a chapter inspiring you to commune with the saints, too.

There are friends who mirror the presence of angels in our lives. In times of need, their support is a heaven sent answer that comes wrapped in their friendship. I have collected friendship quilts over the years, and in researching the history of these quilts, I have come to realize how appropriate it is that friends get together and make a quilt on which all the quilt makers embroider their names. Just like a cozy quilt, good friends keep us warm in the cold times of our lives. Their love and care for us envelops us. I believe that wealth is not achieved by a financial ship coming in; rather a "friendship" that docks in your heart. We have the heavenly friendship of the angels, as well as earthly friendship with people who sometimes can easily be mistaken for angels. At a lecture, someone in the audience asked me if the angels gave me the winning lottery numbers. I replied, "They helped me win the love lottery." I truly believe that being loved by my precious husband, Charles Feldman, who is my best friend, too, makes me the wealthiest woman on earth.

There are angels standing by us who are disguised by their fur. These are our pets who are messengers of unconditional love. Our home – Angel Heights – is at times sheer madness with three Jack Russell terriers racing through the house, and I only wish I could bottle the joy, happiness and playfulness they radiate. I'm certain you have heard the prayer, "Lord, help me be the person my pet thinks I am."

In serving God together with the angels, I have come to know the connection between angels and the arts. Just as the angels are God's messengers of uplifting energies, the arts inspire our inner creativity to take flight and soar to great heights, angelic heights. The angels once gave me the following message: "Food will sustain you as a human; the arts inspire you to be divine."

In healing times the angels are always near us. Once someone said to me, "I think my angels have quit." I responded, "Not possible. They don't work for you."

I hope the words I have written in the following pages convey to you how cherished you are by God, and that this book reassures you that you, too, have angels standing by your side.

Angelic Blessings,
Jayne Howard Feldman

Chapter 1

DAD ANGEL

I have had many wonderful blessings in my life and one of the most abundant is having angels by my side. Two earth angels that are at the top of the list are my parents, Robert and Martha Howard. I have chosen to write about my dad here because of our similar energies and because his death occurred during the writing of this book. My dad's death has had a great impact on me emotionally more than any other event in my life.

My dad was an only child. Even though I was one of six children, I was the youngest child and because of the age difference between my siblings and myself, I was often treated as, and felt like an only child. Many people comment with amazement when they learn of my siblings, "Oh, I thought you were an only child."

My dad and I had many adventures together as I grew up on my parents' farm in Upperco, Maryland. I would ride along in the farm truck as Dad took tomatoes to the canneries in Baltimore or livestock to the stockyards. Dad and I shared a sweet tooth and so I often made chocolate pudding for us in advance and we would have a movable picnic of yummies as we went off together fulfilling whatever farm chores needed to be done. We had many hilarious experiences together, such as the time we were taking a hog to market. The hog jumped the back tailgate of the truck and leaped out onto Reisterstown Road. Dad was driving an old farm truck at a slow speed down the road only to see the pig running alongside the truck. If someone had been videotaping the two of us attempting to round up a large pig, we surely would have been stars on America's Funniest Videos. Once the pig was back on the truck, which involved using the tailgate as a ramp and convincing the pig to climb the ramp back onto the truck, we laughed non-stop all the way down the road.

Not far from our home there is an annual steam show held the third weekend in September where antique steam driven tractors and equipment are displayed Thursday through Sunday. Since this event was first held at Arcadia Fairgrounds over 40 years ago, I have not missed one year in attending this event and neither had Dad. This will be the first year that my dad won't be there; at least not physically. He loved the steam show. He loved the smells of the steam engines and the sounds of the whistles. He loved the old-time threshing machines. He loved the root beer sold by the Amish at their food booths. He loved buying homemade candy, especially fudge made by the church ladies. In fact, Dad was such an excellent customer that some fudge was always held in reserve for him.

Dad was a hard worker. He milked a herd of dairy cows two times a day. I learned my work ethic from my folks. He also knew how to make the little bit of time that was available for fun incredibly special. I have fond memories of Dad making homemade ice cream after church on Sundays. He also dammed a creek on the farm in order to create a small pond for us to swim and play in. He took an old barrel and wooden boards and created a boat for me to push from one side of the pond to the other. I was a regular Huck Finn. In later years he would have a large one-acre pond constructed on the farm, which took recreation to a whole new level in my life.

I shared with my dad a love for roller coasters. He and I would go together on nickel day to the amusement park in Baltimore and ride the roller coaster again and again. We couldn't get enough.

Dad loved photography and I inherited this love from him.

Dad was my Rock of Gibraltar through my divorce. And it was his humor that many times had me laughing when I really felt like crying. He always had a joke to tell.

In the past few years his health took a turn for the worse. His quick pace slowed down to almost a crawl. I hated seeing it because Dad was so independent. He loved climbing in his pickup truck and heading to the local hardware store to chat before purchasing whatever item he needed to complete a job on the farm. As his health deteriorated, I would have royal battles with him over his continuing to drive. Everyone in my family attempted to get him off the road because his hearing and his sight were greatly diminished. Our prayers were answered when he had a traffic violation in which he did not yield the right of way and had a small fender bender. Fortunately, no one was hurt and very little damage done to either vehicle. Even more amazing was that when my dad hit the fender of the other car, he stopped and pulled over and waited for the police who had been called to the scene. However, Dad had to go to the bathroom more than he had a need to wait for the police. So he drove his car up to the nearby town to use a restroom only to be followed by a police car in pursuit. The benevolent policeman, in meeting Dad and hearing of his reasoning, only gave him a ticket for failing to yield the right of way. Additionally this compassionate policeman set into motion the revocation of my dad's license. I was greatly relieved when the Department of Motor Vehicles took this course of action until I shared the story about Dad's license being revoked with friends who own the local diner, Elmo's. Nedy called my husband aside and said, "I don't know how to tell Jayne this, but her dad was just up here this morning riding his tractor." When I confronted my Dad, and told him a revoked license means no driving on the roads, he remarked that he had been driving for 70-plus years and having that many years of driving experience granted him special privileges. He even told me that in his 20's he had a motorcycle license and he was quite certain that still enabled him to drive a motorcycle. Fortunately he didn't own a motorcycle so that theory was never tested. Dad had in his younger days drove a motorcycle to Washington, D.C. to see Lindbergh honored in a parade following his successful crossing of the Atlantic in The Spirit of '76. My dad loved to tell the story of how he was so close to Lucky Lindy that he could have reached out and touched him.

The need to confront Dad, who had become a driving menace, disappeared because he rapidly lost movement in his legs. It became extremely difficult for him to walk and he was having falling spells. All of his children tried to convince him it was time to leave the farm for his own safety. Whenever we would bring the topic up, he would get terribly angry with us and tell us to mind our own business. He had lived his entire 93 years on the farm that had once belonged to his grandparents, and he wanted so very much to die on the farm. During the last six months of his life he sold the farm to a large farming family of Maryland because he knew they would keep the land as he knew and loved it – for farming and not development. The contract allowed Dad to live on the farm rent-free until his death.

One evening my husband and I stopped in to see my dad and he had fallen on the kitchen floor and was unable to get up. His body felt like dead weight in our attempts to lift him. I said to Dad, "I'm calling 911. You have to go to the hospital. You need help." He replied, "Let's wait until tomorrow and see how I feel then." I knew he desperately wanted to stay put and also knew I had to call 911. As I watched the medics load Dad's aged body into the back of the ambulance, I whispered, "I really wanted you to have what you wanted, Dad. I wanted you stay on the farm until God called you home." I knew that Dad would never be returning to the farm and I knew that my life would never be the same as I saw the doors of the ambulance close and drive up the hill of the homestead. Chuck and I followed the ambulance to Carroll County Hospital.

After several weeks' care Dad was moved from the hospital to a rehabilitation center. He was released from the rehab center to the assisted living where my mom, who has dementia, resides. Because of my mother's loss of memory, she is in her own world filled with happiness. Every day is a happy day for Mom; every meal a "happy meal". My Dad, however, wanted so very much to get better and return to the farm. On some level however he must have known this wasn't to be, because he was plagued with infections and each bout weakened him more and more until finally we were dealing with multiple urinary tract infections all at the same time. His body refused to accept the antibiotics for the infections. He was taken from the assisted living back to the hospital. His doctor informed us after Dad had been in the hospital for almost two weeks with the infections continuing, that we had to remove him from the hospital because he surely would get additional infections if he stayed. We moved Dad from the hospital to a rehabilitation center and began a new regimen of antibiotics in the hopes that they would allow for his deteriorating health to turn around. My husband and I went to see Dad every day he was at the hospital and rehab center. On the majority of the days we were there, Dad wasn't awake or alert. He was in a sleepy, dream-like state most of the time. I remember one morning, which I will always treasure. Chuck and I walked into his room and Dad was wide awake sitting up and said to me, "I couldn't be any happier to see you if you were Jesus Christ himself walking through that door." He was filled with such joy to see us. We had a wonderful visit filled with Dad's usual joking and cutting up about his stay in the hospital. I had my dad back – even if only for a day. I cannot begin to thank the doctors and nurses that helped my father during his final months on earth. In his alert moments, he would express a need to get back to the farm to check on it. We would reassure him that this was being done by the family members and the new owners.

I also have to thank my precious girlfriend, Celeste McDonald, who is a nurse. Celeste would call to check in on how my dad was doing and in those conversations she would always slip in a statement that she felt was going to be coming my way and prepare me for decisions that were going to have to be made. I remember one evening, when we talked about how nothing was healing the infections and the doctor had told me that Dad's prognosis was not good, Celeste said to me, "The doctor is going to ask, after several attempts to get the body to heal with the antibiotics, 'Do you want to continue with antibiotics?'" I discussed this with my brothers and sisters and we all came to the agreement that if Dad did not respond to this regimen of medicines, we would change the care to keeping him comfortable and not continue the antibiotic program. I remember Friday, January 24, 2003 after the doctor told me that Dad's body was not responding to any of the treatments that had been given faithfully for over two weeks, he asked me what care he was to give Dad. I replied, "Comfort care only."

When Dad was moved from the hospital to the rehabilitation center, I was thrilled that Dad's room had a window. It was a large window that looked out over the beautiful Carroll County countryside. My Dad loved the light when the sun shone in upon him. He had been a country boy for 93 years who loved being outdoors in the daylight hours. My brothers and sisters all came to visit my dad on Friday and Saturday. Around 3 a.m. Sunday morning I was awakened. I suddenly felt ill. After getting up and going to the bathroom, I wasn't able to get back to sleep. I felt as if I was going to be sick and yet I wasn't. My husband was awakened by my restlessness and asked if I wanted him to call the rehabilitation center. I said I did. When we called we were told that we should come immediately as Dad's breathing had changed.

Fortunately we lived only about 20 minutes from the rehabilitation center. The nurse who was caring for Dad was truly an angel. She had his room and his bed looking heavenly. She had Dad groomed and ready to greet heaven looking very dapper. Because my dad loved my Jack Russell, Benny, and referred to Benny affectionately as his "grand-dog" I had decorated Dad's room with pictures of Benny. I also had made a large sign that read: WE LOVE YOU DAD – Your children. I had these directly in view from his bed. I had placed behind his bed a wonderful painting of Jesus. My dad lived his life with Jesus always near him and I knew it wouldn't be any different in his dying experience. I had even brought in a Wishbone Jack Russell stuffed animal. The nurse had placed it near Dad's head. Benny was watching over Dad, too.

Years ago, my father had a brush with death when he had to be operated on for cancer of the throat. Jesus appeared to Dad in a vision and assured him he would recover. I knew Jesus had appeared to him then, and knew when Dad closed his eyes to earth, Jesus would be ready to greet Dad with open arms. I was certain that all of Dad's relatives were already gathering on the other side to welcome Dad home.

My husband and I were alone with my father during his last moments until the angels came en masse around 5:30 a.m. I felt a heightened presence of angels in the room at this time. I could feel their enveloping presence and love around my father. The frequency shifted at 6:05 a.m. and the light weaving of the room began. The best way I can describe "light weaving" is that the angels created a doorway with light through which Dad would leave earth and enter heaven. The angels built layer upon layer of light. It looked like a vortex of light energy filling the room.

While the light weaving was occurring, an Angel Choir came in and sang the most incredible song. The words are as follows:

"He's got his eyes on heaven; he's got his eyes on heaven.
The pearly gates he can see.
He's got his eyes on heaven; he's got his eyes on heaven.
With Jesus he'll soon be.
He's got his eyes on heaven; he's got his eyes on heaven.
No more earthly worry or strife.
He's got his eyes on heaven; he's got his eyes on heaven.
He'll sleep with the angels tonight."

I was singing out loud to Dad the words I was hearing the angels sing. The angelic sing-a-long continued until just after 7 a.m. At that time the angels changed the words:

"He's breathing in heaven; he's breathing in heaven.
His lungs are filled with eternity.
He's breathing in heaven; he's breathing in heaven.
One with Christ he will forever be."

The angels continued to sing that song to me and to my dad through me until 7:23 a.m. when Dad took one final breath on this side of earth and I know exhaled in heaven. He was finally breathing in heaven. It was incredibly peaceful in the room. In fact, the peace in the room was awesome to experience. After remaining by Dad's side for a short while longer, and having the nurse come into the room to officially document that this physical life was no more, we left the rehab center. We went outside and beheld the most glorious sunrise. It was the only glimpse of sunshine that we would see that entire day. That was especially comforting to me. As a child my dad would sing to me, "You are my sunshine, my only sunshine. You make me happy when skies are grey."

On the way home I telephoned my brothers and sisters to tell them of Dad's passing. I met later that day with two of my siblings to arrange for the selection of the casket and make funeral arrangements. When we were in the casket room and quite frankly overwhelmed with the selection, I whispered in my heart: "Dad, help us to select a casket quickly." I did that because we were all missing him so very much. Just then I turned and saw a casket with a sign that read: Poplar. Dad's farm property included a piece of land with a gorgeous tulip poplar tree. Dad sold that land to me because he knew how much I loved this tree and how many hours I spent contemplating life beneath this magnificent natural wonder. I turned to my siblings and said, "It's this one." They both were a little stunned by my conviction but quite happy that a decision had been made.

My family asked that I compose and deliver the eulogy for my dad. At first I doubted that I would be able to break free from my grief and come up with even one word. And yet I felt so truly blessed to have the opportunity honor Dad. I share with you here that eulogy.

On behalf of my mother, and my brothers and sisters and our families, I would like to thank everyone for your cards of sympathy, flowers, and donations made in honor of our dad, Robert Gill Howard. God bless you for your kindness and thoughtfulness.

As I honor my dad this morning, I would like to do so by weaving into my words the lyrics of a few gospel songs. Dad loved gospel music and he would often share with us stories about the lyricists who wrote the songs he loved. My father especially loved to tell the story of Frances Jane "Fanny" Crosby, a hymn writer who was blind from the age of six weeks. Known as America's hymn writer, she wrote more than nine thousand hymn lyrics, many of which were favorites of our dad, including "Blessed Assurance," "Safe in the Arms of Jesus" and "Tell Me the Story of Jesus."

Dad would look forward to attending the Mt. Zion Church summer picnic because the church would have a musical program, and Dad was always on the lookout for inspiring Christian entertainment that he would then book for the annual Glyndon Men's Bible Class banquet. For many years Dad lead the program committee for this event. I know the Bible Class members will always remember that before introducing the entertainment, Dad loved to lighten up the evening by telling a few jokes. Dad loved making people laugh. If our family was attending an event and got separated from Dad, all we needed to do was follow the laughter.

Dad was a country boy. Even as a man of 93 years of age, there was a country boy inside who loved nature and wanted to die on the farm on which he was born. *This is my Father's world, I rest me in the thought of rocks and trees, of skies and seas. His hand the wonders wrought.*

Dad was born July 28, 1909. He was the son of the late Rosa Mary and Fred T. Howard. Dad inherited the farm from his grandparents William

Thomas and Anna Upperco Gill. The farm had been in the family prior to 1734 when the will of Steven Gill was probated. Just a few years ago Maryland recognized my dad as one of Maryland's century farmers; someone whose farm has been in continuous family ownership for more than a century. Dad and Mom's farm was the second oldest farm of continuous ownership in Maryland.

Dad loved the outdoors. I know many of you who lived near the Howard farm would often times see him early in the morning working on his roses, or later in the day mowing or plowing fields. You could see him wearing khaki pants and shirt and pith helmet. In later years, the pith helmet was replaced by a grey Huntingfields baseball cap given to him by my sister Ginny and her husband, Frank. He was always busy serving God by acting as caretaker of the farm he loved so very, very much.

Dad was a wonderful steward to the land because he loved the earth. Up until his final days on the farm he was still concerned about the pipe being clogged with mud that connected the stream to the farm's pond. He could hardly walk, but he wanted to make certain water was still flowing freely to the pond. As I reflected upon this in writing this eulogy, I thought to myself – what a wonderful message for living life: It is important that we don't allow "muddy" worries to clog our pipelines to God; we must always make certain that our lives are flowing freely with God thoughts.

You could also find Dad in his orchard and the garden behind my parents' home. I would find him there in the morning, and it reminded me of his gospel songs favorites: *I come to the garden alone…while the dew is still on the roses…and the voice I hear falling on my ear, the Son of God discloses.*

I want to share that Dad was a wonderful guardian to animals, too. I will never forget when my Mom's pug was dying of old age. Wonton was held and comforted in his last days by my mom. Little Wonton's body grew weaker and weaker. Dad was often hard to find during Wonton's final days, and when Wonton died my Dad brought out a little wooden coffin he had been building for Wonton. When Wonton's health began to wane, Dad began the task. He knew how much my mother loved this dog, and he wanted to comfort her in her grief by this act of kindness for little Wonton.

Dad sold his farm to the Lippy Brothers this past summer and it brought great peace of mind to turn the farm over to a family that he greatly respected and to know that the land would be farmed.

Dad was a crop farmer, dairy farmer, and turkey farmer. Up until he was 85 years old he would milk a herd of 30 cows himself every morning and every evening. Additionally, during the Roosevelt era Dad supplemented the family income by helping to build Byerly Road.

Dad had a creative side. In the morning in his milking barn he would listen to WBAL radio. He loved the Don Spatz program and to hear Mr. Spatz's five-minute commentary, which always ended with the words "Make this a good day." Dad believed in that same philosophy for all of his life. Sometimes WBAL would have a creative writing contest and Dad won several of these with his delightful poems. In February, 1994 he wrote and won the Carroll County Times' Most Romantic Valentine. Here's part of the poem:

If you were a rose on some lonely lane
And I were a dew drop, behold,
I would never want to part,
But stay close to your heart

He was an amateur photographer. He loved seeing God at eye-level through his camera. My brothers and sisters and I can remember the hours of entertainment he provided us with his family home movies. He was also always ready to take his projector and screen to any church meetings or youth groups that needed a film for the evening's entertainment. He was a supporter of Methodist youth groups and whenever a tractor was needed to pull a float in a community parade, or take a bunch of kids on a hayride, Dad was there.

He was an inspirational speaker. Dad acted as a lay minister for Boring United Methodist Church and a teacher at the Glyndon Men's Bible Class. He shared with us stories of speakers that had inspired him with their messages such as Billy Sunday. In the evenings after a day's work was done, he would often listen to ministers delivering sermons on the radio. He loved doing research for his own future sermons and our house was filled with many books on the study of the Bible.

Of course, Dad was a family man. Dad and Mom, Martha Wisner Howard, celebrated 72 years of marriage last November 8th. They were both together at Look About Manor Assisted Living at that time. Mom and Dad were married in the Boring Parsonage in 1930 by Reverend Chandler. Dad was a wonderful, loving father to six children – Virginia, Charles Robert, James, Rosemary, Joyce and me.

Dad has six grandchildren; seven great-grandchildren and just recently became a great-great grandfather. And Dad's family extended out into the community to include his many, many friends. His neighbors on Byerly Road– the Bosleys, the Rogers, the Abbotts, the Wicklines…just to name a few; his friends at the Boring church (and Emory and Pleasant Grove churches, too because at one time these were all part of one circuit) and friends at the Glyndon Bible class, Elmo's Restaurant, the bank, the Arcadia post office, local garages and hardware stores. And I don't want to forget his friends in the farming industry – farming families - Bowman Feed, Southern States, Walsh Fuel.

He lived a life filled with a richness money cannot buy – a long and happy marriage, six children whom he loved and who will love him forever, working with God's good earth, going to church and Bible class, serving on committees. The pleasure of making homemade ice cream on Sundays after church; working hard in his dairy barn on a hot summer day and taking a break to reach into the tank that kept the milk cans cold and pulling out a bottle of cola; going to the local church's oyster suppers in the fall; sitting on our screened porch with Mom at the end of the day – both in their rocking chairs – reflecting on the day's events, all of this was a part of his life.

And most importantly, Dad was a Christian. In his life here on earth, he loved Jesus and I know he now can show his love to Christ eternally. *Blessed assurance, Jesus is mine! Oh what a foretaste of glory divine!*

Whenever we had a family dinner Dad would say the grace and he always ended every prayer thanking God for the gift of Jesus and salvation through Christ. *What a friend we have in Jesus, all our sins and griefs to bear…what a privilege to carry…everything to God in prayer.*

As I shared, my father would often give sermons at Boring Church as a lay minister, when the pastor was on vacation or at conference. I can remember Dad weaving into his sermons stories of how people had died unexpectedly perhaps through a tragedy. Dad would use these stories to emphasize the truth that we do not know the hour we will be called home. Yet we do have the ever-present now in which to accept Jesus and love Jesus. *Why do you wait, dear brother? Oh, why do you tarry so long? Your Savior is waiting to give you …a place in His sanctified throng. Why not? Why not? Why not come to Him now?*

My husband and I were by Dad's bedside when he died. As he took his last breaths here on earth, his eyes were focused on heaven. His eyes were focused on Jesus. As he breathed in the last breath here, and I know exhaled on heavenside, a wonderful peace filled the room and enveloped both of us.

I know it was Dad's way of saying to all of us – friends and family – alike: *Christ just called the roll up yonder. And it's time for me to be there.*

Amazingly, Dad died almost exactly at sunrise on Sunday morning, January 26th. When Chuck and I left Westminster Nursing Home we witnessed a glorious sun rising up from the horizon and we stopped to soak in the beautiful light. *"Oh there's sunshine…blessed sunshine…when the peaceful happy moments roll; When Jesus shows His smiling face, There is sunshine in the soul."* The rest of that Sunday was cloudy and snowy.

I would like to share a brief video from a local television program that featured our dad and his roses. Dad had many varied interests but his passion for roses was well known and enjoyed by all who passed by the farm.

As you watch now, know in your hearts Dad thanks you for being here today and says to each and every one of you: *God be with you till we meet again.*

The video ended with the interviewer smelling Dad's gorgeous rosebushes and reminding viewers of one of my Dad's mottos for life: every day we should stop and smell the roses.

Shortly after learning of Dad's passing, Tom Wright, husband of Rosemary Ellen Guiley and a dear friend, sent me the following poem he wrote In Memory of the Passing of Robert Howard:

Gates and Lights and Pearly Whites
Are Nothing Beside the Soul.
Eternity breaths and eternity weaves
Into all our incredible whole.
No soul can pass
Without a mass from all they've left behind
And we're not that far
The door's ajar
When God's Angels take us home

Several weeks after Dad's passing, I had a dream. Dad and I were walking together on the property of his farm. We were talking and laughing. Dad was telling me all about the wonderful food in heaven and expressed his desire that I know he's back to being able to do all the things he loves. It was the happiest dream. I awoke feeling wonderful all over from the dream experience. I couldn't wait for Chuck to awaken so I could tell him of my visit with Dad. After sharing with Chuck my dream, I opened the Carroll County Times and saw a poem that a family had printed to honor a loved one in heaven. I knew that not only was this an honoring of their family member, but a blessing for me.

I dreamed about you last night
We talked and laughed a long, long time.

We talked about the day you left,
When God called and carried you home.
You told me God has many plans,
For those you hold so dear.
And that one day we would understand
So we are not to shed any more tears.
We talked and laughed until you said
"It's time for me to go."
I said, "I'll love you always,"
And after that, You were waving and saying, "but I love you most."
Then you had to go.

Dad died the week of my 52nd birthday. When my birthday rolled around on Friday, I didn't feel like celebrating. Chuck is the most wonderful husband and wanted to get me out of the house and create a happy birthday memory. Chuck drove me to Boyds Bear Country outside Gettysburg, Pennsylvania. It's an incredible place for anyone who loves teddy bears. I love teddy bears passionately. I will share in the next chapter the heart connection between angels, teddy bears and humans, especially children.

There are three floors of bears there and adorable displays with bears. It was a rainy day and not many people were visiting Boyds. Chuck told me to just wander at my own pace and was sincerely hoping I would find a birthday present I wanted in this land of bears.

As I walked around I saw a sign that read: You are only here for a short visit. Don't hurry. Don't worry. And be sure to stop and smell the roses. I knew Dad was watching over me.

I took the escalator to the third floor of Boyds Bears and as I entered one of their display areas I saw a large bear with a brown fedora hat. That bear stopped me in my tracks. I had created a collage of photographs of my dad for sharing at the viewing, and one of my favorite pictures was Dad decked out in a fedora. This was truly Bob Bear.

I found Chuck and asked if he would find out the cost and if it was reasonably priced, purchase it as a birthday present. Wouldn't you know it? This was a display bear – for display only – and no amount of money could purchase this bear. Boyds has special display bears manufactured for their display use only. My precious husband offered to purchase the entire display. He talked to the powers that be at Boyds Bears and said he knew they wouldn't want the display broken up by selling just one bear, so he was willing to buy all the bears, including the bench they were sitting on. The answer was still no. Even though I felt initial disappointment in not being able to buy that particular "Bob Bear", I was grateful that we also weren't bringing the entire display home either. To this day I get a hoot when thinking about my husband in negotiation for Bob Bear. Chuck is truly a loving angel by my side.

I found a large bear at Boyds that would do nicely as Bob Bear and we purchased it for my birthday. When I got home, I found and won on EBAY for $10 an identical Fedora to the one my dad wore in the picture. I dressed Bob Bear in one of my dad's favorite woolen sweaters. I placed Dad's driving registration card in his hand. Bob Bear sits on a table next to our bed. Each morning I wake up and see Bob Bear smiling at me I can hear Dad whisper, "I'm never far from your heart."

As I shared in the first paragraph of this chapter, Dad's death has had a major impact on my life. I have been close to my parents all of my life. I lived under their roof until my first marriage at age 20. Shortly after marrying, my husband and I bought land from Mom and Dad and built a home directly across from my parents' farm. At the time of my divorce, I bought the house and property from my ex-husband and I continued living across from Mom and Dad. When I married Chuck in 1999, he sold his former home and together we started a new life at Angel Heights, the property with the 225-year old tulip poplar tree. I interacted with my dad almost daily. I loved knowing what mischief he was getting into. I think one of the hardest adjustments when we lose a loved one is missing their physical presence in our lives. I remember reading a sympathy card I received that said, "It's never easy to say good-bye, to let go of that hand."

Additionally, after my father's death, the new owners of the farm started doing what they had every right to do – making it their farm. They bulldozed down old buildings and made major changes to the landscape. As we come down our driveway, we face the farm. So every morning I would face the reality that Dad was no longer there, and the farm no longer looked as it did when Dad was there. Quite frankly, I felt as if my heart would break with sorrow. Yet I know that change is inevitable in all our lives. I also know that even though Dad moved his residence from an earthly to a heavenly address, he is always near me.

Rosemary and Tom, whom I mentioned earlier, also shared with me a wonderful Eskimo legend about the stars being openings in heaven that has been of great comfort to me. "Perhaps they are not the stars, but rather openings in heaven where the love of our lost ones pours through and shines down upon us to let us know they are happy." I know Dad is happy and wants me to be happy, too.

A few months ago, Chuck came home from a ham radio meeting and shared that the National Railroad Society was going to hold its national convention in Baltimore City the first week in July. Chuck and I are both train enthusiasts and I immediately felt like I was re-living the movie, "Meet Me in St. Louis". The character played by Judy Garland remarks how wonderful it is to be having the World's Fair in her own backyard – right in St. Louis. I felt the same way: How wonderful that this convention was in Baltimore. Chuck and I got so excited about it that we quickly became members of The National Railroad Society and signed up for all the train excursions that were being offered that week. We were so blessed. We had no hotel expense. We had no airfare expense. We got up each morning, rode a metro near our home to downtown Baltimore, walked across the street from the metro station to the host hotel and met the excursion bus that drove us to the train depot. We had signed up for all the one-day excursions. There were descriptions of all the train rides, but because we were late in getting on board with the convention, we just signed up for those that were still open.

When we picked up our tickets and information packet on Monday, June 30th, the Society provided a detailed outline of every mile marker on the route, every town we would ride through and pointed out railroad stations, and important facts about the areas we were to see from aboard the train. We sat down together and read over the itineraries of the trip. I still can remember the chills that came over me as I read the details for the Blue Mountain Limited train ride that we would be riding on Sunday, July 6th. I could hardly get the words out to tell Chuck what heaven had in store for us. My dad had often told me stories of how when he was a boy, he and his grandmother boarded the train at Fowblesburg. They would ride the train through Glyndon, and continue downtown to Camden Yards where they would disembark and spend the day in Baltimore. The Blue Mountain Limited was going to recreate that same route, which had been discontinued many, many years ago. In fact, the train ride would begin at Camden Yards and head north through Maryland and weave through the countryside, going into Pennsylvania and heading up at New Oxford.

The day of the train ride the weather was perfect. It was a comfortable summer day with bright blue skies. Chuck and I were probably the most excited people on board. We sat next to the windows like a pair of kids sits by the chimney on Christmas Eve. We didn't want to miss a single sight as we were passing by because we knew these were the same "rails" Dad had ridden with my great-grandmother. The train provided was a MARC train double-decker and we found a seat on the second level with an absolutely spectacular view of the countryside we traveled through. When the train clickety-clacked through Woodenburg…Boring… and then Fowblesburg, we looked out the window together and saw the road we live on – Byerly Road. We saw Dad's former farm. And we didn't see the changes made in the farm by the new owners. Instead we saw the land – lots of land being loved and cared for. The landscape was gorgeous with its furrowed fields. And that is what was important to Dad. My dad loved the land and the land loved Dad back. The train ride made me realize that although things have changed, such as buildings and barns being bulldozed down, the ideals that Dad lived with his life-stewardship to the land, and responsible guardianship to the earth-were still being abundantly maintained by the new owners. Dad's legacy to the land continues. And those same ideals are alive and well in both Chuck and me. We are stewards and guardians to Angel Heights. Our eyes filled up with tears because we both felt Dad looking over our shoulders enjoying every sight with us. When we passed a field of green, lush corn, we could hear within our hearts Dad commenting on how tall and healthy the corn looked. Dad was with us every moment of the ride. At the end of an absolutely perfect day, we disembarked at Camden Yards and headed back to Fowblesburg by metro and then by car. We both felt that Dad had made a divine connection at an ethereal train station where a conductor called out: "All Aboard for the heaven-bound Angel Express."

Chapter 2

TEDDY BEAR ANGELS

Even though historians may not regard Teddy Roosevelt's refusal to shoot a helpless bear as one of the truly great moments exemplifying his leadership capabilities, I would put it at the top of the list. In November of 1902, President Theodore Roosevelt came to Smedes, Mississippi to settle a state border dispute and to hunt. On November 14th, he refused to shoot a captive bear. President Roosevelt even remarked that he could not face his children if he had shot the bear.

Clifford Berryman drew a political cartoon which appeared in The Washington Post depicting Roosevelt turning his back on a small bear and holding up his hand up to indicate no harm would come to the bear. The cartoonist was making reference to Roosevelt settling a minor boundary dispute between Mississippi and Louisiana. This first themed cartoon of Roosevelt and bear appeared in the newspaper on November 16th, 1902 and was followed by subsequent cartoons with the two teamed up together. As additional cartoons were created, the bear was drawn with more wide-eyed innocence, making the character even more lovable.

The bear quickly achieved star quality by the readership of the newspaper and the image of the bear continued in Berryman's cartoon depictions of Roosevelt. In fact, on Roosevelt's inauguration day in 1905, the newspaper featured the Roosevelt bear on the front page.

Morris Michtom was the owner of a candy and toy store in Brooklyn, New York. Having seen the drawings of Roosevelt and bear, he and his wife, Rose created a brown plush bear. They placed bear and cartoon in their store's front window and identified the bear as "TEDDY". Almost as soon as the bear went on display, it was sold. The Michtoms repeated the process time and time again with each new plush bear assembled, placed in the front window, and immediately sold and on its way to a new home. The Michtoms realized their bear creation had struck a chord in the hearts of the public.

Rose Michtom supposedly even wrote Roosevelt requesting permission to call their plush bear: Teddy's Bear. Roosevelt gave them his blessing with the added remark that he couldn't fathom how his name would make a difference in the sale of bears. One additional point of interest is that Mrs. Theodore Roosevelt wrote a letter of condolence to the Michtom family when Morris Michtom died. Newspapers across the country called him "The Father of the Teddy Bear."

My friend Paula Matthew has shared with me the exercise of remembering one's earliest childhood memory. She believes that this gives an individual a glimmer or glimpse of our mission here on earth. My earliest memory is as a very young child sitting nestled next to my dad, holding my beloved teddy bear, Goldie, close to my heart and both bear and me being entertained by Dad's wonderful storytelling. I remember Dad whispering the stories to me, which made me feel special, that the stories were for my ears only, and of course Goldie's, too. When Paula was teaching me this "first memory" exercise to share with others she mirrored to me that in this life I would place myself close to my "Father" in heaven. I would be empowered by God's messages of inspiration that would come in the form of divine whisperings. I would live a life in which I kept near to me those influences which nurtured my life and I would treasure these healing influences like gold. I encourage you to use this exercise for yourself to tap into a childhood memory that is divinely connected to your life's purpose.

As I got older I never lost my fondness for teddy bears; in fact, I have the Will Rogers approach to teddy bears: I've never met a teddy bear I didn't love. Chuck will attest that he shares Angel Heights with me, the angels, three Jack Russells and a collection of teddy bears. I feel truly blessed for having so many angels by my side: Chuck, my Jack Russells – Benny, Riot and Jackie, my teddy bears, and of course God's wonderful angels.

As I thought back on my childhood memories of having afternoon tea parties with Goldie, I remembered a recording that to this day I still can sing with most of the words. The song is called Teddy Bears' Picnic. In August of 2002 I led a group on one of my annual spiritual tours of the world – known as both "inner outings" and Angel Tours. We went to Scotland.

While in Aberdeen, Scotland we had a few hours of free shopping time. My husband Chuck retreated to the hotel to relax and I ventured into a store called Past Times with a number of my angelic girlfriends. What a divine experience! Shopping with girlfriends! I just about levitated with joy when I saw a CD that featured the original version of Teddy Bears' Picnic. The lyrics were written by Jimmy Kennedy. If you have a child in your life, I highly recommend that you introduce them to this precious song.

"If you go down in the woods today, You're sure of a big surprise. If you go down in the woods today, You'd better go in disguise. For every bear that ever there was Will gather there for certain because Today's the day the Teddy Bears have their picnic."

To this day the song immediately conjures up images of teddy bears with picnic baskets romping through the woods together. It is a song that makes my heart resonate with pure joy. As I thought more and more about the vision of teddy bears having a picnic and the joy and healing that teddy bears bring to children of all ages on the earth, I was inspired by the angels to wrap all that celebration energy into a special day on which everyone in the world could take time to have a picnic or tea party with their teddy bear. Just as the angels are healing guardians, so too are teddy bears.

There's a book called CHASE CALENDAR OF EVENTS that is published annually and through the Chase organization you can promote your own celebrated annual events by listing them in this calendar. Libraries, community organizations, nursing homes, radio and television stations are some of the businesses that purchase this book and look monthly for events that may be of interest for their particular public following. I came to know about Chase in the promotion of BE AN ANGEL DAY (August 22nd annually), followed by INSPIRE YOUR HEART WITH THE ARTS DAY (January 31st annually). The first Saturday of August, 2004 will be the first annual celebration of TEDDY BEARS' PICNIC/TEA PARTY DAY. It's a day to take your favorite teddy bear on a picnic or to afternoon tea. Why not? I consider Teddy Bears my best friends. They are truly healers. When you hold a teddy bear, you are immediately comforted by the way they feel. I love the poem by Eula Smith-Zimmerman:

I love my little Teddy Bear,
He's such a friendly fellow,
His fur, beautiful and soft
Is neither brown or yellow
He plays but never quarrels with me,
And keeps me gay and jolly,
And I don't have to punish him

As often as my Dolly
He's such a quiet little chap,
No impish schemes he hatches,
He never barks, he has no fleas,
At least he never scratches.

In my healing ministry with the angels, I have come to recognize the support teddy bears bring to children who are suffering. There are many wonderful organizations on the planet that deliver teddy bears to children so that they can have a special friend by their side and they don't feel alone. In chatting with members of one of my classes about the healing energies of teddy bears, a woman shared that a hospice organization in Ohio had given a teddy bear to her grand-daughter when this woman's grandson had died as an a infant. It was a gift of nurturance and comfort in a time of sadness and loss and came in the form of a fuzzy bear that the little girl could hold because the baby brother that she loved holding so much was now in heaven. Teddy bears are like the angels. They are messengers of love. For me, teddy bears are divine healers disguised in furry bodies.

Many wonderful organizations have put these divine healers in the hands of individuals in need of healing. Sojourn Bear, Inc. of Treasure Island, Florida is one of these organizations. This healing ministry was founded by Jan Burlew in June of 1995. Jan was recovering from breast cancer and found comfort and healing from her own collection of teddy bears. She was inspired to provide similar comfort to other cancer patients. The mission of Sojourn Bear, Inc. is to provide comfort, inspiration and support to cancer patients with the gift of a uniquely handmade teddy bear. From the beginning, Sojourn's goal has been to give a teddy bear to every cancer patient throughout the United States. What a glorious vision started by one woman being comforted in the midst of a health challenge by her teddy bears! The bears are sewn solely by volunteers of all ages. Participants range in age from nine years to 90+ years. These wonderful earth angels distribute Sojourn Bears through local hospitals and cancer centers. Their motto is "Making Cancer Bear-able"TM.

Another wonderful organization is Operation TeddyCare located in Half Moon Bay, California. The "Dad Bear" of this organization is Dr. Bob Baker, a retired trauma psychologist who spent years in trauma care and is familiar with the best and most credible trauma care providers in the world. "Mom Bear" is Barbara "Ms. B." Moran, who is an author/educator. Their son CJ is the chief bear groomer. The organization delivers bears to traumatized children, such as the children who survived the Oklahoma City bombing and children impacted by the events of 9/11. This project began as a family's mission of love in 1995 when CJ asked his family how they could help the survivors of the Kobe earthquake in Japan. The family decided to collect and send bears. Their efforts resulted in 10,000 bears being escorted by Dr. Bear to Japan. This wonderful family shares one of my beliefs. Teddy bears are an American symbol of love. Teddy Bears are used to help comfort children. They are used in storytelling, role playing and other therapeutic ways. TeddyCare believes the teddies they deliver are ambassadors of love and healing. The organization works closely with counselors, social workers, therapists, medical professionals and members of rescue, fire and police agencies. TeddyCare believes it is important that kids and adults in crisis be treated appropriately. It fills my heart with joy to know that teddy bears represent a symbol of the healing energy and power of the American Spirit. We are a nation of citizens who truly care about people. In Bobbie Moran's own words shared in a Los Angeles Times article written by Cara Mia DiMassa - "Helping Kids in Need Bear Their Burdens," "There' something magical about a teddy bear...there's something about that face that says, 'I understand; I am listening. If you need a hug, let me give you one.'"

In my service with the angels of healing, I have come to recognize that there are grid networks of energy that are utilized by members of similar healing activities. One example is the Reiki grid network that vibrationally connects and supports all the Reiki healers on the earth. All Reiki healers have an invisible support network. Additionally, there is a teddy bear healing network that connects all the beautiful organizations that gift teddy bears as healings. Many police officers keep teddy bears in the trunks of their cars until they are called into service to comfort a child. Teddy Bears That Care, located in New York is an organization that gives bears to children affected by domestic abuse, illness or the death of a parent. Good Bears of the World is a non- profit organization which provides teddy bears to children of all ages, where love, solace and comfort can make a difference. Annually they give out over 20,000 bears to children in need, including the victims of floods, tornadoes, hurricanes and domestic violence both in the US and abroad. They give bears to many sick, injured and underprivileged children as well as lonely seniors. Good Bears of the World was founded in England in 1969 by the late journalist and radio pioneer James Theodore Ownby. Good Bears of the World was the first group to donate teddy bears to police departments in the early 80's. Mr. Ownby died in 1986 but his dream lives on in this healing organization that continues to place teddy bears in the hands of those who need the comfort a bear can bring.

Some organizations focus on gifting bears to children in pediatric wards; some to family shelters; and the list goes on an on. The names of these organizations – Good Bears of the World, Teddy Bear Care Foundation, Operation Bearlift - mirror to the world the common bond of this network which is the warm and fuzzy wonder of the teddy bear. Bears are universal messengers of friendship. They are a security blanket with personality. A security blanket with fuzzy-wuzzy arms and legs. Huggable healers. I love Bobbie Moran's description: "Teddy bears help kids bear adversity."

Operation Bearlift shares in their literature research that confirms that for approximately one child in four, the teddy bear is their favorite toy.

Dr. Mira Kaplan, physician of holistic and western medicine, is the author of "The Teddy Bear Guide to Self-Healing," and the creator of eight different healing bears. She is truly an earth angel who shares the message that teddy bears can improve well being. She maintains a beautiful website: www.teddybearandfriends.com. I encourage you to check it out because she offers 15 ways to use your teddy bear to reduce stress. Here's a couple of Dr. Kaplan's teddy bear healing techniques:

"Meditate with your teddy bear. Imagine yourself going with your teddy bear to a beautiful, serene place in nature.

Take your teddy bear into your world of sweet dreams at night or when taking a healing nap."

What makes a Teddy Bear so adorable and lovable? Soft fur? Open, welcoming arms inviting you to get closer and give 'em a hug? The comforting twinkle in their eye that makes you feel they understand everything you are experiencing in your life? The good vibrations that they give us, telling us that they are just waiting to share a life adventure with us? For me, it's all of these statements and more.

As a lover of teddy bears, I have a collection of teddy bear books. Books on the philosophy of teddy bears, the love of teddy bears, collecting teddy bears, and so on. One of my favorite books is In Search of Teddy by Joan Greene. Tweed Roosevelt, great-grandson of President Theodore Roosevelt wrote a quote honoring the book. "This book is warm and cuddly, should be held often and will be remembered fondly by all who come in contact with it."

In Joan's introduction she shares a story that happened when she opened her store "Bears to Go" in the spring of 1981. A local newspaper ran a feature story on her new store with a picture of a bear included in the article. A woman came into the shop holding the newspaper article in her hand. She was an elderly woman who had managed – after seeing the article a month prior – to find someone who was willing to drive her to the bear shop.

The woman shared with Joan how her heart had stopped when she saw the bear that was like her childhood bear. She asked Joan,"Is he German?" "Yes, Steiff," replied Joan. The woman then said, "Then he will understand me." I can still remember reading those words. The woman summed up for me my heart belief about teddy bears. They understand the "me" in all of us. There are times I believe no one understands me like my teddy bears.

This precious woman's family had fled Germany when she was a little girl. They left everything behind. Her only solace was her teddy bear. Her teddy bear comforted her through all the life-altering events of her life. Teddy was always right beside her, like an angel, speaking softly in sweet German. The woman shared how she had cried herself to sleep in the new place they lived. Everything was unfamiliar, dark, strange, scary for her as child. But Teddy was there to gather her tears. The woman went on to share that everything was gone in her life – her home, her family, her friends, and through the years she had even lost Teddy. "I have outlived them all." The woman's residence was now an assisted living home. She only had one room. She only had her memories.

When Joan handed her the little Steiff, the woman held him close and exclaimed, "Oh Teddy!" She kept repeating those words over and over. She began to speak to him softly and gently in German. Joan wrote, "I would swear that the teddy looked right into her eyes with an understanding nod. After all, he was born German too, and it was probably like music to his little teddy bear ears to hear his native tongue being spoken."

She gave Joan a hankie with money inside and told Joan she had been saving since seeing Teddy in the newspaper. "Three dollars should buy a nice teddy, don't you think," she asked as her eyes pleaded. "Will I get change back?"

In reading this story, I wanted to bestow upon Joan Greene angelic sainthood. St. Joan replied, "Yes, forty-two cents." Joan goes on to share she doesn't know where she came up with the forty-two cents. I have a sensing that the "42" was a message coming through connected with 1942, approximately the time period when the woman was fleeing Germany. Joan wrote that it was just a number that came to her mind. She removed the price tag of $78 and thanked the woman for her purchase.

You don't have to be a rocket scientist to figure out Joan lost money on the sale of the Steiff bear. Joan expresses that she would have given her the bear; however, her father told that she should never take away a person's pride. The woman needed to buy this bear and $2.58 is a fortune when all you have is $3.00 in your purse. God Bless Joan Greene for being an earth angel of goodness. Just as we cherish teddy bears for their healing powers and unconditional love, the teddy bears of the world cherish people like Joan because she was a wise woman who recognized there was healing service to be done by this bear. A 21-bear hug salute to Joan!

One my joys as an author is receiving letters from readers. Many readers have shared how they resonate with my writing and feel like they know me. That brings me great joy as it is my heartfelt desire to create friendships through my books. In an effort to continue my mission of sharing, I would like to tell you a little about my own collection. As I said earlier, I am someone who hasn't met a bear she doesn't love. I am a big fan of Boyds' Bears and have a membership in their bear club known as The Loyal Order of Friends of Boyds (FOB). I am fortunate enough to live close enough to visit Boyds Bear Country in Gettysburg, Pennsylvania often. This is the "world's most humongous teddy bear store" which opened in October 2002. It measures 100,000 square feet and includes a free museum. The store features three floors of Boyds Bears. The company's logo is an oval paw print and the inscription "Bears and Hares You Can Trust." If you are a lover of teddy bears, I highly recommend visiting this barn of bears. My husband always comments about what an incredible marketing department Boyds has because there is something wonderful always going on at Boyds. You can check this out for yourself at www.boydsstuff.com. I have to also share that as a member of the Loyal Order of Bears, when you visit Boyds Country you can ask for a pass code that allows you to get into a special clubroom for members only. The first thing we do when we arrive at Boyds Country is to get the pass code for Chuck. He loves going into the clubhouse and relaxing, playing on the computer, while I am poking around, seeing what's new at Boyds.

It is through my collection of Boyds Bears that I express my "changing of the seasons" creativity in our home. For Christmas, the house is adorned with Christmas bears – snowman bears, angel bears, Santa bears; for 4th of July and Memorial Day the patriotic bears – dressed in red, white and blue come out to play. In the fall the bears dressed as pumpkins and wearing autumn colors are liberated from storage. There are even bears that love the summertime. I make a pretend beach for them complete with sand and they come out into the sunshine wearing swimsuits and little inner tubes around their bodies.

Years ago when I lived by myself and had a massage practice in my home, I had a client remark to me, "Why do you decorate your house so extensively for different holidays when you are the only one living here? Why do you go to so much bother?" I found that an interesting remark because he was standing in my house when he said it and he had obviously noticed the decorations. I also found it interesting because I am never alone. My home – as is my life – is filled with angels…an abundance of angels.

And equally important is doing things for me...even when it's just me, myself and I. That's quite a trio in itself. I replied to him, "Because it makes me happy!" I didn't give any more thought to the discussion until a month or so later when the man returned for another session and indicated he had been visiting his daughter in New York City. He lived at home alone and while in NYC he saw a whimsical holiday item and purchased it for himself to decorate his home...even though he would be the only person seeing it. Watch out! Happiness is contagious!

Additionally I collect Hermann-Spielwaren bears. Hermann-Spielwaren GmbH is now based in Coburg, Germany and run by Rolf Hermann, son of Max Hermann who set up his own family toy business in Neufang, Germany in 1920 and in 1923 moved to Sonneberg. His trademark was "Maheso" from the first two letters of Max Hermann Sonneberg. His son Rolf joined him in 1947. They later founded Hermann & Company in the US-occupied Coburg, near Soviet-occupied Sonneberg. Fearing East Germany's Communist regime, Max and his family fled to Coburg in 1953 where they relocated their company. Max died in 1955, and Rolf took over the company with his wife Dora-Margot as designer. The company was renamed Hermann-Spielwaren GmbH in 1979. Rolf died in 1995 and their children Urusla and Martin are now running the company. As you research the Hermann family you will find that the two bear-making companies in existence now that have the name Hermann are both descendants of Johann Hermann, a Sonneberg toymaker who first founded a company in 1907. Johann and his family were busy making wooden fiddles for children in the early 20th century. When buyers from large American department stores came to Germany in search of "teddy bears" it didn't take long for Johann to recognize that making instruments would play "second fiddle" to the manufacturing of bears. Max Hermann was one of Johann's six children. Since 1993, all Hermann-Spielwaren bears have been signed with a "neckmark" which shows the traditional green triangle and bear with a running dog. Max Hermann designed this logo in the 1930's. Each bear has it own individual number on a certificate as well as on the foot of the bear itself.

I am enchanted by Hermann-Spielwaren bears. They have chosen to create bears for people and characters that I love. I have bears that honor Leonardo Da Vinci, Mozart, Van Gogh, Monet, King Arthur, and Princess Diana, to name a few that compose my collection. In fact, my desk has a book shelf above it and their furry faces are beaming down upon me as I work at the computer inspiring me to fulfill my life's service just as the people they honor did.

I find when I am writing I weave a vibration that becomes magnetic and everything and everyone around me begins to resonate to whatever I am researching or writing about. Just yesterday I went into the nearby Boscov's Department Store and there was a table of ladies' nightshirts for sale. There was a teddy bear nightshirt on the display model. Even though there were about seven different nightshirt designs to select from, the teddy bear design was sold out.

This morning I was at The Light at the Top of the Stairs to meet Mary Mabe who had arranged for an angelic harp blessing for herself and her friend. When Mary came into the room she handed me a gift she had bought for me. It was an adorable white bear with wings. The bear was manufactured by Holy Bears, Inc. and had the word WINGS on the front of the bear. Mary shared with me that the bear reminded her of me and the organization I created some years ago with the same name to support women who were going through divorce. She remembered reading about WINGS in my first book Commune with the Angels.

I looked at the tag affixed to the little white angel bear and saw the bear promoted an organization entitled Texas Wings. The front of the tag has a pink ribbon on it – the symbol of support for those touched by breast cancer. Their website is www.texaswings.org. The healing they are promoting through the furry messengers is "To honor all those whose lives have been touched by breast cancer." They are women "involved in nurturing, giving, sharing." The little bear has the pink ribbon on one foot and a halo on the other foot. I thanked Mary Mabe for being a messenger to me about this organization. Texas Wings is just one more marvelous example of people serving God with the help of some furry friends. And how precious that the bears' manufacturer came up with the divine concept that bears are "holy bears".

I would be remiss to write a chapter about bears and not mention Winnie the Pooh. Winnie is without a doubt my vote for the best-known fictional bear in the world. Dorothy Milne, wife of author Alan Alexander Milne, bought a teddy bear at Harrods in London in 1921 for their son Christopher Robin's first birthday. The bear's name was actually Edward Bear and first made a public appearance in 1924 in A. A. Milne's When We Were Very Young. The name would be changed later and was derived from Winnie – the name of a black bear in the London Zoo that was the mascot of a Canadian regiment from Winnipeg, and Pooh was the name of Christopher Robin's favorite swan; thusly Winnie the Pooh came into being. The original Winnie-the-Pooh is now in the New York Public Library at the Donnell Branch.

One other example of how bears are healing guardians is Smokey the Bear. In the 1940's the U.S. Forest Fire Prevention Campaign selected a bear, a resident of forests, as a messenger to the public that "Care will prevent nine out of ten fires." Smokey was named after Smokey Joe Martin, who worked for the New York City Fire Department in the 1920's. The original artist who drew Smokey was Albert Staehle, an artist with "The Saturday Evening Post."

Americans fell in love with Smokey the Bear. He gained even more stardom when in 1950 a bear cub that had been wounded in a forest fire in New Mexico's Lincoln National Forest was named Smokey and given a permanent home at the National Zoo in Washington. For the remainder of his years he was visited by children who wanted to see the real "Smokey the Bear." Smokey the Bear is one bear that has Congress behind him. In May 1952 Congress passed the "Smokey Bear Act" protecting the name from exploitation. All fees from the manufacturing rights of Smokey products go towards prevention of forest fires in America. Smokey's message is an inspirational one that I know the trees of this great land truly do appreciate: Take Care! Only you can prevent forest fires.

Teddy Bears have even made space history. In Janet Wyman Coleman's book Famous Bears & Friends, Kumataro is recognized for being the fuzzy assistant of Dr. Chiaki Mukai, a heart surgeon and the first Japanese woman in space, on the Space Shuttle Discovery's mission that was launched at 2:19 P.M. on October 29th, 1998. Kumataro – derived from the Japanese words for bear "kuma" and "taro" a common ending for a male name was the name selected after 20,000 responses were given to Dr. Mukai'satellite request for name suggestions for the first bear in space.

Janet's own heart connection with teddy bears began when in 1993 she witnessed first-hand "the great 1993 Rhode Island Teddy Bear Invasion," when cartons containing thousands of teddy bears swept off a barge were washed ashore with the next high tide. As Janet shared, "Thirty-thousand teddy bears, all in argyle sweaters, washed up on the beach in Rhode Island…and I've been amused and interested in the teddy bear world ever since." I sometimes scan E-Bay for teddy bears. I remember once reading a description written by the seller of a teddy bear in which she explained that she had recently remarried and her new husband told her she was too old for teddy bears and because of this she was selling off her bear collection. A part of me wanted to write her and encourage her to keep the teddy bears and get rid of the husband.

In the mid 1990's I was on the road a lot, living out of a suitcase. I refer to my existence during that time as living on a wing and a prayer. It was through the incredible generosity of friends that lived in the vicinity of my appearances that I had lodging I could afford; namely, free. I remember one such experience when I was in the Vienna, Virginia area doing workshops and private consultations. A long-time angel friend, Sharon Shreve, was so very gracious to invite me to stay with her and her husband, John. When I had completed my day's work, I headed to Sharon's home and when I pulled up I saw a young boy seated under a tree in their front yard. I would later be formally introduced to Shane who is Sharon's grandson.

I got out of my car and immediately this young man said to me, "I have been waiting for you. I have been wanting so much to meet you. I want to help you with your bags." I didn't even have time to respond before this young man had opened the car and taken a piece of luggage, which was almost bigger than he was, out of the car and was heading towards the house. I tried to get him to let me carry the bag but he wouldn't hear of it. Into the house with my bag he went where we both were greeted by Sharon. Up the stairs went Shane with my bag to the room that Sharon had so graciously prepared for me.

Shane took it upon himself to help me unload my car for my stay at Sharon's. Shortly after I had settled in at their gorgeous home, Shane came and asked if I would follow him to his bedroom. I walked down the hallway to his room and as I stepped into the room he said to me, "I want you to have anything you want in this room. Anything. It's yours." To this day I am amazed at the generosity of this dear young man. I said to him, "Shane, these are your things. I don't want to take them." I thanked him over and over for the offer and the more I thanked him the more he was determined that I choose something as a gift from him to me. He wasn't letting me leave without a gift in hand. So I looked around for something small and sweet and my eyes landed on a teddy bear. The bear's name was Snuggles. Shane was delighted with my choice as it turned out that Snuggles was a favorite among Shane's belongings. I can still see Shane beaming with joy over my selection.

Snuggles became a traveling companion. If I was in the car, he was with me. If I was working at home, he was by my side. We went everywhere together. He mirrored to me God's desire for our lives: "I want you to have anything you want in this life." Snuggles was a messenger during a time when I would feel alone and uncertain. I was divorced. Walt Blatt, whom I met following my divorce, and whom I wrote about in my first two books, had transitioned to heaven. It was a lonely time. I felt Snuggles was an angelic messenger telling me that in my own future there would be a special man who would say those same words to me, "I've been waiting for you." That man did come into my life in 1999. Charles Feldman and I were married August 6, 1999 at Angel Heights.

When I led a spiritual tour to Turkey in 2000 Snuggles insisted on going with me. Snuggles shared with me that this would be a farewell tour for the two of us. It was time for Snuggles to go back to Shane. Snuggles and I kept a photo journal of Snuggles' adventure in Turkey and I shared it with Shane. I know Shane liked seeing the pictures, but even more he liked seeing his bear buddy Snuggles back on the shelf in his room. I wouldn't be surprised if years from now, when Shane meets that special woman he wants to ask to marry him, he doesn't wrap the engagement ring on a ribbon around Snuggles' neck.

Susan E. Schwartz shares in her book Teddy Bear Philosophy, "Things My Teddy Bear Taught Me About Life, Love, and the Pursuit of Happiness." One of those things is to let yourself be adored. Precious Shane and his sidekick Snuggles taught me that lesson.

Susan's wisdoms also include, "He who says he has no need of a bear…is the person who needs one most; Software will never replace a soft bear; when life knocks the stuffing out of you, be sure to put it back in." But the Jayne favorite of all her wonderful inspirations is: "Men are from Mars. Women are from Venus. Teddy Bears are from heaven." There are words from an old lullaby that remind me that teddy bears are heaven-sent and teach us how to cuddle and be cuddled:

Go to sleep my Teddy Bear,
Close your little button eyes,
And let me smooth your hair.
It feels so soft and silky that,
I'd love to cuddle down by you.
So, Go to sleep my darling Teddy Bear."

Just as Snuggles had been an angelic messenger, an angel by my side, encouraging me to let love come into my life again, there have been bears that have been like a compass that have guided me on the path of my life's service. One such bear is a special black mourning bear with red felt behind its shoe-button eyes. This bear was produced by Steiff in 1912 to commemorate the Titanic disaster and is known as The Mourning Bear. I came across a replica of this bear and the minute I laid my eyes on this bear I knew this bear was in some way saying to me, "Follow me. There's a world I want to show you." I named my little mourning bear: SOTLO. The letters stand for "SPIRIT OF TITANIC LIVES ON" and Sotlo's promptings and inspirations have been truly angelic. In fact, I have Sotlo to thank for introducing me to the incredible adventure of researching the stories of the Titanic. The world Sotlo opened up to me is the one that is shared with people who have heard the spirit of the Titanic call to them. I wouldn't be surprised if those who find my book in their hands haven't already been touched by the spirit of the Titanic. Sotlo was my angelic guide; and with your permission I would like to be yours. An adventure with the spirit of the Titanic is waiting to unfold in the next chapter.

Chapter 3

ANGELS OF THE DEEP

As I mentioned in writing about my relationship with my dad, we would attend the local steam show held on Arcadia's fairgrounds together every September. In addition to seeing all of the steam engines on display, I loved to wander through the flea market looking for treasures that would call out to me. One year while "flea marketing" at the show, I bought a copy of the book Wreck and Sinking of the Titanic – The Ocean's Greatest Disaster, edited by Marshall Everett with a copyright of 1912. I was intrigued with the book, not only because of its musty smell creating the aroma that suggested it had been stored inside of someone's steam trunk, but also because of the numerous photographs included in the book of the great ship, some of the survivors and some of the those not so fortunate.

I can remember watching the movie "A Night to Remember" based on Walter Lord's 1955 bestseller about the doomed Titanic and then wanting to go to my personal library again to read my "flea market find" one more time; my one and only Titanic book.

My interest in the story was again tweaked in 1997 when James Cameron's epic production "Titanic" was at the movie theaters and I went to see it at a matinee showing. The movie won 11 Oscars, including best picture and best director. Within two years, the film had taken in $1.826 billion in box office revenue. It is the most successful film of all time. I sat in a darkened theater crying my eyes out as the credits rolled.

In 2000, Chuck and I celebrated our first anniversary in Atlantic City, New Jersey at the Tropicana Hotel. We were there because Chuck's mother, Mildred, loved playing the slots and we loved Mildred. So we drove to Atlantic City together. While Mildred played the slots, Chuck and I toured an exhibit that was debuting at The Tropicana displaying artifacts from the Titanic wreckage. It was called TITANIC: The Exhibition. Elegant china and silver plates, an assortment of bottles, exquisite jewelry pieces such as a man's pocket watch and a woman's gold nugget necklace, an oil lamp and megaphone were just a few of the hundreds of items exhibited. We even saw a part of the ship, called "The Big Piece" in a tank outside of the hotel.

Some years later this same exhibit would come to The Baltimore Science Center and Chuck and I would again tour the artifacts. Each time we toured the exhibition, I got the sense that the Titanic is an icon of our times and that she was designed and built to be a masterpiece; a ship that was a floating work of art. I went away from each experience feeling a sadness for the lives lost and yet a peacefulness in knowing that the Titanic exhibitions help us to remember the spirit of these individuals by being able to transcend time through looking at the photographs of their lives.

In 2003 James Cameron directed an IMAX movie entitled, "Ghosts of the Abyss," in which the audience wears 3D glasses to view the underwater exploration of the wreck of the Titanic. It was during that experience that I met the "Angels of the Deep" and was given the assignment of researching the Titanic. I have a sensing that vibrationally when I first bought "The Wreck of the Titanic" at the flea market, first watched James Cameron's Titanic and came across Steiff's Titanic Mourning Bear, I was on some level connecting with the Angels of the Deep; however, they made their presence known as I sat in the Baltimore Science Center's IMAX Theater wearing 3D glasses and was mesmerized by the underwater explorations of the robots Jake and Elwood into the interior of the Titanic. My feeling of the Titanic as a floating work of art was confirmed when I saw in the IMAX light being shone through the leaded glass windows of the Titanic that amazingly remain undamaged. For the first time, since the sinking of the Titanic in 1912, we are able to experience a glimpse of the incredible beauty and artistry of this great ship. Thanks to James Cameron and his brother Mike and his Dark Matter team, Remotely Operated Vehicles (ROV's), we are able to see images of the interior of the Titanic not witnessed by human eyes since the night of April 14, 1912.

In a press release booklet, Cameron shared the excitement of the historic filming of the Ghosts of the Abyss: "We went into every space on Titanic that was big enough to permit the ROV to enter…We went into staterooms, saw their beds, their sinks, their mirrors; we knew who was in each room and we found their clothing, their personal effects. We went into the hold and looked at the cargo; we went into the dining room and saw the beautiful leaded glass windows that are still there, intact. The elegance of Titanic still exists."

The feeling I had earlier at the exhibitions is expressed when Cameron goes on to state, "Seeing it this way, there's no way to think of this but as a human tragedy. It's a very large canvas, but there's an amazing human connection....it's the things that people touched that bring history to life." The Titanic is a body of art and it writes its stories in people's hearts; it continues to touch people and bring its history into the present day arena.

When I am given an assignment, it is not as if someone places a piece of paper in my hand on which the assignment is written. What occurs is that the energy of the assignment is radiated to me on a cellular level. I become the assignment and this results in my energies becoming magnetic to everything that will be in support of my fulfillment of the angelic assignment. Even though I have had this experience on numerous occasions, it is still a bit unnerving because I become totally consumed with whatever I am assigned to research. This "consuming" energy then draws into my sphere of awareness items that I purchase for our home to surround myself with the images of the project; it draws books into my sphere of awareness that I purchase to create a library of research materials. These items and books enhance my quest as I move forward with the angels I serve together with on the project. Whatever I am called to delve into by my angel team, and in this experience, a presence of angels known as Angels of the Deep, I feel like my life changes and I am breathing, eating, sleeping, and dreaming the research.

Our home began to be filled to the rafters with Titanic books and Titanic-related items. Chuck is used to this bizarre behavior on my part, and it doesn't bother him. However, on one occasion being in the midst of the "consumption energy" and yet not able to fully realize how this assignment was going to unfold, I said to the angels, "Please reassure me that I am not out of my divine mind." I asked for a sign from the angels that this obsession with the Titanic was what God wanted me to be doing and I was on the right track.

I shared with Chuck that I had asked for clarity of assignment, because a part of me that had surrendered to the project felt totally out of control and I needed to know that this "total abandonment" to the project of researching the Titanic was what God wanted from me.

I told Chuck about my request to the angels as we were driving up Route 30, the Hanover Pike into Hanover, Pennsylvania. We were cutting through Hanover on side streets to get to Gettysburg to attend a function at

Boyds Bear Country for members only. We had taken a day off from working out of the offices in our home to have a play day at Boyds.

As Chuck was driving our car on a small two-lane country road he suddenly said, "The sinking of the Titanic!" I turned my head toward him and said with puzzlement, "Why did you say that?" He pointed to what was on the side of the road to the left of our car. I stared in total disbelief. There on a high school parking lot was a huge inflatable Titanic balloon that was part of a carnival that had been held at the high school perhaps the week prior. The carnival company was deflating this humongous balloon and just as we arrived the Titanic balloon was in the exact position of sinking. Chuck looked at me and said, "There's your sign." We both were flooded with amazement. Chuck pulled the car off the street and we got out and took pictures of the sinking of the Titanic. As I snapped the camera repeatedly, I kept saying over and over, "I cannot believe this!"

Later that day on the drive home from Gettysburg, we stopped at an ice cream parlor to get ice cream cones. We walked into the parlor and were greeted by a large sign: Try our latest ice cream treat: THE TITANIC. We stopped at Spring Meadow Farms, a produce market near to our home, to buy fresh vegetables and saw a tent where fireworks for the 4th of July were being sold. As we walked by the tent, we both saw a particular firework called: THE TITANIC. Chuck remarked, "Hey, Jayne, if you doubted it before today, be assured you are definitely on the right track!"

The Angels of the Deep inspire us to delve deeply into the mysteries of life. They inspire us to read books, study, research, explore and unlock mysteries. I honor all the individuals who have dedicated their lives to research: The archaeologists, scientists, and explorers, to name just a few. There are many who have focused their research on The Titanic. Because of their tireless efforts, there is a wealth of information on this great ship.

In my own research there were certain stories that spoke to my heart immediately. One of these is the story of Vittorio Gatti, a little boy who gave his mohair teddy bear to his father for good luck, when Gaspare Gatti departed to work as the manager of the Ritz Restaurant on The Titanic. Mr. Gatti carried the six-inch bear in his waterproof tobacco pouch. Unfortunately, Mr. Gatti was not one of the survivors of the Titanic. When his body was recovered and buried in Nova Scotia, his wife received his belongings. When Edith Gatti opened the tobacco pouch, she found her son's teddy bear. The teddy bear was indeed an angelic messenger of love and comfort from the Angels of the Deep to both Edith and her son.

Robert Douglas Spedden, known as Douglas, was a six-year-old survivor of the Titanic. Before the Titanic voyage, he had received from an aunt a Steiff bear from FAO Schwarz. The bear was named "Polar". A photograph was taken of Douglas by Father Brown before Father Brown disembarked the Titanic in Queenstown. It is a famous photograph where Douglas is seen spinning a top on the aft saloon deck. His dad is seen standing on the left side of the photograph encouraging him in his efforts. James Cameron recreated this actual scene in the movie Titanic. Interesting enough, in this scene the father, Frederic Spedden, was played by Don Lynch, a leading Titanic historian.

When the Titanic collided with the iceberg, Douglas was awakened by his nurse, Elizabeth Burns. Ms. Burns told Douglas that they were taking a "trip to see the stars."

Douglas, and his bear Polar, his mother, his nurse and his mother's maid all entered Lifeboat No. 3 just before 1:00 am. Douglas' father and some other men were also allowed to board the lifeboat because it was not full.

Douglas slept most of the night but awoke at dawn. After seeing all the icebergs surrounding the boat he exclaimed, "Oh, Muddie, look at the beautiful North Pole with no Santa Claus on it."

For Christmas, 1913 Douglas' mother, Daisy gave her son the Christmas present of a book she had written and whose cover she had illustrated, about the family's escape from the Titanic. The book was written from the perspective of Douglas' Steiff bear "Polar" and the title was "My Story." Leighton H. Coleman III, great-grandnephew of Daisy Spedden, discovered the story in an attic trunk. In 1994 he republished the book with illustrations by Laurie McGaw and included in the book photographs of family members, postcards and mementos. The book is entitled, "Polar the Titanic Bear," and is an absolute treasure. In Leighton's words, "When the Speedens were able to book passage to America on the Titanic, in April 1912, they considered themselves very lucky. The Titanic was the biggest, newest ship in the world – a floating palace that contained every modern convenience and luxury. Douglas and Polar stepped onto the most magnificent passenger ship built in a state of great excitement. They never dreamed that they would soon be part of the most famous sea disaster of all time."

I feel so blessed that the Angels of the Deep introduced me to this bear who survived the Titanic. His story is enchanting and the illustrations and photographs are heart-warming. In looking at the photographs taken by Daisy of the family's world travels, I was amazed to find that the family had stayed at Reid's Palace in Madeira. In <u>DUI Angels</u> I wrote of how Chuck and I had the joy of having afternoon tea on the balcony of Reid's Palace. There is a photograph of a view of the beautiful harbor of Madeira from the balcony of Reid's in "Polar the Titanic Bear." Chuck and I both agree that Madeira is one of the most beautiful places we have visited.

In the Epilogue of "Polar the Titanic Bear" Leighton writes, "Sadly, the Titanic disaster was but a foreshadowing of deeper pain to come to the Speddens. Just three years after the sinking of the ship, nine-year-old Douglas was killed in a car accident near the family's summer camp in Maine. It was one of the first automobile accidents in the state. No one knows what happened to Polar the bear."

After reading volumes on The Titanic, I have created for myself a statement of inspiration. I say to myself whenever I need motivation, "I must rally like Rostron!"

In a later chapter I share Rudolph Gulliano's message about the importance of preparedness. There is no finer example of a hero in action in the Titanic saga than the preparedness of Captain Arthur Rostron, Captain of the Carpathia.

The Carpathia was a Cunard ship that was 58 miles away from the Titanic at the time of the sinking. The Carpathia was heading east to the Mediterranean. At the time the Titanic was sinking, Carpathia's wireless operator, 21-year-old Harold T. Cottam's shift was over. He had worked almost 17 hours and was preparing for bed. He kept his headphones on because he was hoping to get a reply to a communication he had sent earlier to the liner Parisian. He didn't get a reply, but while he waited he retuned to the Cape Cod frequency and picked up several messages intended for the Titanic. He jotted down the messages and planned to pass them to the Titanic's operator. Before turning in he had an impulse to send a fun message to The Titanic to see if he could get any response. He tapped out "MGY" which were Titanic's code letters.

Just as quickly as he sent the code letters, he got a quick response of "K" which means to proceed or "Go ahead." Cottman sent his fun message, "I say, old man. Do you know there is a batch of messages coming through for you from MCC (code for Cape Cod)?" The response came back: "MGY (Titanic) CDQ CDQ SOS SOS. Come at once. We have struck an iceberg. Position 41.46N, 50.14W. CDQ SOS!"

Cottman immediately conveyed the message to the officer of the evening watch and the two men rushed to Captain Rostron's quarters to report the fate of the Titanic.

What happens next is why I inspire myself with the words, "Rally like Rostron!" Captain Rostron not only rose to the challenge, but transcended the challenge. It is as if he had been preparing himself all his life for this night of incredible service of rescuing the passengers of the Titanic.

He immediately set Carpathia on her new course to assist the Titanic's passengers. He began issuing orders to prepare the ship for the receiving of the survivors of the Titanic. He made certain that none of the Carpathia's passengers knew of the drama until it had been completed. All assignments of preparedness were to be fulfilled in silence; any passengers of the Carpathia that were seen walking around were asked to return to their cabins and stay put.

In "1912 Facts About Titanic" author Lee W. Merideth compiled this list of Captain Rostron's orders: "Every crewman was to report to duty at his normal duty station, and each was to be fed and served all the hot coffee he wanted to help keep him awake and warm. Crew members from the steward's department were to gather up all of the blankets, towels and extra crew's clothing to hand out to survivors and to prepare all the public areas with beds. The cooks were to prepare hot coffee and food for survivors. The Third Class passengers were to be placed into one section of the Third Class area so that there would be room for Titanic's survivors. All empty cabins and all officers' cabins, including Rostron's, were to be readied. All cabins with passengers but with empty beds were to be identified so that the empties could be utilized. There were three ship's doctors on board Carpathia, an Englishman, an Italian and Hungarian. Each was told to prepare for the arrival of the survivors, one doctor for the First, Second and Third Class passengers. After the lifeboats were readied, all gangway doors were opened and all stewards, pursers and extra crewmen were to remain by them to help people onto the ship. At each gangway, the crew slung a chair there which could be lowered so that survivors could sit in it while being lifted onto the ship. The crew readied canvas bags and cargo nets to be used to haul people aboard. Ladders for survivors to climb up on and powerful lights were hung over the sides of the ship. Oil buckets were lined up at the forward toilets. If the seas were rough, oil would be poured into the toilets and dumped into the water to calm the water. When Carpathia passengers noticed a change in direction for their ship, stewards were placed in every corridor to answer questions without giving out too much information and they asked all of the passengers to remain in their cabins and keep the corridors clear."

All of the Captain's meticulous orders were being fulfilled as the ship steamed forward to its rescue mission and while doing so it passed many icebergs. Captain Rostron later commented, "When day broke, and I saw the ice I had steamed through during the night, I shuddered, and could only think that some other Hand than mine was on the helm during the night." Just as Rudy Guilliani stated when confronted with the tragedy of 9/11, you do what you have vigorously prepared yourself to do, and trust God will take care of the rest.

When the Titanic survivors were on board, Captain Rostron arranged for an Episcopal pastor to lead passengers of both the Titanic and Carpathia in a service to remember the dead and thank God for the lives of those rescued.

In purchasing Titanic books on EBAY, I made friends with Patty Miller. Patty's email ID is "luvthecarpathia." I inquired about her unique email ID and what inspired her to choose the name. Patty sent me the following answer:

"The name luvthecarpathia comes from the rescuer ship of the Titanic. But my email should have been luvtheRostron, because I admired this man (Captain of the Carpathia), who was humble, a lover of God and because of his bravery in rescuing the Titanic survivors. Rostron was an unassuming man who had such a love of God, he prayed over the victims, before returning the survivors to New York. He also did not, except at the Senate Hearings of the Titanic tragedy, speak of the Titanic sinking in order to become famous or make money. I have for years been intrigued with the Titanic, because of the harsh conditions to which the survivors and victims were subjected to. But until I started searching, out of curiosity to begin with, for what Arthur Rostron had to say, I really did not start accumulating Titanic books. I have always admired and respected the silent heroes, the people who do or did things which have no monetary gain. I admire people who help others with no motivation in their hearts, except that they are caring people.

And I am intrigued with the Titanic story, because of all the silent heroes, the men who gave up their lives, the women who helped others, the Carpathia passengers who gave up what little they had for the comfort of the Titanic survivors. This speaks to me, because I so wish the world today was not so hurried, that people would take time to help the more unfortunate. I try to do what I can to help people who don't have what I have.

Plus, I am intrigued by the Titanic, because the victims not only had to deal with the harsh ocean, but the temperature as well. I, too, at one time was freezing in the cold wet weather and even as the years pass, my heart goes out to the suffering those people went through." Patty is someone who has a heart connection with the Angels of the Deep, Guardians of the Titanic.

In Ghosts of the Abyss, Don Lynch makes a comment that one of the reasons we are intrigued with the story is that we wonder if we had been on board, and realized our life consisted of only 2-1/2 more hours, how would we live those last hours?

Just as we witnessed in 9/11, the best of humanity rises up in an emergency. On the Titanic, the engineers maintained their posts fueling the generators in order to keep the lights on to the very end. They could have tried to save themselves; however, they knowingly gave up their lives in an attempt to do what they could to help save the lives of others. The thirty-four engineers and assistant engineers were released from duty by Chief Engineer Bell. There would still have been time for them to reach the upper decks and attempt to save themselves. Not one man left the engine room. Can you imagine when this group of courageous men were escorted by the angels to meet St. Peter at the pearly gates, the welcoming heaven gave to them for their selfless sacrifice to keep the lights on for others?! There probably was a heavenly ticker tape parade! Here on earth, His Majesty King George V decreed British marine engineers would wear their rank insignia on a royal purple background in honor of the engineers of the Titanic who made the choice that the Titanic would have power and lights to the very end.

In the Broadway show "Titanic: A New Musical" (music and lyrics by Maury Yeston), the character of Thomas Andrews sings the song, "In Every Age" in which he expresses, "Our task was to dream upon and then create a floating city!...floating city!...A human metropolis...a complete civilization. Sleek! And fast! At once a poem and the perfection of physical engineering." Though lives were lost, and the Titanic was a tragedy of epic proportions, the dream was not lost. The vision of a floating city can be found in the aspirations of our space program. I believe the Titanic was a stepping stone to the space station, and the visions we hold of floating cities in space.

The community of Pompeii, once lost, was found and unearthed from beneath the ashes. We have learned so much from the recovery efforts that when you visit Pompeii you step back into history. The remains of the floating community of the Titanic was lost two miles beneath the ocean and we only have twenty years or so until the ocean will totally eliminate all trace of her for eternity. We learn about ourselves when we delve deeply into the lives of people of the earth who lived before us because we are all connected. In the words of Chief Seattle, "Man did not weave the web of life, he is merely a strand in it." And the strand of our lives in the here and now is connected to the strands of lives of the past. Through research we expand our consciousness of our connectedness with those who lived before, those who live now and those who will live in the future. Whenever the past is rediscovered, I truly believe it helps us to have a better understanding of our lives in the present. Lawrence Beesley, a Titanic survivor, wrote in The Loss of the SS Titanic, "Our legacy from the wreck, our debt to those who were lost with her, is to see, as far as in us lies, that such things are impossible ever again." I believe our debt is never to forget in our hearts and minds all the heroes and heroines who have gone before us on the earth. By remembering them and learning about them in researching their lives of greatness with the inspiration of the Angels of the Deep, we instill within ourselves a respect for courageous, unselfish choices.

There is a spirit to the Titanic and the Angels of the Deep are its guardians. The spirit called to all those who embarked on the Titanic for her maiden voyage. The spirit continues to call to the hearts of so many people, including myself, and inspires us to learn about the ship, its crew, passengers, life on board, final hours and more. It calls us to watch movies, visit exhibitions, and join historical societies.

Part of my service with the Angels of the Deep is to compile stories on how the spirit of the Titanic touches people's lives, such as the story shared by Patty. Perhaps you are someone who has been touched by the Angels of the Deep and feel a special heart connection to the Titanic. If you are willing to have your story included in my book, which has the working title of Angels of the Deep – Guardians of the Titanic, please feel free to send me your story.

In my research I have found people who believe that they lived a past life as a passenger on board the Titanic. One such individual is Monica O'Hara-Keeton, who under hypnotic regression recalled being Lucy Latimar. I enjoyed reading this book because of the incredible detective work Monica did. I'm certain the Angels of the Deep inspired her to follow the clues that were given to her in hypnotic regression. In her book, I Died on the Titanic, Monica writes, "While she (Lucy) never actually named Titanic as the ship on which she was sailing to America, the dates and all the circumstances of the regression made it impossible to be any other vessel. The extreme cold and the shivering which she – I – felt when regressed to the night of April 14/15, 1912 were VERY real." Lucy shares her final moments: "The freezing black water had now reached my knees, my thighs, my chest. Breathing was becoming increasingly difficult as my lungs filled with water. It was rising at a terrifying rate…reaching my neck, my mouth, my nose, until I was gasping for breath. It was horrendous. Just when I thought I could take no more, fate stepped in, as I believe she frequently does on such occasions. At that very moment, I noticed what I can only describe as a beautiful fairy castle ahead. Tall, sparkling like crystal, it beckoned to me." As I read the words "fate stepped in," I felt a peacefulness come over me that God's angels that are with us at the time of our death had been there for Lucy. What had been a "horrendous" scene just a moment before, was now replaced by "a beautiful fairy castle" where her true love, who also died on the Titanic, was waiting for her.

The theory that truth is oftentimes stranger than fiction can be applied to the Titanic and one of its passengers, W. T. Stead. I was especially interested in Stead when I learned that he was on his way to America to speak about peace at a conference. In Waiting for Orders, The Story of Alexander James Littlejohn, Steward to W.T. Stead told by his grandson, Philip Littlejohn, Philip writes: "Stead was a powerful figure; on his way to America, to address a meeting on world peace alongside President Taft of the U.S.A., when he lost his life on the Titanic. He talked with world leaders, such as the Tsar of Russia, and through journalism sought to influence and promote the cause of world peace." As an "earthangel4peace," I wondered if the Angels of the Deep were inspiring me to learn more about this fellow peacemaker and so I delved deeper.

Stead was a well-known journalist and editor and had written a story in 1882 about the sinking of an ocean liner in the mid-Atlantic. An iceberg was the cause of the sinking. He wrote the story 33 years before his fateful passage on the Titanic. In the 1880's Stead also wrote an article for a magazine called the Pall Mall Gazette about a ship that sank in the mid-Atlantic and he ends the article with a warning. "This is exactly what might take place and what will take place, if liners are sent to sea short of boats." He continued to promote this warning and even gave a lecture in 1910 in London in which he spoke of the importance of having enough lifeboats on ocean liners to safely protect the number of passengers on board. In this lecture he pictured himself in a shipwreck resulting in his being in the ocean, calling for help. In his imagination a corner had been turned, and the script now included him as the victim.

Obviously something within Stead caused him to be preoccupied with the ocean and the liners that sailed upon the oceans as well as the danger proposed when there aren't enough lifeboats on board a ship. In 1892 an article he authored in Review of Reviews was again the story of a fictional shipwreck. The story tells of a ship that collides with an iceberg. Only one passenger survives and is rescued by a White Star liner called the Majestic. At the time he wrote the article, there was a ship sailing the oceans called the Majestic. Her captain was Edward J. Smith, the would-be captain of the Titanic.

Stead was interested in the world of spiritualism and believed in being able to communicate with people in heaven. Following his death, numerous mediums received messages from Stead. I didn't find it surprising that a man who had spent a good part of his life making contact with people on "the other side" would be continuing the communication when he himself was on "the other side."

I especially loved Philip's story about Mrs. Jean Cambridge, who in 1975 was the owner of Holly Bush House, which formerly was Stead's home on Hayling Island in the United Kingdom. Mrs. Cambridge "went into one of the upstairs bedrooms and discovered a large wet patch on the carpet. Nothing had been split, there were no leaks, and the room felt very cold. There was nothing to explain where the water had come from…It was just as if a wet, dripping figure had stood at the spot for some time."

Stead wasn't the only author to write a story that mysteriously paralleled the Titanic tragedy. Morgan Robertson, an American author, wrote a novel in 1898 about the sinking of a great liner, which he named TITAN. He begins Chapter I with, "She was the largest craft afloat and the greatest of the works of men. In her construction and maintenance were involved every science, profession and trade known to civilization." The novel's tragedy unfolds with the first sentence of Chapter VII: "Seventy-five thousand tons – deadweight – rushing through the fog at the rate of fifty feet a second…hurled itself at an iceberg…nearly 3,000 voices, raised in agonized screams." I have always believed that there really is no such thing as coincidence; it is merely God working anonymously. My interest in connections with the world of the psychics and the Titanic would lead me to the discovery of the book <u>The Titanic – The Psychic and the Sea</u> by Rustie Brown. Ms. Brown wrote this book after ten years of researching extensively the stories of premonitions, "coincidences", and psychic events around the tragedy. I discovered a copy of the book being offered on Ebay. I was very excited because for a few days my bid was the only bid offered. It seemed as if this book would soon be on its way to me. Then just minutes before the end of the auction, a skilled bidder came in with a bid a dollar higher than mine and the book was his. When I got notification that I had been outbid, I knew the auction was closed. I wanted so much to read the book. I was a little stunned by the "outbidding" until the Angels of the Deep inspired me with these words: "check out used and out of print books." Immediately I went to Barnes and Noble's website and clicked on their "used and out of print books" department. I found the book offered for sale at amazingly the same price I had bid on EBAY. I bought the book and waited for its arrival at Angel Heights. I was very anxious and thought to myself that I wish books could be teleported because I wanted it sooner than later; in fact, I wanted it NOW; I was that anxious to read it.

The evening following the purchase of the book on-line, I was teaching my spiritual development weekly class and a dear angel friend, Anne Collins walks into the gathering holding a book. She stops in front of me and says, "I shared with my sister your research interest in the Titanic. My sister went to her book shelf and asked me to show you her most prized possession. It's an autographed copy of <u>The Titanic – the Psychic and the Sea</u> signed by the author Rustie Brown." I held the book with the utmost respect and said, "Tell her THANK YOU! I am waiting for my own copy, but if she doesn't mind I would LOVE to start reading her copy tonight." Anne indicated that her sister really want me to keep the book as long as I needed to for my research. That evening I read the book cover to cover, and again the next day. Finally my own copy showed up at my doorstep, and I gave Anne the book to return back to her sister wrapped in my heartfelt thanksgiving of being an answered prayer to my impatience, "I want it NOW!"

I knew the book, even before reading it, was going to be filled with research on the weaving of the energies of the paranormal into the story of the Titanic. I wasn't disappointed; in fact the book led me to other books written about the Titanic viewed from the concept of a "bigger picture" at play. Ms. Brown's book led me to Alan Vaughan's Patterns of Prophecy in which he states, "The coincidences or synchronicities that link our lives are manifestations of a universe so highly organized that literally nothing happens by chance. Like some incomprehensibly complex clockwork, the universe unfolds in time and space its inner plan that does not allow for accidents...Chance is but an illusion fostered by our incomplete knowledge of the universe's greater plan."

Daniel Allen Butler includes in his book Unsinkable a poem by Thomas Hardy, "The Convergence of the Twain," from Collected Poems. Hardy was a good friend of William T. Stead. The poem eloquently defines the presence of God as the "Spinner of the Years" in the convergence of the Titanic and the iceberg:

"The Convergence of the Twain"

In a solitude of the sea
Deep from human vanity
And the Pride of Life that planned her, stilly couches her.
Steel chambers, late the pyres
Of her salamandrine fires,
Cold currents third, and turn to rhythmic tidal lyres.
Over the mirrors meant
To glass the opulent
The sea worm crawls – grotesque, slimed, dumb, indifferent
Jewels in joy designed
To ravish the sensuous mind
Lie lightless, all their sparkles bleared and black and blind.
Dim moon-eyed fishes near
Gaze at the gilded gear
And query, "What does this vaingloriousness down here?"...

Well: while was fashioning
This creature of cleaving wing,
The Immanent Will that stirs and urges everything.
Prepared a sinister mate
For her – so gaily great
A Shape of Ice, for the time far and dissociate.
And as the smart ship grew,
In stature, grace and hue,
In shadowy silent distance grew the Iceberg, too.
Alien they seemed to be:
No mortal eye could see
The intimate welding of their later history.
Or sign that they were bent
On paths coincident
Of being anon twin halves of one august event.
Till the Spinner of the Years
Said "Now!" and each one hears,
And consummation comes, and jars two hemispheres."

The first time I read this poem, it reminded me of my experience at 11 years old when I unknowingly was part of the jarring of two hemispheres – my world and the world of the angels. I would later use King Arthur's words from the movie Camelot, "I stumbled upon my own destiny" to describe my first encounter with my guardian angel.

In some way when the Titanic collided with the iceberg, it was colliding with its destiny. I believe the jarring of two hemispheres continues as the Angels of the Deep – Guardians of the Titanic touch people's lives with their inspirational energies and jar people to merge their world of the now with the hemisphere or world of the Titanic. It is Titanic's destiny to be remembered.

My research has now led me to explore the story as told by the survivors' survivors. I'll See You in New York and Raised on the Titanic – An Autobiography were authored by David Haisman, who heard the Titanic story told to him on numerous occasions by his mother, who, at the age of 15, survived the disaster. Edith Haisman was old enough to have total recall of the voyage and tragedy. Prior to her death in 1997, and more than 80 years after her father died in the Titanic disaster, Edith Haisman was presented with the gold watch her father was wearing when the ship went down. Mrs. Haisman, 97, was 15 when she and her mother were put in a lifeboat by her father with the words: *"I'll see you in New York."* She never saw him again. A company salvaging the wreck of the ship on the bed of the

Atlantic presented her with the blackened watch her father had worn on a gold chain. At the time of the presentation, frail and in a wheelchair, Haisman recalled the horror when the Titanic sank off Newfoundland in 1912 with the loss of 1,500 lives after hitting an iceberg on her maiden voyage from Southampton. Her father, Thomas William Solomon Brown, had been taking his family to Seattle to start a hotel business. Haisman said: *"I remember everything and it was terrible."* She said that as her lifeboat pulled away she could hear cries from people left on the ship and in the water. *"There were lots of bodies floating. We kept on rescuing people and trying to cover them up against the cold. We were in the lifeboat nine hours."* She later married an architectural engineer in South Africa and they had 10 children. Her family said the watch would probably go to a museum in Southampton.

As I read David's book, I'll See You in New York, I remembered a documentary I had seen, titled "Child's Eyes: September 11, 2001". Children of various ages, religions and backgrounds shared their thoughts on the national tragedy. One little boy named Yedidya, who is 7 years old, said "Everybody who was killed here had a family. Every family who had a person that was killed lost a loved one…a loved one." The sinking of the Titanic and the loss of lives was one of the worst disasters in the 20th century. The attack on the World Trade Center and loss of lives on 9/11/01 was a horrific national tragedy of the 21st century. One thing they have in common is that loved ones were lost.

In that same documentary a young 7-year-old girl named Katy shared the following, "This is for some of the kids who lost family in the World Trade Center. I know mostly how you feel. Because I lost my dad. The few days after my dad died I didn't play. I just sat at the bottom of the step and I just sat there thinking about my dad. We had lots in common. We both liked the smell of marigolds. He's in heaven. But sometimes I think he is having a bad time and is missing me and I think he wants to be down here. When you have a worry, you take two pieces of clay and you roll them in a ball together. (She then takes a toothpick and makes a hole in the center of the ball.) And then see how there is this in the inside (she shows the opening made by the toothpick). Then say your worry into the center (she whispers her worry into the center of the bead). My worry goes into the bead. And when you bake it, it means the worry is stuck in there. Some times the worry does leak out but….rarely. Now I can talk about my dad, but it is always going to be very hard. It is like a mountain of sadness and then after lots and lots of years it gets smaller and smaller and smaller until it all evens out. But it's still like a little bump…I still have that bump and it will probably stay there for the rest of my life."

I wrote an email to David Haisman honoring his service of keeping the memory alive of those Titanic passengers who lost their lives and the survivors and their incredible stories. David lectures worldwide and is always willing to tell his mother's story and answer all questions posed to him about the Titanic. After reading his books, I asked him if there was anything else, after publication of his books, that he wanted to add. As I read his reply, I know that his mother, Edith, in heaven was beaming with pride and love.

"There is much more one can write about such a strong and loving woman than in my books. As the youngest of ten children, I was always amazed throughout my lifetime at the way she favored none of us children more than the other. When in company, right up until the time she passed away, I was always referred to as "her baby", knowing how much I hated it as a young person and illustrating her sense of humor.

"Throughout the war years she worked extremely hard, baking bread, scrubbing floors and starching and sewing umpteen shirts and socks and never complaining. In the late afternoon, she would finish her chores, go upstairs to wash and change in order to look fresh and clean for my father when he came home from work.

"She went to a convent as a young girl and was brought up as a lady and never forgot it throughout her lifetime. Being brought up in the Victorian style, she was strict with her children but we knew she loved each and every one of us. She made my father go to night school at the age of 26 to further his career. One could go on, but quite simply, she was a wonderful woman and I look upon e-mails such as yours as a continuing tribute to her. Thank you once again for your interest, Yours Sincerely, David Haisman."

I am someone who promotes the message that we are all members of a "family of God." I think when a tragedy occurs where there is a loss of life, a part of us is saddened that these individuals were lost so soon that we never had the chance or opportunity to know them. I think that stirs inside of us a burning desire to read about them, learn about and remember them.

After the sinking of the Titanic, changes were made in an attempt to insure that such a tragedy never occurred again, such as laws that prohibited ocean liners from traveling where there were icebergs, and of course the absolute necessity of having lifeboats enough for all passengers and crew on board. Yet no matter what changes we make after hard lessons are learned through tragedy, there is one lesson that rings true through all of life's experiences. We never know when our last day on earth is going to be. It's important to make time now to tell our family members and friends that we love them. It's important to live each moment abundantly and joyously.

As I shared in DUI, I serve with the Angels of Transition by reading the daily obituaries and praying for all those who have died. My prayer is that they are one with God's peace as they transition from earth to heaven. A few weeks ago I opened the obituary page of The Baltimore Sun and saw the incredibly handsome smiling face of Patrick J. LaMoure. He was a trial lawyer from the US Department of Veterans Affairs who counseled injured victims and their families after the September 11, 2001 terrorist attacks. He died of colon cancer at the age of 40 years old. He was a judge advocate in the U.S. Army Reserve, where he held the rank of major. It was through the Reserve that he advised critically wounded September 11th Pentagon victims on such legal matters as wills and powers of attorney. "There were cases where people were severely burned, and he had to take care of their legal and business affairs," said his father, Thomas E. LaMoure. "There were families in a state of shock. There were people not knowing whether they were going to live or die," said Mr. LaMoure's wife.

As I continued to read the obituary I came across a comment by Elisabeth W. Brake, a family friend: "Pat didn't just see the glass half-full. For him, it was Waterford crystal and full of champagne. He truly believed good things were in store."

I have often heard the question asked, "Do you look at your life as a glass that is half-empty or half-full?" Yet, Elisabeth's remark about Patrick gave a whole new option in answering this question. Rather than half-empty or half-full, see your life, as Patrick did, as a glass that is of the finest crystal, filled to the brim and overflowing with goodness and the joyous energy of celebrating life with your family and friends. I have a sensing that Patrick is in heaven being toasted by the angels at a celebration where he is the guest of honor. The celebration is for his life, though only 40 short years, was well-lived here on earth.

Chapter 4

SAINTS AND ANGELS

Years ago, when I visited my friend Mary Jane Oref in Arizona, she gifted me a private reading with a woman who used the most amazing spiritual tool to assist her in the reading. This woman had a large array of antique holy cards. Holy cards are small cards that depict a saint on the front of the card, usually with a beautiful prayer asking for assistance from the saint on the back of the card. I remember to this day being more interested in who these people were on the cards than the messages she was giving to me. I truly felt that this was a divine appointment in my life; it was as if the angels were saying to me, "Jayne, get to know the saints. Commune with the saints."

As a result of that life-changing reading, I began a quest of not only accumulating holy cards but also learning about the saints. This quest has introduced me to the Catholic saints as well as saints of other religions. One humorous incident regarding my learning more about the Catholic saints through holy cards occurred while I was fulfilling an angelic assignment in Portland, Oregon. I stayed in the home of Hilda Kemp, a dear woman whom I know truly brightened heaven with her presence when she died a few years ago. Hilda's home was within walking distance of The Grotto in Portland, Oregon, a beautiful sixty-two acre Catholic Shrine and botanical garden maintained by the Friars of the Order of Servants of Mary.

Every morning for twenty-one days I would go to the Grotto for prayer and meditation. On my way back, I would stop at the shrine's gift shop and spend some time looking at their incredible display of holy cards. I would read the cards and often buy cards that I didn't have. I was enchanted with the lives of the saints. I felt as if I was looking at family photographs when I looked at the holy cards. I remember one day asking the clerk if she had a card for a particular saint. I hadn't been able to find the card in the display. I didn't realize that the store staff had recognized my passion for the saints by my daily ritual of looking at the display. However, I soon learned when she laughed and said to me, "You would know better than us!" I smiled and laughed when I replied, "I guess you're right. I do have these memorized."

As I shared in Driving Under the Influence of Angels, I have a heart-shaped basket in which I keep my holy cards honoring saints. Whenever I am working on a project with the angels, I will often reach into the basket while asking, "Who serves with me?" The card that I draw is a message from God of who will be assisting me in fulfilling the angelic assignment. Through this simple ritual I have come to know the saints as precious friends. I truly feel God wants me to spread the message that not only do we have the angels supporting us in our daily lives, but we have the saints helping us, also.

I want to share the blessing that Ebay, the Internet auction site, has become in my life. Chuck lovingly refers to me as the Queen of Ebay. Many times families who are selling estate items will offer someone's collection of holy cards. I love watching for these because the energy of love for the saints that the person who once owned these cards had radiates from the cards and is truly inspiring. It's also wonderful knowing that person is now residing with the saints. I feel blessed to be guardian of their holy cards which I purchase and often pass on to someone whom I am inspired to educate about a particular saint through a message of inspiration from that saint. A wonderful book filled with inspirational messages from the saints is Rosemary Ellen Guiley's The Quotable Saint – Words of Wisdom from Thomas Aquinas to Zita.

In addition to learning about saints through holy cards, I also love to learn by visiting shrines that honor saints. My husband, Charles, is Jewish. He is also truly an interfaith person because he has so willingly agreed to go to all the shrines, cathedrals and churches that I have felt drawn to explore in our travels. Chuck jokes that he has seen the inside of more cathedrals than any other Jewish person on earth. I think he's right. Additionally he said he's going to get a bumper sticker that reads: We brake for shrines. I am so blessed as Chuck does this because he knows of my love of the saints and angels and it makes him happy to see me so joyous. Many of my friends refer to my husband as St. Charles because of the many ways he supports my service with the angels.

When Chuck and I visited Italy, because there were so many sacred places that the angels wanted me to experience personally, I hired a driver to literally drive us up to each church and wait for us to come out and take us to the next sight. Our driver was Pepe and he was truly hand picked by the angels because he had a love of the angels and saints equal to mine. I remember one afternoon we had just finished a whirlwind tour of churches in Rome and while inside one of the churches, I approached Chuck, who was seated chatting with two American women he had just met inside the church. As I came closer to Chuck I heard him say, "Would you believe this is my sixth church today?!" I smiled and walked outside to Pepe and said, "This will be a wrap for today." Like I said, Chuck is truly a saint when it comes to his support of my research and angelic assignments.

During the years before I met Chuck and I was totally on my own, I found comfort in the support of St. Joseph. Joseph was the husband of Mary, mother of Jesus. I have a great devotion to St. Joseph. In my travels, whenever I would visit a Catholic church I would light a candle and say a prayer to St. Joseph that if it be God's will I would love to meet someone with St. Joseph's energy. He was a man who loved God, a hard worker, a good provider, and a wonderful family man in his caring for Mary and Jesus. I found a beautiful antique painting of St. Joseph holding Jesus in his arms and I placed that painting in a prominent place in my home. Whenever I would pass by it, this painting reminded me that if it be God's will I would meet a man who would be open and receptive to angels, just as St. Joseph was. After meeting and marrying Chuck in 1999, I still pay visits to St. Joseph's altar when I visit Catholic churches. I go there in thanksgiving to God for bringing me my own "St. Joseph".

I think it is no coincidence that the circle of Catholic nuns at The Spiritual Center in Windsor, New York that I have grown to love as angel sisters are, in fact, sisters of St. Joseph.

In Driving Under the Influence of Angels I shared how I traveled across the United States to serve in cooperation with the angels in weaving an energy grid to be of support to the children that were to be born. There have been books written about "indigo children" and "crystal children". In my service the angels referred to them as "angel babies". Wherever possible, I stayed in private homes of people who were willing to help me by providing me the use of one of their spare bedrooms. Whenever that wasn't possible, I would be open to God guiding me to where I was to stop for the evening. I remember when driving through Indiana, the angels said that I would be sleeping near a church. When I heard this message, I immediately thought to myself that perhaps an inexpensive hotel would be located next to a church. As I approached Ferdinand, Indiana I saw a sign promoting the Monastery

Immaculate Conception. The monastery is a place of residence for Ferdinand Benedictines, one of the largest Benedictine communities of women in the United States. The women were like angels to me. They made me feel so loved and welcomed during my stay at the monastery. They invited me to participate in their prayer services, which I did with great joy. I also had the opportunity to explore the monastery and was in awe of its architectural beauty.

The dome of the monastery chapel rises 87 feet from the floor and is 13-1/2 feet in diameter. Angels are depicted in the 16 stained glass windows around the dome. The angel motif is evident throughout the chapel, 94 angels at last count. Literature about the chapel includes the following quote, "The architect seems to have taken a cue from the Rule of St. Benedict, in which Benedict says, '...We gather to worship and praise God in unison with the angels.'" My entire adult life has been dedicated to spreading the message that we are here to serve God together with the angels. I felt as if I had come home at the Monastery Immaculate Conception.

There are two beautiful statues located in the vestibule to the sanctuary. On the right is the Pieta, which serves as a source of comfort to those who have lost a child or loved one. On the left is a statue depicting the death of St. Joseph in the presence of Jesus and Mary. It is the only statue I have ever seen of St. Joseph's death and upon seeing it for the first time I openly sobbed because it is so very beautiful and moving.

I encourage you to visit the monastery if only via the Internet. Their website is www.thedome.org and at this site you will find a "Tour du Jour" which is a different photograph of the monastery each day and "Fleur du Jour" which is a different photograph of a different flower or cluster of flowers each day from the thousands of flowers on the grounds of the monastery. You might want to also check out their online gift shop: For Heaven's Sake. These women are truly earth angels.

Sometimes I feel as if there is a homing device inside of me and it draws me to places where I find people who resonate on the same frequency I do when it comes to my love of the saints. One such place that I was drawn to is the Oratory of St. Joseph on Mount Royal, in Montreal and the person I resonate with is Blessed Brother Andre.

I "discovered" the Oratory when in Montreal to attend a conference organized by Drs. Marilyn and John Rossner, founders of the Institute of Integral Human Sciences. In-between conference activities I went exploring in Montreal and learned of this incredible shrine. The Oratory is the largest shrine in the world dedicated to St. Joseph. Equally incredible is the man who held the vision of the shrine – Brother Andre, a priest who became known as the miracle-worker of Mount Royal, the mount on which the shrine is built.

When you enter St. Joseph Oratory on the walls are hundreds of crutches and canes left behind by people who were cured. The Oratory was built because of the energy of Brother Andre. His great devotion to Saint Joseph inspired him to recommend to all those who were sick and came to him for help to enlist the support of St. Joseph. As the crutches and canes attest, many people were healed. Because he wanted to honor St. Joseph, Brother Andre began the construction of a small chapel in 1904. It quickly became too small and in 1924 the construction of the basilica began and was completed in 1967. When Brother Andre died on January 6, 1937, over a million people filed before his coffin. In the heart of the Oratory is a vessel where the heart of Brother Andre is preserved.

Two books I recommend for those who wish to explore monasteries are: A Guide to Monastic Guest Houses by Robert J. Regalbuto and also Sanctuaries: A Guide to Lodgings in Monasteries, Abbeys and Retreats by Jack and Marcia Kelly. Sanctuaries includes listings for numerous faiths.

In a later chapter I am going to share how the icon angels came into my life and the inspirational and devotional blessings that icons bring to our lives. In my travels with the angels I discovered a treasure at Mont Angel Abbey located in Mount Angel, Oregon There I found a wonderful icon gallery with icons written by Br. Claude Lane, O.S.B. Brother Claude Lane is a member of Mount Angel, a community of Benedictine monks, founded in 1882 from the Abbey of Engelberg, Switzerland. I might also add that if you visit Mont Angel Abbey be sure to visit the gift shop where you might find an Engelbear for sale! Engelbears are bears dressed like monks.

The Spiritual Center in Windsor, New York, which is maintained by the Sisters of St. Joseph, is also available for individual and group retreats. About four to five weekends each summer I visit The Spiritual Center to co-teach spiritual development weekends with Sister Paula Matthew. I love The Spiritual Center experience. There's the art gallery which features Paula's glorious wood carvings where you can meditate with the inspirational art; the peaceful energies of the land; the fabulous bodywork sessions that are available, i.e. massage, reflexology, facials, etc.; and the nurturance provided by the sisters in the meals they prepare and prayer support they provide. Paula is opening an art studio where she will be giving private carving lessons that will be tied into spiritual development, i.e. students will be taught how to carve an altar for their own private use in their home. It's important to allow ourselves sacred time experienced in sacred space. I believe we all should gift ourselves at least one retreat weekend a year, if not more. As an added bonus Transfiguration Benedictine Monastery is across the street with a chapel that has extraordinary icons. There is a golf course adjacent to the property of the monastery. If one of the golf balls stray into the border of the monastery, they are cleaned, put into egg cartons and sold to the world labeled "Holy in One."

I have not been alone in my pursuit in getting to know the saints up close and personal. My dear girlfriend, Celeste McDonald, has joined me on many of my angel tours of the world. Years ago when I led a women's retreat at Walt Blatt's retreat home, Leaf Lake Lodge, located in West Virginia, I was inspired by the angels to offer the weekend to 12 ladies only. The weekend provided the participants an opportunity to commune with the angels and in particular the archangels. I didn't know the women who signed up for that retreat prior to meeting them that weekend; however, the friendships and funship that evolved inspired me to call the ladies the Angelic Sisterhood. There would be other such weekends that followed at Leaf Lake Lodge with many of the same original angel sisters participating. Sometimes things we do, believing we are the ones offering the service, result in God setting us up to be served. I believe this about the Angelic Sisterhood because so many of these great women have remained in my life as dear friends including Sue Ernst, Sandy Milczarek, Judy Stipanovich, Lucky Sweeny and Martha Vineyard.

One of the dearest friends is Celeste. Prior to meeting Celeste at a retreat weekend, I was told by the angels that someone special would be coming and I would know this person was special to me because she had a message for me regarding Our Lady of Knock. At that time the angels were beginning to feed me clues about a group tour I was to organize to Ireland and one of the sights would be Knock Shrine.

During one of the free times during the retreat, Celeste and I found ourselves talking together and immediately knew we were "two peas in a pod" when it came to Jesus, angels, saints, the Madonna and so on. We were finishing each other's sentences. I shared inspirations the angels were giving me, in particular the vision of going to Ireland. Upon hearing this, Celeste showed me a necklace she wore about her neck with what appeared to be a multitude of holy medals. As she unfastened the chain and took off one particular medal she said, "I have a holy medal I want to give you. It's a blessed medal of Our Lady of Knock." In 2001, many years after our first meeting in West Virginia, Celeste would join me when I took a group on a spiritual tour of Ireland. That tour was the result of an angelic inspiration that I was to bring a group to Our Lady of Knock on Mother's Day in May, 2001. Our tour guide nicknamed our angel group "The Irish Green Angels."

The tour of Ireland was filled with blessings from God and reminders that God knows what we need long before we know we need it. As I stated,

I was told that the tour was to be developed around the group arriving at Our Lady of Knock Shrine on Mother's Day 2001 to receive a blessing from the Holy Mother. I followed the inspiration I was given. Another precious woman on the Irish tour who was part of the Angelic Sisterhood that originated back in West Virginia is Sharon Shreve. In November of 1999 Sharon's beautiful daughter Melissa was murdered. Sharon's incredible faith helped her somehow cope with this horrible tragedy. Mother's Day 2001 fell on Melissa's birthday, a fact I didn't know until Sharon told me. I know the angels helped to orchestrate this trip to be a blessing of comfort to Sharon. Who better than the Blessed Mother to comfort someone who has lost a child?

I have had amazing experiences with the saints on my angelic tours. Before leaving for Ireland the angels gave me the inspiration that the tour should be called "The Grace Tour." When we arrived at Our Lady of Knock shrine, our guide met us and extended her hand and said, "Hello, I am Grace." Prior to going to Ireland, I always thought of popular Irish names for women as being Kate and Mary, for example. It seemed on our trip, everyone was named Grace. Additionally, the first day of our trip to Ireland our bus driver who knew nothing of The Grace Tour selected a roadside restaurant for us to dine at which just happened to be called "Grace's".

While we were in Ireland the relics of St. Therese were being shown throughout the country. The tour of the relics was called "The Grace Tour." We did not know that ahead of time. Celeste and I are lovers of religious relics. Celeste and I found out when we were visiting a Catholic church in Dublin via a large banner outside the church that the relics of St. Therese would be at this particular church the following week. Because of our devotion to St. Therese, known as the Little Flower, we couldn't believe we were a week early. We stood outside of the church and expressed our sorrow that we were a week too early to see the precious relics. Just then a man came up to us and said simply, "She's here." We asked in unison, "Who's here?" He said, "St. Therese's relics are here in Dublin down the street at St. Therese Church." Our feet had wings as we ran several blocks to this church. As we walked into the church a monk wearing the typical brown robe approached us and said, "She's been waiting for you." Now it may be that he made that statement to everyone who came through the door to see the relics of St. Therese; however, Celeste and I felt especially blessed by his kind words.

Another angelic sister is Barbara Daire who, too, has been blessed by the presence of the saints in her life. One day I received the following email from Barbara:

I was in court today, Jayne, with a Band of Justice Angels. My attorney told me the Judge to whom I presented my case for an ex parte order last week told him I presented my case well and I was very organized. Today, frankly, I felt most of the time I was going to throw up, since my "ex" was there. Bill (Barbara's husband) was a witness and my attorney presented my case with the journal, tape recordings and police reports. The Judge ordered a Protective Order for a year, the longest possible time. He declared that the "ex" has "massive anger management issues" and indicated that I had not only proven my case with clear and convincing evidence, I had cleared the hurdle of "beyond a reasonable doubt." There was even an angelic Marshall who kept the "ex" from harassing me, which he tried to do as soon as the Judge left the courtroom, and who warned me to be very careful. As I sat on the witness stand for part of the time during this hour and a half trial, I noticed the light fixture above the tables where counsel sits. There was a huge, round, light fixture, larger across than a person, with a smaller round "hub" in the center and "spokes" going out of the hub. At one point, when I was faltering a bit on the stand with the "ex" staring me down, I saw the Wheel of Light and felt the presence of beloved St. Catherine of Alexandria. I believe you told me many months ago it was meant that I would walk into a court and hand justice to my "ex". I felt much lighter. I give thanks to God for my Divine Helpers who assisted me in crossing the bridge I crossed today."

Catherine was a beautiful princess who lived in Alexandria and converted to Christianity after having a vision of the Blessed Mother and Baby Jesus. Catherine was a woman who declared her faith openly and spoke out against Emperor Maximinus who was persecuting Christians. Maximinus gathered fifty philosophers together in an attempt to change her beliefs. She converted all fifty to Christianity. They were executed because of this conversion. Because she rejected Emperor Maximinus' attempts at seduction, she was thrown into jail. She was condemned to death, to be placed on a wheel spiked with blades. When she was placed on the wheel, the wheel exploded and flew into many pieces. The pieces killed her executioner and many spectators who came to watch her die. She later died when beheaded with a sword. Angels carried her body to Mount Sinai where later a church and monastery were built in her honor.

Saints have inspired me with their prayers, their teaching and preaching, with their service to God, and most importantly, with their being human. Many of the saints' lives ended in imprisonment and martyrdom. In reading these accounts, I always ask myself, "What would I have done?" Would I have been true to my faith in the face of a violent death?

When I was in Bosnia I visited the Franciscan monastery at Siroki Brijeg, about 45 minutes from Medjugorje. On February 7, 1945, Communist soldiers burned to death 30 Franciscans. Communist soldiers came to their monastery and said to the Franciscans that they would be allowed to live if they renounced Christ. One by one the Franciscans stepped forward and kissed a cross that the Communists had thrown down on the ground after ransacking the church and one by one they affirmed their eternal allegiance to Jesus. All of the men, ranging in age from those in their early 20's to the elderly, were thrown into a bunker together and burned to death. I walked down into the bunker and stood there thinking again of their last moments on earth. I had read of martyrs who died hundreds of years ago. This was martyrdom that occurred just three years before I was born. While standing there, the angels brought into my awareness a book I had just recently discovered. It is called The Cloud of Unknowing. This book on contemplation was written by an unknown author in the second half of the 14th century. The "cloud" refers to that which is within each of us that unites us to God. In my reading of this book I remembered my pondering upon the thought that those who hurt and mistreat us are to be regarded as "best and special friends" because their actions are catalysts that cause responses in us that afford us the opportunity to be seen for what we truly are. I have to admit that when someone is unkind to me, my first thought is not usually, "Wow, you are such a special friend for saying that." Yet this book gave me an appreciation of Jesus' message of turning the other cheek. I knew that the Communists who put the priests to death would be accountable for their actions and their actions clearly let the world see "what they are". In short, evil. The Franciscans never took their eyes off Jesus. I feel certain that the bunker was filled with much more than fire and smoke. I feel that there were angels with these incredibly courageous and God-loving men, angels who guided them into the wide-open arms of Christ. The last moments of their lives may have been painful; however, they now live joyously with Christ for all eternity.

Since very early in the history of the Catholic church, the remains of a saint or holy person were called relics, a term that was derived from the Latin word for remains: Reliquiae. There are three classifications of relics. First class relics are parts of the bodies of saints. Second-class relics are objects sanctified by close contact with saints, such as articles of clothing, objects they used in their life, or in the case of a saint who was martyred, the instrument of their torture. Third-class relics are objects or cloths that touched either a first- or second-class relic.

The Bible describes in Acts 19:11-12 that God performed miracles at the hands of Paul. People who were sick and had cloths that touched the skin of Paul were cured or freed of evil energies.

The Old Testament tells that after Elisha died and was buried a dead man's body was thrown into the grave of Elisha. When the body came in contact with the bones of Elisha, the dead man came back to life.

I do not worship relics. I love the energies that the relics radiate. These are people who absolutely adored God when they were alive. Every part of their being was energized with adoration for God. That same adoration radiates through their relics.

In October 1999 I led a group of ladies to France. The trip was planned around many of the places in France that made up the life experiences of St. Joan. Driving Under the Influence of Angels was dedicated to the spirit of St. Joan because her words "Forward With God" have been of great inspiration in my life.

Additionally we toured the childhood home of St. Therese, and the convent where she lived and the Basilica built in her honor. I will never forget being with all my angel sisters as we toured the Martin home in Lisieux. A gentle rain was falling outside. When we all stepped outside into the garden area, overhead the most magnificent rainbow appeared. We have been blessed with a rainbow appearing on each and every one of the angel tours. Additionally, while at the Carmel in Lisieux, France we got to see the gorgeous cascade of hair shorn from St. Therese when she entered the convent. Her father saved the hair. Interestingly, St. Therese thought of herself as a "new Joan of Arc," dedicated to the rescue not only of France but of the whole world. She declared: I was born for glory. She knew at an early age that she wanted to be a nun. She appeared before Bishop Hugonin of Bayeux to ask to be allowed into the convent. He asked her, "You are not yet fifteen and you wish this?" She replied, "I wished it since the dawn of reason."

We have her sister Pauline, who became prioress of Lisieux Carmel, to thank for ordering Therese to write her autobiography. As a result, the world is blessed with The Story of a Soul. The book was published in 1898, one year after Therese's death. The first printing of 2,000 copies swelled to millions of copies. The book has been translated into over 40 languages. Therese thought of herself as a little wild flower growing in a forest. The little flower that survives all the seasons and blooms and flourishes is a lot hardier and stronger than one might think from its appearance only.

Therese had a sensing that her service after death would extend beyond her autobiography. She remarked that she would be very unhappy in heaven if she couldn't continue to do little favors on earth for those she loved so much. She stated that upon her death her mission of "making God loved as I love him, to give my little way to souls" would begin… "Yes, I want to spend my time in heaven in doing good upon earth." She died at 7:20 pm on September 30th, 1897. Months before she wrote a letter in response to someone's concern and anxiety over her illness: "I am not dying. I am entering into life." St. Therese has taught me that when we close our eyes to earth, and open them to heaven, our service continues.

During the angel tours, Celeste and I get together in the evenings and look over the maps and guidebooks of the country we are visiting to make certain we haven't missed someplace that we can add on. Yes, I know. I am a bus driver's worst nightmare. A woman who adds on to the itinerary. Fortunately I have been blessed with the most divine bus drivers. France was no exception. Our driver and guide Francoise was sent from heaven.

As we traveled through France I kept hearing in my head the song sung by Andy Williams, "The Village of St. Bernadette." I've always loved that song. Because the song was so persistent, I knew there was an angel clue coming through to make a connection with the visionary of Lourdes. The Virgin Mary appeared to Bernadette a total of 18 times. I shared with Celeste that I believed St. Bernadette was calling to our group and we starting looking through the guidebooks for the St. Bernadette site we were being guided to add to the trip. Celeste and I realized we were going to be close to Nevers, France, something we hadn't realized before. When I received inspiration in planning the trip it was always around Joan of Arc and St. Therese. We met with Francois and asked if it would be at all possible to make a quick stop at Nevers. He was willing to do it but it would have to be a short visit and we had to sacrifice a lunch stop.

The next day the angel tour pulled into the chapel of the Convent of St. Gildard. Thirty years after her death the body of St. Bernadette was discovered incorrupt, during an official recognition of the relic as required for the Cause of Beatification. Incorrupt means that her body had not decomposed. In 1925, the body, with the face and hands now covered with wax, was moved to the chapel of St. Gildard. It can be seen in a glass-sided reliquary. Addtionally, at St. Gildard in Nevers you can see the armchair on which the saint sat at the time of her death along with many other items that belonged to Bernadette.

When in Assisi, Italy Chuck and I viewed a handwritten blessing to Brother Leo that St. Francis had penned as well as a habit worn by St. Francis. St. Francis is a saint known and loved by people of many faiths. It was such a precious experience to be able to see these items and to be able to walk in the fields that Francis had loved so much. Francis died on October 3, 1226 after uttering these words: "I have done what is mine to do;

may Christ teach you what is yours to do." What an empowering deathbed blessing for our lives. Do what is yours to do! Sometimes we get entangled in the thought that the doing, i.e. that which is ours to do, has to be accomplishing something big. In Jean Vanier's words, "We don't have to be heroes…We don't have to do big things, but to live each day in love, doing little things, learning to welcome one another, particularly the weak and those in pain."

As I mentioned, I absolutely adore Padre Pio and wrote about this precious man in Commune with the Angels. My heart was elated when he was canonized as a saint on June 13, 2002, which happened to be Father's Day. A behind the scenes saint in Padre's life was Mary Pyle. Mary was born in Morristown, New Jersey. She met Padre Pio in 1924 and because of the powerful effect on her life from that divine appointment she was inspired to immediately make her permanent home in San Giovanni Rotondo, Italy where Padre Pio lived because she knew he was the spiritual director for whom she had prayed for so long. That would be her home for the next 44 years of life up until her death in 1968.

In talking about that eventful meeting, Mary said, "We just looked at each other at first, then I fell to my knees and said, 'Father'. He placed his wounded hand on my head and said, 'My child, stop traveling around. Stay here.'"

She was known as "the American lady in the pink castle" because she built a large home of pink bricks just three houses away from the monastery. Mary was fluent in five languages. She answered much of the correspondence received by Padre Pio and was of tremendous help to the thousands of visitors who came to visit him. Mary was organist and choir director for Our Lady of Grace Church. She opened her home to all visitors. She exemplifies a person who lives their life doing little things every day that when woven together create a tapestry of a life lived serving God. A priest once asked Padre Pio about Mary: "She is a marvelous creature, isn't she?" Padre nodded and said, "The earth is much more beautiful because of her presence."

I would like to point out that when I visited San Giovanni Rotondo in Italy and toured the home of Padre Pio, I was amazed that Padre Pio had saved every letter ever written to him. I remember walking into a particular room and seeing stored behind glass thousands and thousands of pieces of correspondence. This made me appreciate Mary even more when I thought of her helping Padre handle his correspondence, the scope of which was mind-boggling.

Under the spiritual guidance of Padre Pio, Mary asked the Superior of the Capuchins for permission to wear the "penitential habit". The following year when her novitiate ended, Mary was accepted into the Profession of the Third Order of St. Francis. Her life was dedicated to service, charity, simplicity, and goodness. I feel a special love for Mary because I once met a family member of hers. This individual knew of my great devotion to Padre Pio and was inspired by the angels to give to me a holy card of Padre Pio with a hair from Padre's beard. This individual had been given this card by Mary Pyle. This is one of my most precious possessions.

In the Basilica of St. Peter in Rome Chuck and I witnessed the chains that were worn by St. Peter, and thorns from the crown that Christ wore when being crucified still exist on the earth. I have seen Christ's crown thorns in Santa Croce in Jerusalem in Rome, too. For me my spiritual path is to find ways to place myself as close as possible in God's energy. In Commune with the Angels I wrote about the importance of prayer time and meditation. Placing myself in the presence of relics allows me to experience a healing vibration.

When I was in Egypt, I visited the Convent of Saint George. I was allowed to enter and view mosaics and paintings of Saint George. The art was inspiring. The nun who walked with me as I toured the convent spoke no English. She showed me some very old chains and even wrapped the chains loosely around me. I don't know exactly how, but I conveyed to her that I wanted simply to pray on my own, and she honored my request. I later learned from reading that you can, in fact, allow yourself to be chained to the wall of this convent while the nuns recite prayers on your behalf. I am certain it is a very beautiful ritual but I have to admit that without someone translating what exactly was going on, this farmer's daughter from the cornfields of Upperco, Maryland would have been a little shaken if nuns had started chaining me to a wall. That is a perfect example of the grace of God, somehow conveying that I wanted to pray alone rather than being chained to the wall.

There is one place on the planet that may quite possibly have as many relics as the Vatican. It is St. Anthony's Chapel in Troy Hill, Pittsburgh. On the roof of the chapel is a statue of one of my favorite saints, St. Anthony. I have always remarked to my girlfriends that when I die I hope to be able to track down St. Anthony and personally thank him for keeping me sane. St. Anthony is the patron saint who helps us find lost items. Whenever I misplace something, which seems to happen frequently, I call upon Anthony to help me by chanting a prayer that people who love St. Anthony know: Saint Anthony, Saint Anthony, please come around, Jayne has lost something that must be found." I really cannot remember a time that Anthony has not helped me find what was misplaced or hidden from sight.

Father Suitbert Goedfried Mollinger was a pastor with a special devotion to St. Anthony. This devotion prompted him to build the Chapel of St. Anthony in the 1880's. Father Mollinger loved St. Anthony and many other saints and because of this made numerous trips all over the world to collect relics. Father Mollinger had received an inheritance from his family and he spent most of this fortune on the chapel and its relics. There are over 4200 relics in St. Anthony's Chapel. These relics are contained in 800 cases known as reliquaries with 525 accompanying documents which give dates, names and identify the seal of a Bishop or postulator of the saints' causes, attesting to the authenticity of these relics. Additionally the chapel's exquisite stained glass windows were made in Munich, Germany. The chapel makes a wonderful spiritual pilgrimage destination in order to experience the energies of over 4,000 relics gathered under one roof.

For an individual to be recognized by the Catholic church as a saint, four steps are involved. The life of the person must be examined and they must be deemed a "Servant of God." After further examination and scrutiny the person is called "Venerable". This term denotes that their actions on earth are worthy of imitation and revered for their holiness. Two miracles are needed to declare that the person as "Blessed." This is not necessary in the case of an individual who is martyred.

In a quote from Making Saints the author Kenneth Woodward describes the miracle process as having to establish (a) God truly performed a miracle – nearly always a physical healing – and (b) the miracle occurred through the intercession of the Servant of God.

After the two miracles are confirmed, the individual is Beatified. Then two more miracles are needed to declare them a saint for the imitation of the Whole Church. With that, the saint is officially canonized, recognized as a saint by the Catholic Church.

I have taught a class entitled "Commune With the Saints." In my class I share that the word saint is derived from the Latin "sanctus" which means a holy or godly person. I share my understanding of the word "saints" through assigning these inspirational messages to the letters in the word:

S - Serves God in the world
A - Attains God-consciousness through inner attitude and meditation
I - Integrated with God's energies of love through prayer
N - Natural state of Samadhi*, resides in a
T - Trusts in God; surrenders to God daily
S - Sweeps soul clean daily with spiritual discipline

* Samadhi is a Sanskrit word which means enlightened bliss state.

I have created an exercise in which you can recognize people who radiate the "sanctus" vibration to you. This exercise consists of the following thoughts and questions:

Someone whose life message inspired your life. What was their life message?

Someone who showed you how to "lighten up". How did they do this?

Someone who inspired you to think. How was your thinking changed or expanded

Someone who helped you feel safe, secure in a scary time of your life.

How did they do this?

Someone who helped you tap into your inner child's goodness and creativity.

How did they do this?

Someone who helped through healing. What was the healing you received?

Someone who showed you the best of humanity. Someone who mirrored a God quality or ideal to you. What quality or ideal did you see in this person?

Someone who helped you through a dying experience. How did they help you recognize a birthing was occurring, too?

Someone who showed you the view from a higher vantage point, i.e. the bigger picture. How did this change your own vision of life?

Someone whom you consider a master at what they do or did when here on earth.

How did they inspire you to embrace your own mastery?

Someone who embodied service to others, i.e. a real team player. How did they impact your life?

Someone who embodied true courage. How did they strengthen you?

I'd like to share the insights I received for myself when I did my own exercise. Joan of Arc is someone whose life message inspired my own life's message. Her words "Forward With God" and "I was born to do this" truly lift my spirit in challenging times.

Charles Schulz and Snoopy showed me how to lighten up. They remind me to remember to laugh daily. They inspire me to make time for the funny papers.

Albert Einstein inspired me to think. His quote, "I want to know God's thoughts; everything else is a detail," totally changed my consciousness.

St. Joseph helped me feel safe and secure in a very scary time of my life. His energies as a loving man, husband, father and an individual who was open to angels' messages brought me great comfort.

St. Therese's life of goodness always inspires me to do things that keep me in touch with my own inner child's goodness. She truly is an individual whose life of goodness was seeded at birth.

Madame Curie helped me heal my tendency to be impatient. By her life's example she taught me healing requires patience.

Stonewall Jackson taught me the best of humanity. If you do not know about this amazing Southern General, I encourage you to read about him. He taught me that any imperfections in our life, any shortcomings can be changed through discipline.

Padre Pio taught me to discover that which is being birthed in the midst of a dying experience. He also taught me that spiritual tests come with spiritual growth. They are just part of the territory. I learned not to fear the tests, and also learned to expect them.

Sadako Sasaki, the young girl who inspired children of the world to fold origami cranes in the consciousness of peace on earth, taught me that sometimes we start something that others are to finish.

Mattie Stepanek, the young poet who has appeared on Larry King Show, Oprah, and has written numerous poetry books, has reminded me to celebrate every day by letting your heart sing "Heartsongs".

Father Mychal Judge, the priest who died giving last rites to a fireman on 9/11, epitomizes a team player and that we should be serving God with our last breath.

Todd Beamer's final words, "Let's Roll," inspire me to embody true courage in all of my life's challenges.

Additionally you can aspire to be a blessing or saintly vibration with your own life through affirmations. I encourage you to read the following affirmations and fill in the blanks with words that express your own soul's true divine identity. Then utilize the affirmations throughout the day.

I am God's messenger of
I have and share the divine gifts of
I think God's thoughts in my own thoughts of
I feel safe and secure in
I radiate goodness by creating
I am a guardian and steward of
I mirror to others
I desire to be remembered for
I see the big picture in
I glorify God by
I am a blessing to others by
I believe God has asked me to

I love the saints, as by their faithfulness to God and their fellowship with us, they radiate the God-thought that we are brilliant! Like the stars we are here to shine and glorify God with our light.

Just think of yourself as a God-star. Just as the stars in the night sky appear to have darkness around them, we often have darkness around us in our lives. Yet we are here to embody the God-thought that the divine held of us when we first came into being. We are here to be bright and shining through our inner gifts and talents. We are here to warm with our love. We are here to sparkle with our individual personalities. Saints are truly sparkling God-star beings and that doesn't change when they die. They still continue to shine upon us with their friendship, love and support.

I was raised in the Methodist Church. In our services the saints were mentioned in the Apostles' Creed with the words, "I believe in the communion of saints." That was about the extent of the focus given to the saints in the church I attended. I may be wrong in this observation, however, I believe that most Protestant churches have steered away from focusing on the saints. I believe many religions have made the decision to keep all lessons based upon expanding the congregation's awareness of Jesus Christ and living a life of commitment to Christ. I do not believe, however, that learning about the saints and opening up our hearts and minds to their spiritual experiences detracts from our adoration of Jesus because saints are people who were examples of living all that Jesus taught us through his teachings here on earth, his sacrifice for us, and his resurrection into heaven.

I recently discovered that Upper Room Books has published two books that I feel are opening up the Protestant community to the joy of knowing the saints as family members of God. As I said earlier, the saints are not to be worshiped. They are messengers of God's wisdom, individuals whose spiritual lives help us strengthen our own sacred walk here on earth. The books are entitled, The Workbook on Lessons from the Saints and The Workbook on Keeping Company with the Saints, both authored by Maxie Dunnman. I absolutely love the title "Keeping Company with the Saints." What a great God-thought! The books encourage you to create a group study around the material. These books are fabulous spiritual tools and offer chapters such as: "Jesus Was Alive in Their Experience;" "They Believed That Obedience Was Essential;" "They Thirsted for Holiness;" "They Knew Peace" and "Joy That Transcended Circumstances." If you would like to start exploring the inspiration the saints can bring to our lives, you will find a real spiritual treasure in these two books. You can obtain them through http://www.upperroom.org/.

Maxie Dunnam writes about Martin Luther King, Jr., a modern-day saint whose birthday is now a national holiday in America, as a person who passionately sought God. He was a messenger to us to spend our energies on moving ourselves closer and closer to God. Dunnam writes about John Wesley, founder of the Methodist church. Wesley was a man who believed faith had to be practiced daily. Sometimes with the fast pace we live here on earth, we want instant everything, including instant spirituality. Dunnam shares Wesley's spiritual commitment to a life filled with prayer, reading the scriptures, meditating on God's words, doing no harm and purposefully doing good. I always remember my mom making the remark, "The spirit is willing but the body is weak." In researching John Wesley, who has endeared me to my childhood faith of Methodism, I have come to recognize that just as the body is weak at times, there are times the spirit is weary from living life. I find myself denying myself spiritual time that would most definitely provide the healing I desperately need. Wesley wrote that these are the times to pray even more, "not be weary or faint in your mind," not allowing the mind to deny what is truly needed. And the result is in Wesley's words: "...the door of mercy, of holiness of heaven shall be opened to you."

If you would like to focus your exploration of saints on women saints, another Upper Room publication that provides written guidance in aligning yourself to five extraordinary women saints is Under Her Wings by Kathy Bence. Kathy's book provides support for your own life through learning about these precious women. Kathy's writing creates the feeling that they are our mother hens and we their little chicks, under the wings of their life experiences; thusly her husband came up with the title: "Under Her Wings".

Years ago I was introduced to the research of Hilda Charlton, a spiritual teacher and author who has presented lectures at the Cathedral of St. John the Divine in New York City. Hilda recorded SAINTS ALIVE for Sounds True. This is an eight-hour tape program that explores the lives of eight saints: St. Joan of Arc, Pericles, Holy Lady Ammal, Jesus, Sathya Sai Baba, Our Lady of Fatima, St. Therese of Lisieux, Krishnamurti, Sri Nityananda, St. Martin de Porres, Sri Ramakrishna, St. Colette, and George Washington Carver. In Hilda's words saints are "perfected beings, who give up their place in heaven to come to earth and help us....Just call their names, and out of the reservoir of faith they left on earth will come forth a power that will ignite your own power. That is why they descended: to help not humanity in the abstract but, yes, you and me." Whenever I hear her speak these words by listening to her tapes again and again, I feel so blessed and loved by God.

I have already mentioned several abbeys and monasteries that I loved visiting. There are many shrines that are very special to me also. In Driving Under the Influence of Angels I wrote about The National Shrine of Our

Lady of Lourdes in Emmitsburg, Maryland, which is about a 45-minute drive from my home.

In our travels Chuck and I also had the opportunity to visit the Sorrowful Mother Shrine located in Bellevue, Ohio. The Sorrowful Mother Shrine was established in 1850 by Father Francis Brunner, C.PP.S., as a place for spiritual pilgrimages to honor the Sorrow Mother and foster a deeper devotion of the Blood of Jesus Christ.

The Shrine is administered to by the Missionaries of the Precious Blood. This Marian shrine was one of the first in the Midwest. It has 120 acres of beautiful woodlands. The shrine promotes that it is a place where one can truly "...stand still and feel the presence and love of God." There are paved walkways that wind among tall and colorful oak trees and lead to Stations of the Cross and replicas of the Lourdes and Sepulchre Grottos. Additionally there are prayer and meditation spots that honor St. Francis of Assissi, St. Anthony, St. Joseph and the Christ Child, St. Lucy, St. Catherine, St. Therese and many more inspirational grottos, and a beautiful Pieta Outdoor Chapel. Chuck and I both fell in love with the energy of the Sorrowful Mother Shrine experience. After leaving this shrine we continued on our drive westward across the country as I had a speaking engagement at an Angels of the World convention in Wisconsin. At one particular traffic intersection shortly after leaving the shrine, we stopped for a red light. The light changed to green. Chuck didn't move forward. I even remember turning my head to look at Chuck to see why he wasn't driving the car forward. Just as I did I saw out of the corner of my eye a tractor trailer 18-wheeler being driven by a driver who ran through the red light at what seemed 90+ miles an hour. Chuck and I both shuddered at the stark realization that had he moved forward when the light had in fact turned green, we would no longer be alive. We would not have survived the impact of this huge vehicle going at such an accelerated speed. We are both convinced that the energy of goodness that had flooded our souls at the shrine had in fact inspired Chuck to "stand still and feel the presence of God." In my life now, whenever I feel I am living like a "runaway train" I think back to that intersection. I pause and contemplate the words that the administrators of the shrine share in their invitation to the public to visit the shrine: "stand still and feel the presence and love of God."

There are times that the angels and saints have taken over the tours I am leading. One such example was in Ireland. In Driving Under the Influence of Angels I wrote of our precious bus driver and guide, Maurice O'Brien who in fact fell in love with and married one of the ladies in my tour group and the two of them are living happily ever after.

On our visit to the 5,000-year-old Neolithic Newgrange and Dowth, just before leaving the site, the angels inspired me to go back to the information desk as they wanted me to pick up a particular brochure. I did this and was guided to a brochure on the town of Kells. Upon our arrival in Dublin we had visited the Book of Kells, which is on display at Trinity College in Dublin. Many consider this to be the greatest Irish work of art. The book was produced around the beginning of the ninth century and contains a Latin text of the four Gospels plus gorgeous Celtic designs that illustrate the text. There had been some aggravating circumstances around the tour in the morning, which Maurice had jumped into and healed. I said to the angels that we had a long drive ahead of us to Donegal where we were staying for the night and if they wanted to "add on" Kells they were going to have to make it happen because I wasn't going to do it.

I was sitting up in the front of the bus in the navigator seat and Maurice was driving towards Donegal. We were enjoying the Irish cassette tapes he was playing for our entertainment. After awhile Maurice looked at me and said he felt it would be nice to give the ladies a stop and a bathroom break. I agreed. He indicated that the town of Kells would work out nicely as such a stop. I showed him the brochure and said that the angels had guided me to this place, too. Maurice remarked, "You're spooking me now!"

One other amazing coincidence occurred on that trip with Maurice that gave him the feeling we were "spooking him". When we began our travels exploring Ireland with him, Celeste and I who were seated at the front of the bus shared with him how many of the tour members had a deep devotion and love of the saints. Maurice commented that there was only one saint that he had a particular closeness to, and with that he lowered his visor and showed us a picture of Padre Pio. Well, many of us are such fans of Padre Pio that we have been nicknamed by our husbands and friends: Padre's Girls. Celeste wears a Padre Pio watch; we all have stickers with Padre's picture in our cars; we wear Padre medals; and so on. The minute he revealed to us that he was connected to Padre, we literally squealed with delight. Our "group squeal" just about caused him to drive off the road.

Maurice safely navigated us to the town of Kells for the rest stop. In Kells there is a small hut in which St. Columba and other monks lived before going to Scotland. It is believed that the Book of Kells was produced in the monastery of Ceannannus or Kells in Co. Meath, where the Columban community had fixed its headquarters after the Norsemen sacked Iona in 806 A.D. After the Columban foundation came to an end, the Book of Kells was preserved in the Kells parish church. It was later removed for safety to Dublin and presented to Trinity College by Henry Jones, Bishop of Meath.

I was told by the angels that our group needed to experience the energies of the Columba's house as it was an important saint connection. I saw in the brochure that there is one woman in the town who has the keys to the hut. She is the keeper of the keys. We were only stopping for 15 minutes and I said to Chuck that as soon as we got off the bus we had to find this woman wherever she was in the town. Chuck and I quickly moved down the street of Kells when a woman came up to me and said, "Are you looking for the keys?" She dangled the keys in front of me. I tried to grab them, and she said, "Oh, no. They're my keys and I will open the door for you." By that time the ladies had caught up with us and we had an incredible experience with St. Columba's energies. As I came to realize that the angels had guided us to stand in the sacred space where the Book of Kells manuscript had been written, I felt blessed by the energies of all those who have lived on the earth and dedicated their lives to making certain the words of the Bible are never lost. As I mentioned in this chapter earlier, the prayers of saints are divine inspirations for our lives. One of my favorite prayers written by Columba is:

My dearest Lord,
Be thou a bright flame before me,
Be thou a guiding star above me,
Be thou a smooth path beneath me.
Be thou a kindly shepherd behind me,
Today and forever more.

The energies of the Columban community were so powerful in fact and called to our group so abundantly that on the last day of our Irish Tour I knew the following year we were to gather again in Scotland, particularly on the Isle of Iona. For my Angel Tour of Scotland, which we called The Jubilee Angel Tour because it was the same year of Queen Elizabeth's Jubilee celebration of her coronation, I had the divine blessing of having John Begg, owner of Caledonian Tours, as our guide for the tour. John was a walking-talking encyclopedia of Scotland. He is Mr. Scotland himself. He arranged so many surprises for us.

When we were in Scotland, Chuck and I celebrated our third wedding anniversary on August 6th, 2002. We wanted to renew our wedding vows in the presence of all our friends who were on the tour with us and both felt that The Fairy Bridge was a perfect location. The Fairy Bridge is located on the road to Dunvegan Castle where the Fairy Flag of the MacLeods is on display. Legend has it that years ago the Chief of Clan MacLeod met a fairy princess. They fell in love with each other. The King of the Fairies did not want to grant permission for the princess to marry a human. The King knew that humans age and die and the fairies live forever. He knew that one day the princess's heart would be broken. She wept so intensely at the decision, that the King of the Fairies gave in and allowed her to marry with the understanding that she could only live with the Chief for one year and a day.

The Princess and the Chief of the MacLeod Clan were wed and a son was born to them. When it came time for the princess to keep her promise to the King of the Fairies, the entire family went to The Fairy Bridge. Before leaving, the princess made her husband vow that their son would never be left alone or allowed to cry, because hearing him cry would break her heart.

The Chief of the Clan grieved for the loss of the princess. The members of the clan decided a great feast should be planned for the Chief's birthday in an attempt to lift his spirits. It was a great celebration full of music and entertainment. The nurse who was in charge of watching the baby left his nursery in order to listen to the music. She failed to hear the baby awake and cry. The princess in the Land of the Fairies heard her son and immediately appeared next to his crib. She comforted him by holding him in her arms. She wrapped him in her fairy shawl. The princess whispered magic words to him; kissed him on the forehead, laid him back down into his crib with the shawl wrapped around him and returned to the world of fairies.

Years later the son shared the story of this visit by his mother and that she had told him that evening that the shawl was a magic talisman. If ever the Clan MacLeod faced mortal danger, the Fairy Flag was to be waved three times and the fairy kingdom would come to their rescue. The fairy flag could be used three times only. The fairy flag has been used two times to date: once for protection in battle and once for protection against a terrible plague. There remains one more waving.

During World War II members of the Clan MacLeod carried pictures of the flag in their wallets while flying in the Battle of Britain. None were lost to the German flyers.

For our celebration on The Fairy Bridge, I had gifted all my girlfriends bubbles and fairy wands for the festivities. It was a ceremony celebrating all the joys of life, and Chuck and I shared our thanksgiving and joy in being married to each other.

Following the ceremony, we continued on the road to Dunvegan Castle where we actually got to see The Fairy Flag and tour the castle. While we were there, John purchased picnic foods for us. We had thought we would go to a restaurant for lunch as we had done in previous days. John surprised us by having all the fixings for a perfect picnic when we met the bus after the tour, and added to the joy when he shared that we would be returning to The Fairy Bridge for the picnic. We were delighted by his thoughtfulness as it gave us more time to bask in the enchanting energies of the area. It was truly special to be at a place that members of the MacLeod Clan recognize is a doorway to the fairy world.

As part of our tour experience we visited Iona and were able to stand on Cnoc Hill, the hill of the Angels in Iona. The story of Angel Hill was first told in Adamnan's, Life of Columba, which was translated in approximately A.D. 600 from Latin. Adamnan was Columba's biographer, and wrote the biography over 60 years after Columba's death.

Columba was seen by a brethren standing on the mound now known as Hill of the Angels, praying with hands spread open and outwards towards heaven. He was gazing up towards heaven. The brethren reported that a multitude of angels were seen descending from heaven. He described them as clad in white, bright citizens of the Heavenly Country. They encircled him as he prayed. They conversed with him. Then they flew quickly back to heaven.

Columba was aware that even though he had previously asked that no one follow him to the hill, one brother had done so. The man asked for forgiveness for disobeying his request. Columba told him that no mention of the angelic visitation could be made while Columba was still alive. The man only related the account following Columba's death.

Columba was 77 years old when he died. The week prior to his death he saw an angel who told him that he would be leaving earth behind. On the day of his death he climbed the hill above the monastery and blessed Iona. He returned to his cell and resumed his work of copying the 34th Psalm. He stopped this task after he had written these words, "Fear the Lord, all you His saints: for there is no want to them that fear Him" He went inside the church to the altar. He was found by his fellow monks lying on the ground, the whole church bathed in a heavenly light. Even though the monks were saddened to find that Columba was dying, the look of joy on Columba's face gave them cause to believe he was witnessing the angels that came to bring him home. In the Liturgy and Ritual of the Celtic Church, F. E. Warren wrote "And having given them his holy benediction in this way, he immediately breathed his last" – at daybreak on Sunday, June 9, 597 A.D.

When Columba was a child, he spent so much time in church that he was nicknamed Columcille, meaning 'dove of the church'. One of the things I love so dearly about Columba is the fact that he encouraged everyone to make frequent use of the sign of the Cross over every task and job, over every hill and vale, over everything in life. He believed in blessing everything he encountered with God's energy. The Dali Lama is a saintly being on the earth at this time. One of his teachings is that he says internally with everyone he meets, "May you be blessed. May you be free of suffering."

Additionally, as the leader of the monks of Iona, Columba created Columba's Rules. One of the rules was that special saints' days were to be recognized and on these days the community was to display "fervor in singing the office for the dead as if every dead person was a particular friend of theirs." With his wisdom, Columba inspired his community to recognize that the saints in heaven are friends to us here on earth. I consider Columba one of the friends on my own personal Angel Team.

As I mentioned earlier, one of the things that endears the saints to me is their humanness. Just like me, they made lots of mistakes. In his book, Servants, Misfits and Martyrs, James C. Howell writes, "All the saints had their foibles, their dark side, their embarrassing moments. But for us flawed mortals, even their flaws are beacons of hope, that God can use even us, in spite of our inadequacies. We will see that it is often the case that God uses saints precisely through their weaknesses. For us would-be saints, it is hopeful to know that our giftedness can emerge out of that place where we have been wounded."

In The Way of St. Francis: The Challenge of Franciscan Spirituality for Everyone, Murray Bodo expresses a similar thought, "It is easier to rationalize and dismiss Jesus than Francis, because Jesus after all, is divine and so far above us. But Francis is only human like us. What he is, we can become." Just like the angels, the saints do not want to be worshipped. They are God's heavenly cheerleaders and divine mentors who are supporting, inspiring, and encouraging us to stay the course and keep our focus always on God's will for our lives. I have recognized in my researching saints that no one ever became a saint who only served themselves.

In Mother Teresa's words:
At the end of life we will not be judged by
How many diplomas we have received
How much money we have made
How many great things we have done.
We will be judged by
"I was hungry and you gave me to eat
I was naked and you clothed me
I was homeless and you took me in."

Nor did any of the individuals who eventually were recognized and canonized as saints live their lives seeking notoriety or sainthood. They sought God only. Brother Lawrence, a Carmelite monastery cook and cobbler, author of The Practice of the Presence of God, shared in an interview that took place on September 28, 1666, that he had "always been governed by love, without selfish views, and without concern" whether he would be lost or saved…having resolved to make the love of God the end of all his actions.

A spiritual practice I have incorporated into my life is to read out loud the words to the ancient Irish hymn, Be Thou My Vision.

"Be thou my vision, beloved Lord: none other is aught but the King of the seven heavens.

Be thou my meditation by day and night: may it be thou that I behold forever in my sleep.

Be thou my speed, be thou my understanding: be thou for me, may I be for thee.

Be thou my father: may I be thy son; mayst thou be mine: may I be thine.

Be thou alone my special love: let there be none other save the High-King of heaven.

Thy love in my soul and in my heart – grant this to me, O King of the seven heavens.

Beloved Christ, what'er befall me, O Ruler of all, be thou my vision."

If you want to have a sing-a-long, get yourself a copy of Mack Bailey's CD "Why I'm Here." The Jordanaires, the legendary quartet who did backup on many of Elvis' recordings, provide the background vocals for this song. You can purchase the CD at Mack's website www.mackbailey.com. I have a special heart connection with Mack Bailey. When I began my monthly HA HA tape subscription series, I wanted to play a song at the beginning of the tape each month to create the energy of all of the subscribers gathering together, i.e. reconnecting with each other monthly. The playing of a tape theme song would create the atmosphere that we were back together once again. The angels gave me the vision of a house in the country with a large porch filled with rocking chairs, and all the HA HA subscribers gathering on the porch, taking time from their busy lives to rock in a rocking chair and be comforted by the messages the angels shared through the monthly tapes.

The song I was guided by the angels to discover and then use is by Mack Bailey and it is called "Tenderly Calling" and can be found on his CD "On My Way."

On Mack's "Why I Am Here" CD you will find the modernized words of the hymn "Be Thou My Vision." I include them here for your use in singing along with Mack and the Jordanaires.

Be thou my vision, O Lord of my heart
Naught be all else to me save that thou art
Thou my best thought by day or by night
Waking or sleeping thy presence my light.

Be thou my wisdom, and thou my true word
I ever with thee, and thou with me, Lord
Thou and thou only, first in my heart
High King of heaven, my treasure thou art.

Great God of heaven, my victory won
May I reach heaven's joys, O bright heaven's sun
Heart of my own heart, whatever befall
Still be my vision, O ruler of all.

Whether you are saying the words "mayst thou be mine: may I be thine" from the ancient hymn or singing "I ever with thee, and thou with me, Lord," let yourself feel enveloped by the communion of saints who bless you for making time in your life for proclaiming with every beat of your heart and every breath you take what truly is important: your love of God.

There are saints among us, everyday people that respond to life in times of emergency and crisis as true saints or as God's blessings in action. One "everyday person" who inspired me with her "God blessing" action was Kenisha Thomas. In 1996 I heard on either a t.v. or radio news program a story that truly touched my heart and still does to this day. After hearing it for the first time, I knew that it was the kind of news story that People Magazine would report. The following week I went to the grocery story, leafed through the July 8, 1996 issue of People Magazine and sure enough there was a full page devoted to Kenisha Thomas. The article's sub-heading read: "As anti-KKK demonstrators turn violent, a black teen shows her compassion is color-blind."

The incident took place in Ann Arbor, Michigan. City officials had granted permission to 17 Knights of the Ku Klux Klan to have a rally on the second-floor promenade of the City Hall. Most of them wore their hoods. At the same time, 300 anti-Klan protesters were assembling. One of the anti-Klan protesters saw a white male spectator wearing Confederate flags on his vest and T-shirt. The angry demonstrators rushed the man and then things went terribly wrong. The man was hit with a sign by one person as another person began to beat him up.

Kenisha Thomas was there originally to join in the anti-Klan demonstration. She was a high school senior from Ypsilanti, Michigan.

When she saw the man who had fallen and was lying on the ground, the victim of the anger of the protestors, she threw her own body over his. She became a shield against the punches and kicks directed at the man.

When asked why she risked her own life, Kenisha responded, "You don't beat a man up because he doesn't believe the same things you do.... He's still somebody's child." What if we lived our lives treating everyone as "somebody's child," knowing that somebody is God.

I was delighted with the headline People magazine chose for their article about Kenisha Thomas because quite frankly it describes her perfectly: GUARDIAN ANGEL.

Just as I was wrapping up this chapter on Saints and Angels with the message that there are "everyday" saints all around us, I came across an article in The New York Times written by Andy Young entitled, "ART/ARCHITECTURE; Beatified by E-Mail: The Lives of a New Collection of Saints," which appeared on Sunday, August 10, 2003 as part of the ARTS AND LEISURE DESK section of the newspaper. Thanks to the kindness of Andy Young and The New York Times, I am able to share with you the story of how New York artist Josh Gosfield is honoring his friends as saints. I felt an immediate kinship with Josh when I read how the roadside Mexican altars had "infected his artistic mind." I truly believe "angels of a feather, flock together." Here's Andy's New York Times article about Josh:

"Josh Gosfield, a commercial artist living and working in Manhattan's West Village, was going about his business two and a half years ago when he was transported by a vision. It was a saintly vision, the likes of which he had never experienced. Stranger still, it was a saintly vision of an old friend, and it came to him when she stopped by his studio for a visit. He photographed her "for no good reason," he recalls. "I didn't really know what I was doing. Or why." But the Lord works in mysterious ways, and the Muses even more so. Mr. Gosfield found himself playing around with the image - centering his friend's face in a spiky halo, surrounding it with blocks of color that looked like stained glass. Before he knew it, he had transformed her into what he called the "patron saint of Mexican revolutionaries, cab drivers, dog walkers, and zoo keepers." At first, he says, he was drawn to "the visual aesthetics of creating a saint - the closed eyes, beatific expression, airbrushed tones and symmetrically radiating graphics." But something more than aesthetics made him return to the project again and again. He had e-mailed his Santa Isabella to a group of friends, and that direct connection - the ability to show his art to a wide audience of his precise choosing, on his terms and at his pace - got him hooked. Since the beatification of Santa Isabella, he has turned all sorts of friends and strangers into holy apparitions, as well as vehicles for his cultural obsessions, political gripes and artistic experiments. And he has found an ever-larger audience for these experiments, now distributed via e-mail through what he calls the Saint of the Month Club.

Mr. Gosfield might seem an unlikely conduit for Christian iconography. He was raised by atheists in a non-observant Jewish household, and he practices no religion himself. But, as he recalls, "the first time I went to Mexico and saw roadside religious altars, it completely infected my artistic mind." In any case, the messages that his saints convey tend to be defiantly secular - on such topics as Mr. Gosfield's excitement about his wedding, his anger about the war in Iraq, or his belief that people work too hard. "My saints aren't in the self-abnegation category," he says. "They're lusty, hard-drinking, partying saints." In July, a clothing designer and musician became Saint Petra, "an intergalactic space stewardess," who says that when the planet is in turmoil "it's time to get off the globe and go-go galactic." Saint Olga, the zaftig "Gypsy Saint of everywhere and nowhere" - who holds a bottle of wine in one arm, a pug in the other, and suggests we "get drunk, make a baby, and bark like a dog" - was sent out in December 2001 as an "alternative holiday" saint, "in response to all that sadness and smoke hanging in the air after 9/11," Mr. Gosfield says. (One of the few saints he describes as "hectoring" shows a woman - Mr. Gosfield's sister - somberly staring into the camera, amid the words "From Warsaw to Rwanda, From Wall Street to Baghdad, St. Lizette remembers all those who fall to bullets, bayonets and bombs.")

Mr. Gosfield, who has produced illustrations for a wide variety of major magazines, and who once designed a Christmas window for Barney's featuring the author David Rakoff as Sigmund Freud, brings a considerable degree of visual sophistication to his project. He combines references to the kitschy, high-gloss work of the French photographers Pierre et Gilles (without their overt homoeroticism), Barbara Kruger's text-based collages, Russian constructivist collages, and the Latin-American religious iconography that so inspired him. At the same time, they suggest the graphic style of greeting cards, with a cheery, art-of-the-people sensibility. His work also suggests a degree of professional sophistication, as Mr. Gosfield has struck on a way to display his art while bypassing all of the usual channels, and hassles. By using e-mail, he says, "I don't have to ask anybody's permission. I don't have to have a show, get into a fuss with a gallery dealer about what images they want to hang on the wall, or deal with some art director who's going to say, `I don't know about that blue background.'" As a result, he says, "I get to spend all my time making this thing, then send it out into this very intimate environment of a person's computer." He compares the effect to that of "one message in hundreds of tiny bottles."

Over the years, the construction of these messages has become increasingly elaborate, involving props, locations, computer animation and music. "I'm so nervous before I send them out," Mr. Gosfield says. "Is everything spelled right? Is all the animation going to work with different browsers? Is this thing really stupid?"

But they have also become more intimate, reflections of some very private concerns. Last fall, his wife was hit by a truck. She survived, but not before being dragged for a block. "I turned her into a cowgirl who had been dragged under a horse, but survived in great fashion," Mr. Gosfield says. Set to "Happy Trails," an animated Saint Camilla is told by the "Great Cowboy in the Sky" to "Get yer cowgirl self out from under the truck and into the world and preach the gospel of hard ridin' and good times!"

For all his irreverence, Mr. Gosfield still sounds a bit awestruck when he talks about his saints, the figures at the center of all his stylistic and technological experimentation. "I kind of have crushes on them for that month," he admits. "I'm a saint slut." You can sign up for Josh Gosfield's Saint of the Month Club at his website: http://www.joshgosfield.com/ and www.joshgosfield.com/saints.html.

Chapter 5

ART ANGELS

"God gives every bird its food, but He does not throw it into its nest." This quote by J. G. Holland is one that spoke to me on a soul level the first time I read it. I believe the message can apply to almost everything in our life. We have to show up for our life and do our part. I have mentioned that as I have walked my life's path there have been many clues given to me by the angels along the way. The clues give me directional guidance, however, I must have my eyes and ears open and pay attention to the signs on the road. In my service with the angels I have found the signs and signals to be subtle, more often than not.

My childhood memories are not only those of the incredible opportunities I was afforded to be close to nature every day of my life by growing up on a farm, but also the memories of being intrigued with the art that hung on the walls of my parents' farm house. I remember in our dining room was an exquisite painting of Christ kneeling in prayer in the Garden of Gethsemane. Additionally there were prints of Sir. Thomas Lawrence's paintings The Blue Boy and Pinkie in my bedroom and Degas' ballerinas in my sister Joyce's bedroom. I can remember feeling drawn into the world the paintings mirrored to me. In my lectures in which I have shown slides of angel art, many people share remembering seeing the painting of the guardian angel with a small child in their childhood home or the home of their grandparents.

If someone would ask me what do I do in support of my health and well-being, my response would be: I surround myself with art. I give thanks to my mother and father for giving me that message by the art that they chose to have in our family home. Art can be like a pair of angels' wings that envelops us with God's inspiration.

I was recently at an art lecture where the speaker shared the idea of parents changing the art in their homes periodically to give the children new images to contemplate. Children are curious and will observe and study what is in their environment. They are equally aware of changes in their environment. Chuck's grand-daughter Nikole was recently visiting our home, and when noticing a new box in the backyard, which was in reality a generator, asked if it was a "chocolate-making machine."

American youth spend approximately 1,500 hours a year watching TV. They spend only 900 hours in the classroom. The average American youth sees up to 40,000 commercials a year. By the age of 18, the average American youth has seen 200,000 acts of violence, including 40,000 murders through the media.

As I shared in Driving Under the Influence of Angels, I was inspired by the angels to establish an annual day of celebrating the importance of art in our lives. January 31st each year is a day to pause and reflect upon the importance of "Inspiring Your Heart With Art." Art in whatever form – painting, sculpture, dance, poetry, theater, film, and so on, is an honoring of the gift of creativity given to us by God. I encourage you to seek out an art adventure. It may be an adventure where you gift yourself the opportunity to be an artist by signing up for a pottery class, or it may be an opportunity where you are the spectator and observe that which has been created, such as going to an art museum, poetry reading, or symphony concert. Amelia Earhart said, "Adventure is worthwhile in itself." So have an art adventure.

In elementary school one day our class took a field trip to The Walters art gallery in Baltimore. To this day I can remember feeling as if I was Alice in Wonderland as I stood in the room filled with knights' armor, followed by my being guided into a room full of mummies and Egyptian artifacts. It was truly a wonderland of things I had never seen before in rural Upperco, Maryland. The experience awakened within me a yearning to learn even more about art.

This awe and love of the wonder of art stayed with me, and with the support of the angels I was guided to discover specific types of art. My discoveries were not just for my growth, but were to be shared with those I taught or reached through private consultations, tape subscriptions, lectures and retreats. I first researched the angels depicted in art and fell in love with the work of Fra Angelico, including his: A Glory of Angels as well as his many paintings of angels with musical instruments. He was born Guido di Pietro. Fourteen years after his death, the name Fra Angelico was given to him in tribute. The name means "angelic brother". It has been written that Fra Angelico prayed earnestly prior to painting; painted on his knees; and wept whenever painting Christ.

I was guided to seek out art that depicted Archangel Michael, such as Raphael's The Archangel Michael Casting Satan Out of Heaven and Guido Reni's "The Archangel Michael Overpowering Satan." Whenever I had a little extra money, I would have slides made of inspirational paintings of angels to use in my presentations. I wanted everyone to experience the glory of angels depicted in art. I now provide slide presentations on angels, Madonna, cemetery angel monuments, icons and more. I loved giving people the experience of "opened-eye meditations" with art. I truly believe that when you place yourself in front of uplifting and inspirational art, you are blessed by the experience.

It was with great delight that I recognized that the popularity of angels had resulted in angel calendars of all sizes and shapes, featuring great works of art that depict the angels. When interviewed on a radio program, I had a caller question me about the merchandising and commercialization of angels, making reference to angel calendars. I replied that everyone has free will as to how to spend his or her money. However, quite frankly, I was delighted that after years of seeing "pinup" calendars, especially in garages that I visited for automotive needs, I felt the image of angels was a refreshing change in the offerings of calendars.

There have been times throughout my life when I am introduced to something new to me in art and in that introduction I feel once again like "little Jayne" at The Walters art gallery being shown a new wonderland. One such introduction took place in Russia in 1994 when I explored the Orthodox Churches and was exposed to icons. It was a mystical experience standing with worshippers inside Kazanskiy Kathedral in Red Square in Moscow. It was consecreated October 15, 1636. There was a wooden church before, but after it burned down, the tzar ordered to use bricks from the Kremlin palace which had been built at that time. In 1928 it was restored, but all the work was stopped and it was destroyed. Peter Baranovsky, a famous Soviet restorator had drawn detailed plans of the cathedral which make it possible to reconstruct it in 1935.

Inside Kazanskiy Kathedral, hundreds of candles were flickering light upon sacred icon images. The powerful icon art that was surrounding me from all sides, the glowing light of the candles, and the prayers of the faithful created an atmosphere of palpable holiness. As I stood in the midst of this holy energy, it felt as if it were above me, below me, before me, behind me, and to the right and left of me. I knew the holy beings depicted were different in each work of art, yet there was a similarity in the style of the paintings. I would later learn that these paintings were, in fact, icons. I couldn't take my eyes off the art. I felt as if I wanted to merge with the paintings.

The word icon originated from the Greek word "eikon" which means image. At one time icon was a term that was used loosely to describe all kinds of sacred art such as mosaics, painted boards, sculptures, and frescoes. Today it means painted panels that depict holy images of Christ, the Blessed Mother, saints, Biblical stories, and so on. Since the sixth century icons have been used extensively in the Orthodox Church as liturgical art.

Many members of the Orthodox Church not only experience the joy icons can give when they attend churches, they have a family icon corner in their home, where morning and evening prayers are said. There are icons of saints who bless cooking in the kitchen, there are icons that adorn the walls of homes and icons to be used in personal altars. When I read of this, I again felt the warmth that was provided me in growing up in a home that was filled with uplifting art images. The icons are not in the home to decorate the house. They are in the home as an extension of the energies that the family experiences when gathered together in the religious community of their church. The icons bless the home with the energies of holiness and intimacy with God.

Icons are painted according to a prescribed style. An icon is painted on a wooden panel. Cloth is affixed to the face of the panel. Layers and layers of a primer of glue and powdered chalk or alabaster are affixed over the panel. The panel is left to dry. The next step is for a design to be incised on the surface. Once this is completed the painting of the image begins following the incision as guide. Tempera paints, powdered colors mixed with egg yoke, and a small amount of rye beer are used by the icon painters. Dark colors are painted first and when lighter colors are applied on top of them a three-dimensional effect is created. Once complete, the icon is varnished with a boiled linseed oil mixture. This brightens the icon and serves as a protection for the image. Some icons have gold leaf added. The completed icon represents a window opening to another world.

Recently I had the experience of going to John Paul II Cultural Center in Washington, D.C. where the exhibit Windows Into Heaven – Russian Icons, 1650-1917 was on display. The exhibition was curated and catalogued by James Lansing Jackson. While at the center I purchased a copy of the official exhibition guide. The following is Jackson's dedication: "To the anonymous icon painters whose creations grace this exhibition. May you rejoice in heaven knowing your works have survived and continue to inspire all who seek the splendor of their truth..." The title of the exhibition was gleamed from the words of a Russian peasant who called icons: "windows into heaven."

Egon Sendler described an icon as an "image of the invisible" in the title of his book The Icon. I truly believe that energies that are more times than not invisible to us are made "visible" when we meditate with icons. I also believe there is a beauty that is truly divine in that which is holy. Icons radiate a holy connection with God.

Pope John Pall II described iconography as "based on the mystery of the Incarnation in which God chose to assume a human face. In the last analysis, sacred art seeks to transmit something of the mystery of that face...by contemplating icons in the whole context of liturgical and ecclesial life, the Christian community is called to grow in its experience of God, and to become more and more a living icon of the communion of life between the three divine Persons."

Adam Cardinal Maida, Archbishop of Detroit and President of the Pope John Paul II Cultural Center made this comment about the 81 painted panels that comprised the Windows Into Heaven exhibit, "As the Holy Father points out, icons for Eastern Christians – and for all of us – are more than artwork, they are expressions of faith....as we gaze at this wonderful collection, our seeing is truly transformed such that every glance becomes a prayer." What a truly inspirational thought. Every glance we give to an icon becomes a prayer.

If you find yourself in the dilemma of having to buy a gift to commemorate a special occasion, perhaps for a wedding, graduation, or house warming, I think a perfect gift would be an icon, perhaps an icon depicting an angel, God's messenger of blessings, or an icon of Saint Francis whose words, "Lord, make me an instrument of Thy Peace," inspire us to peaceful lives.

Photios Kontoglou, a renowed modern iconographer wrote, "Icons raise the soul and mind of the believer who sees [through] the icon to the realm of the spirit, of the incorruptible, of the kingdom of God, as far as this can be achieved with material means."

I personally feel an icon is a gift of spiritual substance and is so much better than a toaster. Consider gifting sacred art that will "raise the soul and mind".

When I was in Turkey in 2000 with Celeste McDonald, Nancy Schwartzberg, and Chuck, we all piled into a taxi and headed off to visit a particular church that the guide book indicated would be open and accessible. When we arrived, the church was closed. The hours had changed since the guidebook was printed. Our thoughtful taxi cab driver, in seeing our disappointment, asked why we had chosen that church. I indicated that the guidebook said the icons were beautiful. The taxi driver smiled and remarked, "Icons. If you like icons, I have the church for you!" This is commonplace in our angel adventures. One door is closed to us so that we allow for another amazing experience God has in store for us to unfold. I encourage you, whenever you travel, pack trust in your backpack. Our taxi driver drove us to: the Greek Orthodox Patriarchate Church of Istanbul. It is truly the ultimate icon experience. We were the only people in the church at the time of our visit except for a dear man who spoke to us in a language we didn't understand. We did, however, fully understand his enthusiasm for the way in which God was glorified through the icons. Additionally, after communing with the icons, we went outside to the courtyard of the church and had the good fortune of meeting a Bishop of the church who happened to be with a group of young men who spoke English. I asked if the Bishop would offer a blessing and prayer over us, and he was kind enough to stop and do this.

We also had the good fortune of touring the Antalya Archaeological Museum, which has many, many icons in its collection. In fact, a long narrow hall is devoted to icons and is known as The Gallery of the Icons. There are icons narrating the life of Christ: The Annunciation, Nativity, Presentation in the Temple, Teaching in the Temple, Christ and the Samaritan Woman, Healing the Blind Man, the Transfiguration, The Last Supper, Christ Washing His Disciples' Feet, Christ on His Way to Golgotha, Crucifixion, and Two Angels at Christ's Empty Grave. Additionally of the other icon depictions, one is of St. Nicholas of Myra and a small reliquary is nearby containing some of the bones of the saint.

In fact, on all the angel tours we are guided to churches and museums where icons are waiting to be experienced. When icons are created, the last features painted of the individual depicted are the eyes. It is believed that as the eyes are completed the Holy Spirit descends into the eyes of the icon image. Because of this, when someone stands before the icon and experiences the icon as sacred art, there is a blessing that is transmitted from the eyes of the image to the observer of the art.

I shared in Driving Under the Influence of Angels that when I was in Old Cairo, Egypt, after having visited St. George Convent and Church, I saw a store across the street where the shopkeeper was sweeping the front entrance. I walked up to the gentleman and when I opened my mouth, the Holy Spirit took over. Before I knew it, I had asked him, "Do you have any icons." I was amazed as to where the words came from and equally amazed by his response: "Come inside. I am the only store in Egypt that sells icons." There were beautiful icons of Mary and Jesus, and the Holy family. I looked and looked and yet didn't find what I was looking for. The storekeeper said to me, "What is wrong? Aren't my icons beautiful?" They were beautiful, truly exquisite icons. However, I was looking for an icon of St. Michael. It would be a healing for me as I was feeling very depleted. I shared with the storekeeper I was looking for an icon of St. Michael. The man brought out from the back room of his store a contemporary painting of St. Michael painted in the style of icons. The painting was truly magnificent depicting Michael with one hand raised in a gesture of blessing and one hand stretched out extending an image of sacred geometry. I purchased that painting. The icon painting of Michael – God's Messenger of the Sacred Geometry in Creation – has traveled all over America with me. I have even had the painting photographed and have given out thousands of copies of the prints because I truly believe that when you gaze into the eyes of Michael you receive a blessing of God's protection. If you would like to have a free print, simply send a self-addressed stamped envelope to me at Angel Heights/PO Box 95/Upperco Maryland 2115. I will joyously send the icon print to you.

Additionally, if you are looking for a source for icons I recommend requesting a catalog from Monastery Icons, which offers icons created by the Desert Fathers of Light of Christ Monastery. Their website is www.monasteryicons.com.

In the Christian tradition, the first icon was created by Christ himself. There are various versions of the legend, but according to one version, King Agbarof Edessa, which is now Urfa in Turkey, suffered from leprosy. King Agbar sent an envoy begging Christ to visit and heal him. If Christ could not do this, King Agbar wanted his messenger, an artist, to paint a portrait of Christ and bring it back to the King. The artist attempted to make a painting of Christ but his efforts were futile because Christ's face kept changing due to the glory of God he bore. When Christ saw that the artist was unable to paint him, Christ asked for water, washed his face, and wiped it with a piece of cloth. Christ's features remained imprinted on the cloth. Christ sent the cloth to Agbarand Agbarr was healed.

Agbar placed the icon above the gates of his city. His great grandson, who was a pagan, would later attempt to destroy the sacred image. A bishop found a hiding place for the image and walled up the image with a burning lamp. In the middle of the sixth century Chasroes I, King of the Persians, besieged Edessa and discovered the image intact, and that it had been imprinted upon the tile which had concealed it. Thus the legacy of icons created with cloth and tile began.

The legend continues that the icon was brought from Edessa to Constantinople in the tenth century and placed in the church of the Virgin of

Pharos in the Great Palace. After the city was sacked by Crusaders in 1204 the whereabouts of the icon was not known.

The story of Veronica, a woman who stepped out of the crowd that watched Christ carrying the cross on his way to be crucified, tells us she wiped the sweat from his face and his features were imprinted on the head cloth she had used.

There is also belief that the earliest icon of the Blessed Mother was in fact painted by Saint Luke when she appeared to him in a vision. In studying icons I have learned the meanings of posing and positions that the sacred image depicts. In the icon painted by Luke, Mary is shown with a raised open right hand pointing to Jesus. This gesturing is known as the hodigitria manner. The one who is pointing is "showing the way". Mary is showing that our attention should be upon Christ.

This famous icon was a "palladium" or protector icon of the Byzantine Empire. Empress Eudoxia had discovered the icon and sent the icon to Pulcheria, a religiously devout sister of Theodosius II. Pulcheria kept the icon safe in a monastery in Hodgeon. It was believed that the icon radiated special powers and energies and became a protector of Constantinople. It would be brought out and carried along the city's walls during battles. When the Ottomans besieged the capital in 1453, the icon was carried along the city's walls one final time. The icon was then offered to a church in Chora on the island of Ios in Greece.

There is a legend that the icon was not "offered" but rather found among the rocks of the island's seashore with a lighted candle on it. In discovering the icon and realizing the power, the natives threw the icon into the open sea to protect it from falling into Turkish hands, because the Ios was occupied by the Turks. The icon floated back to the coast. The icon was then taken to the church of the Holy Cross, only to be found again the next morning among the same rocks on the steep hillside of Chora.

The islanders interpreted the "return of the icon" as a sign to build a new church to house the icon, but chose not to build on the exact spot where the icon was found because of the inaccessibility. The foundation of the church disappeared every day. The islanders soon recognized that the icon had chosen the spot for the new church, known today as Panagia Gremiotissa, which houses this miraculous icon.

Another icon that has an incredible story of floating at sea is the icon of St. Michael the Archangel that was brought to Sitka, Alaska in about 1813. The community of Sitka was actually founded in 1799 by a group of Russians led by Alexander Andreevich Baranof who was manager of the "Russian American Company." The first settlement that was established was christened “New Archangel Saint Michael.” The name would be changed to Sitka years later.

As the community flourished Orthodox missionaries came to Alaska, one of whom was Bishop Ivan Veniaminov who petitioned to the church in Russian to allow the expansion of church activities in the Russian colonies. Veniaminov was consecrated to the rank of Bishop of Alaska, Alaska’s first Bishop. He was responsible for raising support for the building and dedication of St. Michael’s Cathedral on November 20, 1848.

Icon treasures were brought to Sitka from Russia on the ship Neva, which foundered off Cape Edgecumbe. Of course, the community was greatly saddened over the loss of the sacred cargo that was on its way to their church. About thirty days after the sinking of the Neva, a cargo container from the Neva floated to the shores of Sitka. When it was opened, the icon of Archangel Michael was found inside. Nothing could keep Archangel Michael from his earthly assignment of protecting this precious cathedral that bears his name. The icon is 84% silver and is truly one of my favorite Michael icons of all those I have been blessed to see in my travels.

On January 2, 1966, a great fire caused by a faulty furnace in a business near St. Michael’s Cathedral broke out. The entire community turned out to become firefighters. When it was realized that the Cathedral could not be saved, a “human chain” was formed to remove all the valuable icons and sacred treasures from the church, passing them down the street to a place of safe-keeping. In that fire 23 businesses of Sitka and the cathedral were lost. When you visit this cathedral, which was rebuilt and dedicated on St. Michael’s Day in 1976, you will see how objects that are literally impossible for a human to lift were carried by those who were at the beginning of the “human chain”. I truly believe Archangel Michael was at the head of the brigade of love and was helping to radiate to the people of the community God’s power to help them remove from harm’s way these sacred belongings.

While in Istanbul, Turkey our angel band of four also experienced the icon mosaics of the Church of Hagia Sophia also spelled Ayasofya. Hagia Sophia was built by the Emperor Justinian I in the year 537 AD. Built in only six years, this most magnificent of all the Byzantine churches was designed by architects Anthemios of Tralles and Izidorus of Miletus. This church was the Cathedral of the Ecumenical Patriarchate of Constantinople for more than one thousand years. It was known as the Great Church because of its large size compared to other churches in the then Christian World.

In the icon mosaics of the church, the emperor was also used as a subject. One mosaic depicts the Virgin Mary with the emperors Justinian and Constantine sitting at her sides. Another shows Emperor Leon kneeling before Jesus who is sitting on a throne.

After Fatih captured Istanbul in 1453, Hagia Sophia became a place of worship for the Muslims. In 1934 Ataturk ordered that the structure be used as a museum. The Hagia Sophia is currently being restored with one quarter of the mosaic decorating the magnificent dome having been completed. I believe all of us – as citizens of the world – have a responsibility to support with our prayers and our involvement the preservation of the great art and architecture of the world.

On March 20, 2001 Professor Lowry Burgess presented The Toronto Manifesto: The Right to Historical Memory to the Toronto World Day Roundtable Dialogue. The manifesto was written by Professor Burgess in response to the destruction of the Buddhas in Bamiyan, Afghanistan.

"In the cause of human toleration and understanding, and as a comfort to the world, historical and cultural artifacts require care by all people and societies. In conservation and preservation is assurance of shared meaning, a cooperation and communion in deeper human values, a celebration of high aspirations, and a continuity of memory and love.

Historical treasures constitute a common heritage, and ultimately contribute to an essential repository of living knowledge. Such historical properties gradually become the inheritance of the world, reaching across the boundaries of place, time and culture— ultimately owned by all— a common property. It is from this common value that larger crucial meanings for both individuals and societies can be discerned and wisdom derived for the future creative conduct of the world. Through mutual responsibility for historical memory we affirm humanity and tolerance for each other as individuals and societies.

As global networked communication systems grow in flat simultaneous electronic time, more and more the actual artifacts and monuments from deep historical time increase in psychological and sociological significance. There is a productive balance between the sense of being grounded in locality and global electronic and economic dislocation.

This vital balance between past and future becomes critical to participation in planetary civilization with a sense of value and identity so fundamental to individuals and societies desiring to belong in time and space. The participation of historical artifacts and monuments in this local-global communication and communion is dependent on their continued existence.

To be effective, conservation and preservation must garner economic rewards within the global finance system. Commitments to historic preservation can be seen in global finance as a new form of value- a value that does not move- a timeless value of enormous worth. In the development of such a grounded commonwealth many relationships need understanding.

Conservation and preservation can be structured as part of the dynamic economic reward structure within the global finance system. They can act as attractors for investment as well as conduits for financial debits, credits and multipliers for investment flow.

A global financial framework that motivates and rewards historical preservation and conservation must be integrated within existing financial networks and exchanges. Such economic advantage equates with the survival of culture. In such a structure, preservation and conservation become economically advantageous. In this way, it is possible to foresee a vast inter-net of global historical resources that is as globally beneficial as the creation of the Internet.

Equally, disincentives and punishments need strong enforcement. Individuals and societies, states and countries can be held formally and firmly accountable for destruction or illicit commerce. This condemnation is part of the emergent structure of worldwide human rights and the body of law accruing through prosecutions of the World Court. More specifically, the Right to Historical Memory is an essential building block within the growing body of human rights promulgating itself through future laws, policies and conventions worldwide.

The complexity of designating and conveying responsibility for preservation must not justify inaction nor foster resignation. While destruction and irrevocable loss through hate and greed is easy, the burden of care is great and the effort of education and preservation constant.

Any human without memory is lost. Humanity without memory engenders a frightful retreat into brutal nonexistence. For each moment lost a precious artifact or monument disappears for all time. Any time lost is literally TIME lost. The ongoing destruction must cease. Setting these issues before the world in an urgent and profound appeal is a first step toward remedy and sanity."

Dr. Burgess is as brave as our forefathers who stood up and declared the rights all human beings are entitled to that would become the foundation of our great nation. Dr. Burgess declared the right we all have to historical memory through the arts.

In 1996 I was inspired by the angels to travel to Atlanta, Georgia. As I was operating on almost zero dollars for this angelic assignment, I called upon a woman I had met at a conference in Calgary, Canada who made an open-ended invitation to stay at her home if I ever arrived in Georgia. I took her up on her offer and called her as soon as my angel team indicated there was service to be done in Georgia. While flying into Atlanta, I was reading the airline company's flight magazine and learned that at the High Museum of Art an exhibition entitled "RINGS: Five Passions in World Art" was appearing there. This exhibit brought together masterpieces spanning 75 centuries of human life. The exhibit was held in conjunction with the 1996 Olympics being held in Atlanta. It was organized by the High Museum and The Atlanta Committee for the Olympic Games Cultural Olympiad through J. Carter Brown, the distinguished Director Emeritus of the National Gallery of Art in Washington. It was a one-time-only exhibition and it featured 125 art treasures representing 44 nations and the emotions of Love, Anguish, Awe, Triumph and Joy. I knew I was to be at the exhibit that was opening the same time I was arriving in Atlanta, but without a car, I was going to have to find a way to get to the museum and also obtain a ticket for this incredible exhibition. I said a prayer, "Dear God, I really want to see this exhibition and I am willing to clean the toilets of The High Museum of Art to do it. If it be Thy will, please help me get to see this exhibit."

The woman kindly met me at the airport, and as she drove me back to her home she said to me, "Oh, by the way, I am a volunteer at the High Museum of Art and the Members Only special preview of RINGS: Five Passions in World Art is taking place tomorrow. I thought you might like to help me by working as a volunteer ticket taker at the Members Only event. We'll then get to see the exhibit ourselves after the special event is over." I sat there in wonder at the words she was sharing with me. The amazement melted into pure joy and thanksgiving. I was humbled by God's love for me.

The advertisement in The Atlanta Journal that promoted this incredible event read as follows: "HIGH PASSION - Love, anguish, awe, triumph, joy. More than 125 of the world's greatest masterpieces reflecting the universal emotions. For 12 short weeks, this will be the finest exhibition on American soil. If you have a passion for great art, you won't want to miss it." I felt so blessed to see this exhibit, which included such great treasures as Auguste Rodin's "The Kiss" loaned from France; Luca Giordano's "Saint Michael Vanquishing the Devil" loaned from Germany; Henri Matisse's "Dance" loaned from Russia; and Wellington's "Shield" loaned from England.

Because of my passion for angels and art, I have been fortunate to get advance notice of exhibits. One example of this was the Vatican exhibit: Angels of the Vatican: The Invisible Made Visible. In 1998 a 98-piece exhibit visited five cities in the United States and my beloved Walters art gallery of Baltimore hosted the exhibit during the holiday season. Several people who were involved behind the scenes of this exhibition made me aware of this exhibit coming to Baltimore years before the actual event. I was thankful for this information because for two years I promoted the exhibit in every lecture I gave – no matter what town I was speaking in. I repeated: "The Vatican angels are coming! The Vatican angels are coming!"

The angels have guided me to discover the world of mandalas as artistic expression. The word mandala means "mystic circle". Mandalas represent the soul, the progress of the soul's enlightenment, and the universe. Mandalas have been used in the Tibetan Buddhists' spiritual practices. When sand mandalas are created five monks work seventeen-hour shifts. The mandala takes about four days to complete. Not only are the monks creating a mandala, but they are creating an energy and atmosphere in which peace resides.

Many of the visions of Hildegard of Bingen, a twelfth-century Benedictine nun, were in the form of mandalas.

Joan and Miron Borysenko wrote of Hildegard in their forward for Judith Cornell's MANDALA: "In her vision, light and sound were central. Hildegard said, 'God was and is without beginning before the creation of the world. God was and is light and radiance and life. And God said, "Let there be light," and so were the light and radiant angels created.' When you study Hildegard's mandalas, or listen to her music, you are drawn into the very light of creation itself."

Rose windows in medieval cathedrals were usually made with an image of the Virgin or Virgin and Child in the central pane, and as such were images of love and examples of mandalas. They open the soul and guide the heart of the individual to open further up to God. The Rose Window of Notre Dame Cathedral in Paris is an example of such a mandala of light and love.

Circular in form, mandalas draw in the eye and invite the viewer to wonder. They help us to become "centered". They were created originally in Hinduism and Tantric Buddhism and now are used ecumenically all over the globe in spiritual, mathematical, psychological and artistic endeavors to guide people to self-consciousness. "The more science progresses," wrote St. James Jeans of relativity and quantum mechanics, "the less the universe looks like a clock, and the more it looks like a thought." A mandala is a thought of the whole. It is a circular form with a spiritual content. I encourage you to seek out mandalas of the world religions as well as science and astronomy. All mandalas have the potential to center you and bring a wholeness to your psyche and soul. You can use mandalas for meditation, for healing and for growth.

In classes that I have co-taught with Sister Paula Matthew csj at The Spiritual Center in Windsor, New York, we have given students the experience of creating their own mandala in a weekend retreat and then of learning how to attune themselves to healing self insights from the mandala.

In my own individual service of offering private consultations, I offer mandala readings. People who contract for this reading are sent a meditation tape and a mandala page that is a white sheet of paper with a mandala circle in the middle. They are encouraged to listen to the meditation tape and then to fill in the mandala page I have sent them with colors, symbols, and images. They send the mandala page back to me and I create an inspirational tape interpreting the mandala, including angelic messages. These tapes are produced with the support of the angels of art. The mandala is a divine eye-piece by which you see yourself with light sight. Mandalas open you to your own inner rainbow presence.

I have seen the inspiration of mandalas as created by the Universe in spiral nebula as photographed by the Hubble. Additionally, the Hubble Telescope has introduced me to the world of art in space. The stunning images of the Hubble Space Telescope have opened my soul's eyes to the art of God. I encourage you to go to http://hubble.stsci.edu/gallery. Experience for yourself the images shown in the gallery. Psalms 19:2 inspires us to realize: "The heavens speak of the Creator's glory and the sky proclaims God's handiwork."

If you are doing something creative in your life, and you experience a block, such as a writer's block, just take a look at these breathtaking space images. Allow yourself to stand witness to the work of the Great Creator mirrored to us by the Hubble Space Telescope and hear in your soul Dante's words: "I believe in one God – sole, eternal – He who, motionless, moves all the heavens with his love and his desire…This is the origin, this is the spark that then extends into a vivid flame and, like a star in heaven, glows in me."

Chuck and I attend a free public lecture the first Tuesday of every month at The Hubble Space Telescope Institute in Baltimore. We find that our inner lights are rekindled when we sit in the audience and witness the newest space images captured by the telescope. We sit back and let the scientists fill us in on what's new in the heavens.

Let yourself feel God moving through the heavens and moving through you. Connect with the brilliance of the cosmos and even more profoundly connect with your own inner brilliance. The divine spark that is within you is fired up when you pause to admire the divine sparks of the heavens.

John Milton wrote in Paradise Lost:

"Whether heaven move or earth
Imports not, if thou reckon right; the rest
From man and angel the great Architect
Did wisely to conceal and not divulge
His secrets to be scanned by them who ought
Rather admire."

I believe in all spiritually inspirational art – in the art of the heavens and art of the earth there is that which is concealed and waiting to be revealed to those who take the time to admire it. It's important to take time to appreciate all the good things in your life.

Additional expressions of space art are the crop circles that appear on the planet annually. I want to first clarify that even though I would like to know how they are created to satisfy my own curiosity, it will not change my opinion of them. I want no part of all the energy that has gone into the controversy of whether they are created by aliens or are man-made. If aliens are making them, I want to thank them. If people, I want to thank them, too. I find it absolutely amazing that someone (or perhaps a group) is using the earth as a canvas to create these thought-provoking shapes. Let's just suppose someone is in fact making them as a hoax. I would love to ask them: "What is inspiring you to choose such awe-provoking configurations?"

I have attended numerous lectures in which Drunvalo Melchizedek has shared with us the revelations he has received that the Flower of Life symbol, a fractal flower pattern found universally, contains within it all the encodings for life: "every single mathematical formula, every law of physics, every harmony in music, every biological life form…absolutely everything that's within the waveform universe." Crop circle formations have included all the shapes that are fundamental to sacred geometry including the Flower of Life symbol, the circle, the spiral, the cube, the Tree of Life, and so on.

There was in fact a breathtaking crop circle entitled "Mandala" discovered in Woodborough Hill, England in 2000 made out of 308 triangles of standing crop. It is considered by many to be the best formation ever found and there's a wonderful photograph by Bert Janssen that captures the beauty of this crop circle. Again, whoever did this: BRAVO! I encourage you to purchase a book on crop circles and do open-eyed meditation with these images of sacred art.

Crop circles are beautiful. They are mysterious. And the ancient sacred geometries and mathematics mirrored to us by the crop circles are truly remarkable.

In 1993 I traveled to England to speak on the topic of angels at an ARE world conference. Before I went to the conference, I was given a clue by my angel team prior to leaving for England that I would be making contact with someone connected with "CSETI." I didn't know what the letters meant. I did not have my first computer until 1996 so I did not have the easy research access of the Internet. I remember watching a television program called

SIGHTINGS on the Fox Channel one Friday evening just before my trip abroad. The program featured a story about a group of scientists who were part of an organization called: CSETI – The Center for the Study of Extra-Terrestrial Intelligence. They were doing research on the crop circles in England. CSETI were following a protocol they had established in attempting to make contact with whatever force was creating the crop circles. I remember thinking, "How truly beautiful. They are honoring the divinity in all life expression." They had set up a protocol that they followed faithfully and in one of their experiments they held a group thought-image of a particular geometric design. They held this image in a group meditation. The next morning they discovered very near to where they had held their group meditation, a crop circle of the exact same design had manifested in a field. No one truly knows how it got there. Could it have been the power of their minds that created the image? Could it have been an angelic response to their openness? No one knows. Yet it did appear and was photographed.

After the world conference in London, England, my girlfriend, Ann Bell and I took a tour of some of the sights of England. The bus stopped for lunch at a roadside thatched-roof restaurant. When I walked through the door, I was amazed to find in front of me a bar with cardboard diecuts of crop circles dangling from the ceiling. I turned to my right and over the fireplace was the photograph of the image that had manifested following the CSETI's experiment. The same photograph I had seen on SIGHTINGS. At that point, I felt as if the angels would be humming the theme to "Twilight Zone" in my ear at any moment.

I approached the bartender and asked, "Why do you have crop circles hanging from the ceiling?" He smiled and said that many of the scientists came to this pub after researching the crop circles. I immediately thought of Casablanca, "Of all the gin joints in the world, she had to walk into this one." I decided to probe further and asked him, "Do you know anything about a group called CSETI?" As if on cue, the door behind me opened. The bartender looked at the person who had walked in and then looked at me. "I can't help you, but he certainly can. He's one of the CSETI scientists."

I have been known to have out-of-body/in-body experiences and that is exactly what happened in that pub in Wiltshire, England. I started jumping up and down and hugging this individual, saying, "The angels know about you! The angels know about you." Can you imagine what the poor soul was thinking? He responded, "That's bloody well lovely, ma'am. What do the angels know about me?" I told him I didn't know exactly but felt it was in connection with the honoring of the divinity in all life by the group's practicing a defined protocol in its attempts to determine the originators of the crop circles. Ann and I shared lunch together with George Wingfield and this brilliant man spoke to us of things that were so far above our range of comprehension that we hadn't a clue what he was talking about. He shared that he was a member of BUFORA (British UFO Research Association). However, we felt blessed to be with him and told him we would pray for him and his research.

I have found in my travels that the angels bring into my life people that are far superior to me in wisdom. In the past I would feel uncomfortable in that I didn't have a clue what they were talking about and came away feeling like the biggest dummy on the planet. I have since learned that when we think something is going over our head, it is really a good thing. Over our head is a divine charka. I refer to it as the Christ Consciousness Chakra or Christ Star energy and it is sitting there waiting for us to stretch and allow ourselves to believe in the 98 percent of our mind that is still uncharted territory. I encourage you to once a year, attend a lecture on a topic that you know absolutely nothing about. And if it is centered around something in which you already judge yourself "poor in wisdom", then that is even better yet! We are here to stretch those mind cells. We are here to forge forward using all our mental faculties. We are here to align ourselves with the infinite mind. Additionally, if you do want to learn something and to incorporate the learning into practice in your life and you have a teacher but you just are not getting it, do not give up on the subject. Find another teacher. Sometimes the teacher only knows one way to teach it and that way doesn't compute with the way your brain works. Believe me, there is more than one teacher of any subject on the planet. I learned this lesson the hard way. In junior high school, because of scoring well on a placement test, I was put in an advanced math class. It seemed that everyone in the class breezed through the lessons. I just couldn't comprehend what was being taught. I was failing miserably. The teacher agreed to meet with me after school and as luck would have it another student, who really didn't need the extra help, decided to show up too. Quite frankly I think she had a crush on the teacher. So of course she supported his technique and I continued be in my own world of "What you are saying doesn't make any sense to me." I frustrated him; he frustrated me. It was only by my parents' wisdom that another tutor helped me and I got through the experience. For years I felt like the village math idiot because of that experience and the fact that I couldn't learn like everyone else in the class did. Then one day, through God's grace I had a dream in which I saw myself at a divine university. I was given the opportunity to sign up for whatever classes I wanted to take. There was a registration angel helping me. After selecting a course, I remember saying to the angel, "Who is going to be my teacher?" The angel replied, "Who do you want to teach you? The choice is yours. There are many teachers available for every subject. Make learning an enjoyable experience." I awoke from the dream realizing there ARE many teachers available for every subject and when something isn't enjoyable or after attempting to stick with the class I am still not making any headway in learning the subject, that's a clue for me to seek out another teacher or to approach learning the subject from another direction.

Now the encounter in England was just the tip of the iceberg. When I came home, I learned that Spiritual Frontiers of Baltimore was hosting a woman, whom I had not yet met, named Rosemary Ellen Guiley. She was the president of the North American Studies of Crop Circles. Rosemary gave a slide presentation of the crop circles she had studied in England. That lecture was my first introduction to Rosemary, who is now one of my dearest friends. She is beautiful inside and out; in fact, she's gorgeous inside and out. She is the most incredible writer and presenter. I encourage you to check out the many books she has written. I truly believe the capital "R" in Rosemary stands for research. She is a brilliant researcher. During her presentation I recognized the crop circle image on one of her slides. I didn't know the image as a crop circle, but rather the configurations or geometric shapes were similar to those I had learned in a mystery school I was participating in. I was intrigued. So I scribbled the images in my journal. I went home and applied the musical notes that I had been taught by the mystery school that were connected with each of the shapes. I had an idea. That weekend I was going to West Virginia for a retreat with the Angelic Sisterhood. Wouldn't it be fun to play the musical notes on a child's xylophone, just like they did in "Close Encounters of the Third Kind?"

At Leaf Lake Lodge in West Virginia, I asked the fifteen ladies if they would be open to an evening meditation around crop circles, space, and communication with the many dimensions of God, followed by the playing of the notes. We meditated together and everyone had expansive meditation experiences. Some felt they floated out with the stars; some felt they were having starship experiences. Afterwards we all went outside on the outdoor balcony of the lodge. In the dark, by flashlight, I played the crop circle-inspired tune. I played the tune three times. Then something unbelievable happened. I am grateful there were 15 witnesses. The lodge had a set of wind chimes on the deck. There was no wind that evening. The chimes had been silent and still. As soon as I concluded the tune for the third time someone from somewhere played the tune back to us exactly on the wind chimes. The wind chimes had been created to play only one set of notes. Something occurred where the wind chimes became a messenger in mirroring back to us the sounds I had sent out to the Universe.

We were all stunned. I once again had one of those out-of-body/in-body experiences and started jumping around the deck in joy and celebration. One of the ladies pointed to a brilliant light in the sky and asked, "Is that Venus?" Another woman replied, "Well if that is Venus, it's coming right toward us!" We all watched while the light moved closer toward us. Rather than a satellite that goes from right to left in the night sky, this brilliant light was moving from up above us, down closer towards us. We could only see a bright ball of light. The light came closer, then stopped and then starting doing loops –spirals sideways. One of the ladies laughed and said, "Look, it's imitating Jayne. It's jumping for joy!" Shortly after the spirals or happy loops, the light beamed rapidly out of our sight. It was just there in one second and gone in the next.

I had the opportunity to speak at an ARE Conference in California the week after that humbling experience and I ended my lecture by telling the story. I told the audience I couldn't explain what happened. I simply wanted to share my experience. When I concluded the lecture, a woman approached me and shared that she was the sister of one of the founders of CSETI and was going to tell him the story. She did in fact do that and I received a beautiful letter from the group asking if I would be willing to share my research with them. I laughed as I read the letter and thought to myself, "What do I do? Get an envelope and place the xylophone inside it and mail it to them?" Because that was the extent of it. I did reply and shared with them the simplicity of the "research" and the "findings" that occurred on the balcony in West Virginia. I honor CSETI because communication is an art. These wonderful people are moving forward with their research in finding ways to communicate with "the unknown" of space and they are doing it with the highest integrity, respect and protocol.

Whether your soul is nourished by the art of configured crops of wheat in England or the art of growing a crop of corn in your own backyard garden, make art your friend and art will befriend you in return. The angels inspired me to take the word friend and develop the message that art is a friend that supports and heals you:

F - Foundation symbols and colors are found through art that allow you to connect with and express your inner ideals/values/core truths that center you.

R - Reconnection with God/Spirit/the divine occurs through art. God wants us to awaken the creator energy in each of us and create beautiful expressions of art ourselves.

I - Inspiration for your soul – your heart – your life occurs through art.

E - Energies radiate through art to your spirit. Art puts you in the flow of divine inspiration, blessings, and healings.

N - Nurturance occurs through art. Your heart, soul and mind are fed abundantly by art.

D - Divine light body emerges through art. The multi-dimensional you awakens through art. Just like a sparkling diamond, art supports you in tapping into "facets" of yourself you didn't even know existed. You discover your inner ability to shine.

As I have shared, there are many ways to be an artisan. Participating in the art of friendship is one of the most satisfying. One of my greatest joys in life is spreading the message that we all have "friends in high places". We have family members and friends who are in heaven who love us abundantly in addition to our angelic friends watching over us, too. "What is a friend? A single soul in two bodies." wrote Aristotle. Just as the angels, family members and friends in heaven are blessings and benefactors and providers of goodness in our lives, we have blessings in our good friends here beside us on earth. Just as the friendship of angels is a gift from God, precious human friendship is equally a treasure. Friends are truly angels by our side.

The Dictionary of Word Origins explains the original meaning of the word friend. "Etymologically, friend means 'loving'. It and its Germanic relatives (German freund, Dutch vriend, Swedish frande, etc.) go back to the present participle of the prehistoric Germanic verb *frijojan 'love'." A friend is a gift of love. As I have shared in my prior books, back in 1993 I founded the celebration of BE AN ANGEL DAY annually on August 22nd. In promoting this annual event I encourage people to be an angel and do one small act of service for someone, and to search out ways to be a blessing in someone's life. Additionally I promote a specific inspirational thought for each year. The celebration for the 11th Annual Be An Angel Day held on August 22, 2003 was "Be an Angel. Be a friend."

Having friendships in your life can make your life healthier. Having friends can improve your physical, spiritual, emotional and mental health. Being able to pick up the telephone, call a friend, and talk helps to relieve stress. In writing Driving Under the Influence of Angels, one of my heartfelt desires was to honor people who have truly been earth angels in my life. My friends have supported me through all of my life's challenges. There were times when the going got tough and my friends gave me the feeling that no matter what I had to face, I did not face it alone. I treasure my friends and know I am a wealthy woman when it comes to golden friendships.

Additionally, my friends are the treasure in my life when things are tame. I have found that it is important to see the art of friendship as something that requires a "maintenance program". In maintaining my friendships, I am truly supporting myself in maintaining my sanity in a sometimes crazy world.

My friends represent the most beautiful flowers growing in a garden of love and they need my attention if I expect the friendship to bloom. I deem tending to my friendships as an important priority.

Johann Wolfgange Von Goethe wrote: "The world is so empty if one thinks only of mountains, rivers and cities, but to know someone here and there who thinks and feels with us and who, though distant, is close to us in spirit, makes the earth a garden." I agree with the belief that my friendships, friends of all the kingdoms of the earth, make the reality I share with them a garden of love.

I do recognize that our lives are so very, very busy and the days turn to weeks and then years quickly. Have you ever had the sad experience of thinking about someone, and wanting to make time to visit with them or contact them, and then suddenly they pass away? I have had that happen and I call the experience a "soul shudder". My soul shudders at the thought of a missed opportunity to tell someone while they were here on the earth with me that I care for them.

From "soul shudders" I have learned not to postpone but to make fun dates now with my friends and to continue that practice every month. I think it is one of the healthiest things I can do for myself. We get together for tea or lunch or a movie, and we laugh, and laugh and laugh. It never fails that I learn something new from my friends. They tell me a program to watch, a book to read, or a movie to see. They tell me ways they are improving their lives. I have found that through friendship we can divide and conquer a great deal of information. I don't have to read everything on the planet, because my girlfriends are doing their share and filling me in at our monthly get-togethers.

I recently read a beautiful article about friendship written by Victor Parachin that appeared in The Mayans' Daily Meditation magazine in July, 2003. In his article he listed ways to practice the fine art of friendship. Think of yourself as an artist who is master of the "Fine Art of Friendship." Here are some of Victor's ideas: "Reach out. To make a friend, be a friend. Make friendship a priority. Even though you are busy, schedule friends on your calendar just as you do a medical appointment. Show friends you care. Curb criticism. Remember: Small gestures make big differences. Assess before you invest (before you commit to a new friendship, know it is an investment of time, energy and spirit). Never gossip about a friend. Practice loyalty. Be a foul-weather friend." In the words of Walter Winchell: "A friend is one who walks in when others walk out."

Think about your precious friends often. Make time to keep in touch by writing a letter, making a phone call or sending an email. Let your friends know how much you love them and are grateful for their friendship. And I would be remiss not to honor the friendship we have with the animal kingdom. They are friends who love us unconditionally. So make time for your pets, too. My Jack Russells, Benny, Riot and Jackie, are my bestest buddies. For those of you who read Driving Under the Influence of Angels, which was published by ARE Press in 2002, you may remember at that time I had as pets Benny and Riot. In early 2003 I was telling Chuck about the things I wanted to do in 2003. In the midst of the conversation these words came out of my mouth and where they came from I am not quite certain, "and I want to be a Jack Russell Rescue home." Chuck looked at me and asked, "What is a Jack Russell Rescue home?" I looked bewildered myself when I replied, "I don't exactly know but I am going to find out."

In researching Jack Russell Rescue I learned that we could become a foster home for Jack Russell dogs that were rescued from local pounds. We would keep the dog until someone who wanted to adopt the dog came forward. I talked to Chuck about the idea and we both agreed that since Benny and Riot brought such joy into our lives, this would be a wonderful service, to become a foster home. So I filled out all the necessary paperwork and waited for Jack Russell Rescue to assign a foster dog to our home.

The weekend of March 1st we received a phone call. We were asked if we were willing to take a special case. The dog was named Jackie. She was 12 years old. She was born on March 1st, 1990 and since the time she was a puppy till just recently she had had one owner who was an older man. The man had died. None of his family wanted Jackie. She was taken to the local pound where she was rescued from death by Jack Russell Rescue. We were told she slept a lot because she was an older dog. She couldn't go up stairs because of her age. She ate very little. She had tumors and cataracts. We drove to a McDonald's parking lot in Frederick, Maryland, the meeting point for picking up Jackie. I remember when we placed Jackie in our car. She looked so frightened and scared. I got right up in her face and said, "Precious Jackie, we love you. You don't have to worry about a thing now.

We are going to take care of you." She proceeded to bite that big protruding thing I had stuck in her face, namely, my nose. Ouch! I deserved that.

Chuck and I realized that we now had a third dog for keeps because quite frankly, who goes looking for a 12-year old dog with tumors and cataracts. I soon realized that Jackie's owner was watching from heaven the events taking place, especially the possibility of Jackie's life ending. The owner must have thought to himself, "I have to find a home for Jackie." And so on that day back in early 2003 it was his angel who whispered to me the words that came out of no where and into my mouth, "I want to be a Jack Russell Rescue home." I have told this individual in spirit he is more than welcome to come visit Jackie in our home anytime he wants; after all, Jackie was his best friend for 12 years.

I encourage you to make arrangements now for the care of your pets in case you are no longer able to care for them. Ask your best friend if they would be comfortable acting as guardian to your pets. This is another way of being a good steward to these loving angels with fur who are by our side.

At the same time Jackie came into our lives, I found articles in the newspaper about how single men and women soldiers who were sent to fight in Iraq were facing the dilemma of finding people to care for their pets while they were away. Perhaps a way to support our troops is to offer your services as a foster home for the pets of soldiers overseas. I have to be truthful, however, if I bring one more pet home to Angel Heights, I may be advertising that I need a foster home.

An amazing thing has happened since Jackie came into our home. The dog that supposedly couldn't go up steps, slept all the time and didn't eat much has now been transformed into a dog that races down the steps every morning leading the way ahead of Benny and Riot; she wants to join in all the play, and gets great enjoyment at meal time when she happily gobbles down her food. Plus she's kissing and licking my nose rather than biting it off.

There are many ways we can express the inner artisan energy in our lives. The arts of friendship, cooking, home decorating, feng shui, gardening, painting, dancing, music, theater, and poetry are just a few. In the words of Joseph Campbell, "Follow your bliss."

My bliss or passion for art has grown such that it is now a passion to be a messenger of art to others. My husband and I have made our home, Angel Heights, a home that is filled with art in every room. We love inviting people into our home not only for the enjoyment of friendship, but also the enjoyment of the art we have to share. In all of my seminars and retreats, I show art images to participants to inspire them and give them the opportunity to experience art as a spiritual tool. I gift art as presents. I buy movie gift certificates and enjoy popping them inside a note or card to a friend. I promote art by including mention of important art events taking place in Maryland whenever and wherever I speak. Perhaps there is something that you are passionate about in your own life. You first have to hear the message for yourself. And that's not an easy task with all the annoyances and distractions in life. In my own life, by the grace and love of God I heard the whisperings of the angels encouraging me to discover my soul's passion for art. I pursued this path with a fervor and conviction. Then one day I realized that just as the angels have been messengers to me, I had become a messenger to others. I was an earth angel promoting inner peace through art. I was spreading the divine message that art is one of many glorious ways God has given us to inspire and discover within ourselves our own inner creative abilities.

In Driving Under the Influence of Angels I shared a quote by Jose Arguelles in which he applied to the letters A – R – T the words "A Radical Transformation."

At the World Summit on Peace and Time held at the University of Peace in Coasta Rica from June 22-27, 1999, the following article was included in a Declaration of Calendar Reform developed by Dr. Jose and Lloydine Arguelles, along with other summit participants. I hope you'll read out loud to yourself the following article: Article VII. Commission on Art and Culture.

The time has come for humankind to once again honor the role of Art in the process of healing the soul. When the people's consciousness is connected to the heart, then the potential of Art as Time is recognized, [Global Culture] is birthed from the union of Science, Art and Spirit, awakening unity through diversity, a living model of peace.

We resolve:

- The reinstitution of sacred ritual and ceremony as integral components of cultural unification, acknowledgment of universal holidays or [holy days] in particular, that of a Universal "Day Out of Time", a planetary pause, on the 25th of July each year, as an International Day for the celebration of Arts and Culture. This act of global synchronization, with the focused intention to share in arts and culture has served as an invitation as well as a template for individuals, communities and nations to unify in the spirit of Festival, open to a spectrum of interpretation in form, empowering and enriching all peoples in acts of creativity. This respect for diversity assures peace.
- With the institution of Peace, the creation of a Global Endowment for the Arts, in order to supply materials for the teaching and

demonstrations of art. These funds will be generously applied in projects for the arts within institutions of education, hospitals, rehabilitation centers, industries, and human care facilities in all communities.

- The formation of self-sustainable arts communities, utilizing cooperative lands in the return to a natural rhythm; joining as spiritual families, uniting races and traditions in honoring and respecting the Earth in creative processes of permaculture, hand crafts, and healing therapies.
- The promotion of multi-cultural art exchanges, intuitive art programs and caravans for the Arts to integrate concepts of global peace and harmony with Nature into each and every community of the planet.
- The adoption of symbolic representations of an awakened planetary consciousness, such as flags, monuments, songs and other expressions of love.
- Art is a means to inspire all humanity to its greatest evolutionary potential. Art is not only an external expression, but a way of life in an awakened culture that recognizes that every human being is an artist, creator and co-creator of global peace. The ultimate act of creation is the creation of peace.

In writing this chapter, I asked the Art Angels to inspire me with the message to end this chapter. Shortly after making that prayer request, I was watching the BRAVO channel on cable TV, and saw an ad for "Art. Ask for More," a national arts education public awareness campaign sponsored by Americans for the Arts. Americans for the Arts is the nation's leading nonprofit organization for advancing the arts in America.

The website www.artsusa.org. promotes this message: "The less art kids get, the more it shows. ART. Ask for more." Additionally the website offers suggestions for how all of us can help make a difference in assuring children get more art into their lives and the importance that art plays in children's lives. Did you know that the arts teach kids to be more tolerant; express themselves creatively; promote individuality, bolster confidence; and improve overall academic performance? It's true. The arts can also help troubled youth, providing an alternative to delinquent behavior. Research reported in "Living the Arts through Language + Learning: A Report on Community-based Youth Organizations, Shirley Brice Hearth, Stanford University and Carnegie Foundation for the Advancement of Teaching, Americans for the Arts Monograph, November 1998" shows that young people who participate in the arts for at least three hours a week through at least one full year are:

Four times more likely to be recognized for academic achievement
Three times more likely to be elected to class office within their school
Four times more likely to participate in a math and science fair
Three times more likely to win an award for school attendance
Four times more likely to win an award for writing an essay or poem
Attend music, art and dance classes nearly three times as frequently
Participate in youth groups nearly four times as frequently
Read for pleasure nearly twice as often
Perform community service more than four times as often

Art education truly impacts children's lives in an uplifting way; in fact, it positively impacts people of all ages. It is a message that the Art Angels and heavenly hosts are squarely behind. It was the reason for my angelic assignment of establishing INSPIRE YOUR HEART WITH THE ARTS DAY in an effort to promote a global awareness of how healthy art activities are for us spiritually, mentally, physically and emotionally. There's no coincidence that in the word "heART" you find the letters that spell ART. It's a divine clue that art is good for your heart.

The importance of the arts in our lives is a message that our president stands squarely behind, too. President George W. Bush made the following statements about the importance of the arts: "From music and dance to painting and sculpting, the arts allow us to explore new worlds and to view life from another perspective. They also encourage individuals to sharpen their skills and abilities and to nurture their imagination and intellect."

Make today the day you pARTicipate in the arts.

Chapter 6

TREE ANGELS

In 1997 the theme the angels inspired me to share in promoting BE AN ANGEL DAY was "Have a Tree-mendous Be An Angel Day." In my talks about the annual angel day celebration I was encouraging audiences – whether I was on the radio, or appearing at lectures - to consider the words of an English proverb: "He that plants trees loves others besides himself."

Zoroaster, a Middle Eastern philosopher and religious reformer who lived in the sixth century B.C., taught his students the following law: if you have one child you must plant one tree a month; if you have two children you must plant two trees a month; and if you have ten children you must plant ten trees a month. As soon as the children are grown, it becomes their responsibility to make certain that the multiplying of trees continue so that when these trees grow old, new ones replace them. Zoroaster recognized forests as the greatest natural treasure we have.

The trees are the lungs of the earth. The trees do not exist because of us. We exist because God gave us trees. Marco Polo shared the story that in traveling through Siberia he met a local tribe that believed the king of their tribe was not of human birth but rather was born from the trees. In the Druid culture, highly illumined philosophers and priests were referred to as tree men or trees. Legend has it that Alexander the Great spoke to talking trees. Buddha received his illumination while under the bodhi tree near Madras, in India. Trees are mentioned throughout the Old and New Testament.

In my travels I have seen numerous times the Jesse Tree depicted in religious art and illuminated manuscripts. This symbol is derived from the 11th chapter of Isaiah. In this chapter Jesse is shown resting on the ground. From his loins a great tree rises above him. In artistic depictions of the Jesse Tree numerous figures of his descendants are pictured above the tree. According to St. Matthew this tree was a prophecy of Jesus Christ's genealogy. At the top of the tree is Mary holding the Christ child. Seven doves surround Christ, representing the seven gifts of the Holy Spirit. When I was in Chartres I traveled to the celebrated Jesse Tree Window. Its dates back to 1145 A.D.

Additionally, in the Bible we learn God created two trees in Paradise: the tree of knowledge of good and evil and the tree of life. Adam and Eve disobeyed God, ate of the tree of knowledge of good and evil and were cast out of the Garden of Eden, thus prevented from ever eating from the tree of life. Christians believe that Christ's cross became the tree of life and in the early church a tree was often used to symbolize Christ.

Jung researched the symbolism of a tree as an archetypal symbol of a human's spiritual growth. Jacob Bohme was an earlier messenger of this concept in his book Law's Figures. He described a divine tree in man. "A tree with its roots in the heart rises from the Mirror of the Deity through the Sphere of Understanding to branch forth in the Sphere of the Senses. The roots and trunk of this tree represent the divine nature of man and may be called his spirituality: the branches of the tree are the separate parts of the divine constitution and may be likened to the individuality; and the leaves – because of their ephemeral nature – correspond to the personality, which partakes of none of the permanence of its divine source."

Religious temples were often built in the center of sacred groves because trees were believed to possess divine intelligence and power.

During that "Tree-mendous" theme year I offered the suggestion of planting trees wherever there are children, as a symbolic gesture of supporting the future generations of the earth and our desire to leave the earth in better condition than we found it.

Additionally, I encouraged the public to plant a tree in memory of a loved one in heaven. Life is eternal! As trees are planted for the children of the earth and the memory of children in heaven, we are accepting that the circle of life is never broken. Many people arrange for a tree to be planted in the Holy Land through the organization Trees for the Holy Land, whose motto is "Give trees…Give Life." Israel is the spiritual and religious homeland for three of the world' s major religions. The land of Abraham, Jesus and Muhammad. Trees are planted in the Holy Land of Israel in memoriam, in celebration, for churches and groups, for children.

When I was weaving a Star of David grid energy across the United States, an angelic assignment which I explain in detail in Driving Under the Influence of Angels, I fulfilled the service with the help of archangels, angels, saints, and the kingdom of nature. During the anchoring of the fifth point of the grid in the Northeast United States, I served with the trees of the earth. The trees are the ancient ones on our planet. Trees inspire us to be connected to both heaven and earth for they themselves exist in two worlds. With their trunks rooted solidly to the ground they teach us the importance of similarly having roots that will support us, i.e. the rooted foundation of our beliefs, ideals, and values. Additionally their branches reach upward towards heaven inspiring us to reach upwards to God, to reach high with our visions and our dreams.

Rabindranath Tagore in Fireflies wrote, "Trees are the earth's endless effort to speak to the listening heaven." Have you ever listened to the wind moving through the trees and heard a sound coming forth from the rustling of the leaves? To me it is the "music of the spheres" and I believe the trees are joining in the music-making by accompanying the wind to honor God.

There are Middle Eastern traditions where people practice "Phyllomancy." This is the art of hearing God speak through the rustling of the leaves of the trees. In the Bible in Judges 4:5 we learn of Deborah, a ruler of Israel, who lived under a tree that bore her name. The tree would have been considered an oracle tree, i.e. a tree that had a voice. The tree would share wisdom with those who communed with the tree by living beside the tree. It is a powerful message that those who live their lives where there is wisdom, will hear it.

I love the trees and part of my life's service is in support of the trees here on earth as is it the service of many of the members of the Ha Ha group. All of the angel tours have taken us to the woods and forests where Mother Earth has asked us to bring healing. We traveled to the woodlands of Bosnia, Ireland, Scotland, Turkey, France and Germany to be of healing service to God.

We as humans have oftentimes forgotten that we share the earth with all the kingdoms. We sometimes think only of ourselves and this kind of thinking can create an imbalance in nature. Additionally, we sometimes do things that result in toxins going into the ground, to be shared by the roots of the trees. Many of us in the Ha Ha group have had experiences where we developed unexplainable body rashes. I, in fact, broke out in a rash that formed a tree on the trunk of my body. After visiting the doctor and being told I just needed to wait it out, and that he didn't have a clue how long that would be, I asked the angels what the heck was going on. I was told simply: transmutation on behalf of the trees. The transmutation healing consists of taking the toxins into our bodies, and allowing the healing to occur within us, because we humans are the ones who put the toxins in the earth in the first place. I later shared the rash story with my angelic girlfriends, and was amazed at the number of them who were experiencing similar bizarre rashes. All of our rashes eventually went away. Sometimes we say in prayer to God: Lord, I am ready, here I am, use me. God replies, "Ok, let's clean up the earth. And YOU get to be the filtration system."

Trees are incredible blessings from God. In many cultures such as the Celtic, woods and forests were revered as sacred because of the many blessings they provided. The woodlands provided nuts from the trees; game lived in the forest; wood could be used for kindling and the building of homes that provided shelter. Wise ones of ancient times recognized that trees were sacred and before a tree was cut down a ritual was performed to ask forgiveness from the tree. An old Scottish poem gives the recipe for the nine sacred woods that are to be used for kindling for the ritual of the Beltaine fire, a fire that is burned on the even of May 1st. On Beltaine Eve druids would position themselves on hills and view the rising sun. It was their belief that the burning fires would draw the sun's power to them and would bless their community. The poem goes as follows:

Choose the willow of the streams,
Choose the hazel of the rocks,
Choose the alder of the marshes,
Choose the birth of the waterfalls,
Choose the ash of the shade,
Choose the yew of resilience,
Choose the elm of the brae,
Choose the oak of the sun.

If you are counting the trees listed, you will note there are only eight given in the poem. The ninth was only known if you could talk to the trees and were deemed worthy enough to be told. A forest is a place of many divine gifts waiting to be shared. Fiona MacLeod, a Celtic visionary of the late 19th century whose identity was later revealed to be William Sharp, a man who wanted to express his feminine side, once said, "Where the forest murmurs there is music: ancient, everlasting."

There is a divine order to life that the trees mirror to us through the cycles at work. The wind in the fall drops the autumn leaves to the ground. The leaves resting on the ground soon decay and give nourishment to the roots of the tree that support the new growth of the tree in springtime. Trees teach us that there is a season for everything and to be comfortable with the cycles of our life.

I have seen the angels of nature who are guardians to the trees. They are often taller than the trees that they watch over. I have seen them float from tree to tree in a forest merging with the energies of the tree. They shapeshift themselves into light beings that radiate a rich hunter green ray of light. Once they merge with the tree, and infuse the tree with God's changing energies, the angels' radiating light morphs from the hunter green to become a pure white. I had the sensing that an energy transfusion was taking place. Have you ever walked through a woods and thought for certain you saw a humanlike face or form in a tree?

If you would like to see beautiful illustrations of "Lords of the Trees" find a copy of Geoffrey Hodson's The Kingdom of the Gods. Geoffrey had similar experiences to mine in seeing spirits of trees and described them as follows: "nearly all well-grown trees have attached to them…an advanced nature spirit…the presence of such being through the constant play of its thoughts and auric energies, greatly quickens the evolution of tree life and consciousness."

If there are woods near your home or on your property, learn which tree is the King Tree Devas. Simply ask the angels of nature to guide you to the King Tree Deva or the Father of the Forest. The tree that is the oldest tree in the community or grove of trees. Just as is true with kings of the human kingdom, he projects a regal quality and functions as an "elder statesman" watching over the community. His energies are a stimulating force of God in the woods community and can be translated as a message to the younger trees to "Grow tall! Grow up!" What a wonderful message for human parents to give to their little seedlings: "Grow tall." Additionally the names of the trees were used in the formation of the ogham alphabet. Each letter was named for a tree, and messages were shared by designating leaves for each of the alphabet letters and placing the leaves on a word. Leaves from trees that were not included in the alphabet were considered "space" letters or "blank" leaves to divide words from one another.

Here's the alphabet used by the Druids. The letter of the alphabet is shown first, with the name of the tree that represented the letter in the alphabet, and the Druid name for the tree as it was spelled in the Druid alphabet.

The Consonants

B	Birch (Beth)
L	Rowan (Luis)
N	Ash (Nion)
F	Alder (Fearn)
S	Willow (Saille)
H	Hawthorne (Uath)
D	Oak (Duir)
T	Holly (Tinne)
C	Hazel (Coll)
M	Vine (Muin)
G	Ivy (Fort)
P	Dwarf Elder (Pethboc)
R	Elder (Ruis)

The Vowels

A	Silver Fir (Ailm)
O	Furze (Onn)
U	Heather (Ur)
E	White Poplar (Eadha)
I	Yew (Idho)

I encourage you to think about trees you have loved in your life. Perhaps there was a special tree in your family's backyard when you were growing up. Perhaps there is a beloved tree in your own backyard.

Make time to be with the trees of the earth. Talk to the trees and then listen. Ask the trees what it is like to be a tree.

One of my all-time favorite books is Jeffrey Goelitz's <u>Secrets from the Lives of Trees</u>. Jeffrey shares a conversation with a backyard poplar during which the tree talks about the wind coming:

"When the wind comes, I dance. Dancing in the wind is a very alive experience, especially when the sun is out. When I dance and my branches sway and my leaves shake, the fairies dance right alongside in joy. They are delightful to have around. I'm built to move. My delicate structure allows me to be flexible. It is partly out of who I am and partly out of survival. I can't help it. Isn't it wonderful that dancing in the wind helps me survive?"

Recently when I re-read Jeffrey's book again, I thought of a popular song, "I Hope You'll Dance." The song conveys the message of the songwriter that if you have the chance, it is hoped that you will take the opportunity to dance. After reading the tree's words: "When the wind comes, I dance," I carefully considered these incredible words of wisdom. When the winds of change blow into our lives, let's remember to DANCE! Let's cha-cha right through the challenges; let's tango through entanglements.

It's hard to say that there's a best part of Jeffrey's book, because every page is a treasure; however, my favorite part is in Chapter Eight where there are Modern Contributions from people who have loved and communicated with trees. I have shared the following with many audiences because it is truly a blessing.

The excerpt came from an interview Jeffrey gave with Marcel Vogel. Jeffrey led into the except with an explanation of who Marcel Vogel is, which included this first sentence: "Marcel Vogel was a Senior Scientist with IBM for 27 years until his retirement in 1984, when he formed his own laboratory, Psychic Research, Inc."

Vogel shared this thought in the interview. "The oldest living form on this planet is the Sequoia gigantean. If you approach it with your hands open, you will feel the entire history of this earth plane contained in the tree. It's a record keeper; the patterns of life are stored in a tree. If you draw in your breath, open the thymus and the solar plexus and then embrace a tree, release your breath into the tree and then breathe again, suddenly you and the tree become one. You will feel your body oscillate to the rhythm of the tree and you will go deeper and deeper, you are drawn into the tree. You and the tree become one. As you do this you realize a oneness with all life. That to me is very beautiful."

When I first read that statement, I put down the book and thought to myself, "You, Marcel Vogel, are very beautiful!" Since then I have been introduced to amazing crystals that were developed by Vogel in his laboratory.

In growing up on my parents' farm, I would love to walk across the pastures and cross over Byerly Road to the property that was part of the farm across the street. I would march up the hill to the top and sit beside the huge tulip poplar tree. I would nestle myself into the groove that the roots created next to the tree and spend hours with my friend, whom I secretly called "Old Pop" because it was a very old poplar. I spent many wonderful childhood hours leaning up against Old Pop. Tulip polar trees have a flower that looks just like a tulip. The flowers are pale green petals flecked with orange. The tree can grow to heights of 170 feet. Old Pop is 90 feet tall.

My dad obviously observed the love that existed between the tree and me because after I married for the first time, he took me out to lunch one day and said, "How would you like to buy the land at the top of the hill with the tulip poplar tree?" I remember sitting there across from Dad and experiencing a feeling that something too wonderful was happening to me. Something so wonderful I had never even dared to believe it possible for myself. I am one of six children, and so the property could not be just gifted to me in fairness to my siblings. A fair market price was determined and the transfer of title was made. "Old Pop" and I are still together. In fact, as I am writing this book I can look out the window to my left and see Old Pop standing tall – over 90 feet tall. Old Pop is registered as one of the great trees of Maryland. In 1976 I hoped that Old Pop would be recognized as a bi-centennial tree, and it was at that time I learned that Old Pop was planted a few years after 1776, which means this year Old Pop is celebrating 225 years of life here in Upperco, Maryland. I think somehow that makes Old Pop the un-official Mayor of Upperco. I love when people stand under the tree and say, "If only this tree could talk!" I smile inside and think, "He does!"

One way to support the healing of the earth is to send love and appreciation to all the trees. Greet the trees on your way to work each day. Notice the trees that share your environment. Every tree has its own special energy. Make time to place yourself near trees and experience their different life forces. Talk to trees. Let the answers and messages the trees give to you float into your mind.

Someone who has found a way to honor America's historic trees is Alabaman Stephen Malkoff. In his words: "Trees have been silent witnesses to our nation's history," and Stephen has captured the beauty of America's exceptional trees through his pencil portraits.

Malkoff's vision is to create a portrait of an historic tree in each state and the District of Columbia. Upon completion of this, he hopes to hang them in a venue like the National Botanical Garden. Along the way of fulfilling this vision, Malkoff has been recognized by American Forests, who selected him to be the artist for the National Register of Historic Trees. In an interview for Country Living magazine, March 2003, Malkoff shared that his favorite subjects include, "Arlington National Cemetery's John F. Kennedy Post Oak; General Sherman, a 2,400-year-old sequoia in Central California; and a tulip poplar that George Washington planted at Mount Vernon at the dawn of our nation." Think about the trees you have met during your travels down life's road. As I contemplate the amazing trees I have met in my travels, the banyan tree at Thomas Edison's summer home in Fort Myers, Florida comes immediately to mind. It is the largest Banyan tree in the United States. Thomas Edison planted it as a seedling, which was a gift from Harvey Firestone. Many of us became acquainted with the following poem during our school years. I think it is a perfect way to honor the trees. Take this book out with you when you visit with your friends the trees and read the poem to them:

Trees
(For Mrs. Henry Mill Alden)
I think that I shall never see
A poem lovely as a tree.
A tree whose hungry mouth is prest
Against the earth's sweet flowing breast;
A tree that looks at God all day,
And lifts her leafy arms to pray;
A tree that may in Summer wear
A nest of robins in her hair;
Upon whose bosom snow has lain;
Who intimately lives with rain.
Poems are made by fools like me,
But only God can make a tree.
— Alfred Joyce Kilmer

As Hal Lindsey, columnist for the WorldNet Daily expressed in one of his columns, "Among the losses to society as a consequence of the carnage of the Great War (World War I) was a young poet named Joyce Kilmer. A daring and courageous solider of the famous "Fighting 69th," Sgt. Alfred Joyce Kilmer was killed in action near the French town of Seringes on July 30, 1918. Kilmer was best known for his poem "Trees." Kilmer penned his famous poem on February 2, 1913."

Edmond Bordeaux Szekely founded in 1928 the International Biogenic Society with Nobel Prize-winning author, Romain Rolland. He authored more than 80 books on philosophy and ancient cultures. His work included translations of selected texts from the Dead Sea Scrolls, Essene Gospel of Peace and selected texts from the Zend Avesta of Zoroaster, whom I mentioned earlier. Following his death, his wife, Norma, found a manuscript written in his own hand from his research work. This manuscript shared Essene traditions from original Zoroastrian sources concerning regenerative "communions" with "Holy Streams of Life, Sound and Light." One of the communions is The Morning Communion With the Tree of Life:

The Communion
Brother Tree…Brother Life
"Gray are all the theories, But Green is the Tree of Life." – Goethe
"God is the God of the living…" – The Essence Gospel of Peace

"The Tree is the Law Itself" - Zarathustra

You are floating through the green foliage of a beautiful forest, the sun filtering through the lacy web of leaves, a carpet of velvet green beneath you. You pause before a tall, majestic tree and embrace it. You feel the life-forces of the tree flowing through you. As you breathe deeply, repeat to yourself the word 'Life.' Soon you will feel the tingling of the life-forces of the trees in your spine, and you can direct these forces to the areas of your body which need healing. At the end of this communion say, "Thank you, Brother Tree."

God has blessed us so abundantly with the gift of sharing the earth with the trees. Shakespeare sought to find "tongues in trees, books in the running brooks, sermons in stones, and good in everything."

Think of times when it has been so hot outside and you have sought protection from the sun under a tree. Perhaps you are also protecting your home from strong winds by creating a barrier with trees. Trees have been your playmates when you climbed them, played in them, and maybe even built a house in them.

Think of the subtle way we have recognized the power of trees through the statement we oftentimes say even without thinking, "Knock on wood." That statement evolved from a time when people wanting to cut down a tree would literally knock on a tree to make certain no spirits were residing in the tree.

If you want to open yourself to the trees, I encourage you to follow the same suggestions I offered in Commune with the Angels for opening to angels. First, believe in the trees. Believe in them not as spiritless, but rather your forest friends who support your life by their presence. Read about trees. Two great books for your reading pleasure are Meetings with Remarkable Trees and Remarkable Trees of the World, both written by Thomas Pakenham. If you want to give a gift of love, give someone you care about a seedling tree and one of these books. These are great coffee table books.

Make time in your life for visiting parks, taking walks to where there are trees. Sit under a tree and meditate.

Just as the Boys Scouts do, learn to recognize the different trees. Give endearing names to your favorite trees or ask them what they would like to be called.

Reflect upon trees with "soft-gaze" eyes and allow yourself inner eyes to show you the fairies that share sacred space with the tree community.

In addition to loving art, I also love great architecture. One of the best examples of an architect honoring the environment in which he is building a home is Frank Lloyd Wright's Fallingwater. Wright once said, "Nothing is more difficult to achieve than the integral simplicity of organic nature, amid the tangled confusions of the innumerable relics of form that encumber life for us. To achieve it in any degree means serious devotion to the 'underneath' in an attempt to grasp the nature of building a beautiful building beautifully, as organically true in itself, to itself and to its purpose, as any tree or flower."

When you tour Fallingwater. you will find a home that appears to have been placed over the waterfalls and amongst the trees. Nothing of nature appears to have been disturbed. You will see that the home was built around the trees. Wright wanted the trees to freely rise through the house in witness to the union of home and woods. Edgar Kaufmann, Jr., whose father hired Frank Lloyd Wright to build a weekend home for his family, wrote in his introduction of Frank Lloyd Wright's Fallingwater: "When Wright came to the site he appreciated the powerful sound of the falls, the vitality of the young forest, the dramatic rock ledges and boulders...But Wright's insight penetrated more deeply. He understood that people were creatures of nature, hence an architecture which conformed to nature would conform to what was basic in people...It (Fallingwater) indicates a world in which the works of mankind and the processes of nature harmonize productively." A sign we have posted on our property reads: We live in harmony here on the hill.

Whenever you feel spacey and need to feel grounded, go to the trees for strength. You can go to a favorite tree by actually going there physically, or you can go in your mind. Stand before the tree and greet it as you would a precious friend. You may want to put your arms around the tree and exchange hugs. Then sit down beside the tree with your back to the trunk of the tree. Feel yourself supported by the tree. If you are doing this inside your home, a wonderful way to do this is to sit with your back up against the wall.

Remember the words of Marcel Vogel: "If you draw in your breath, open the thymus and the solar plexus and then embrace a tree, release your breath into the tree and then breathe again, suddenly you and the tree become one. You will feel your body oscillate to the rhythm of the tree and as you go deeper and deeper, you are drawn into the tree. You and the tree become one."

Take long, slow deep breaths. Concentrate as you release your breath into the tree. Feel your body totally relax. Go deeper and deeper into relaxation.

Imagine yourself merging with the tree. The roots of the tree are one with you and you can feel yourself connected to the earth. You feel yourself grounded. You feel the energies of the Mother Earth blessing you and providing nourishment to you. Let the energies flow throughout your body. Have a sensing that every cell, atom and molecule is abundantly fed by the earth. You are one with the tree. One with Mother Earth.

Then see yourself merging with the branches of the tree. You and the tree are reaching up toward the heavens together. You reach higher and higher. You feel a oneness with the tree and a oneness with Father Heavens. Let yourself flow with the divine energies from the heavens.

Feel the flowing of energies from below you and from above you. You are perfectly balanced in oneness with heaven and earth, soul and spirit. Your male and female energies are in balance, too. You are breathing divine energy.

In this place of peace, give thanksgiving to God the Creator for your oneness with heaven, your oneness with earth, and your oneness with the trees that connect us to heaven and earth. In this sacred space, ask God how you can be of service. Ask how you can help to root God's love solidly on earth. Be still and listen for God's answer. Ask how you can become a messenger of the importance of "reaching for the sky;" reaching up for God. Listen for the answer. Ask how you can be a blessing to the trees that are a blessing to you. Listen for the answer.

Let your focus and attention return to the tree you introduced yourself to; the tree you greeted and hugged. Become aware of the tree, its roots, trunk, branches. Become aware of your body, your arms and legs. Focus on your body and open your eyes and feel a joy in your heart for God's tree-mendous love for us shown to us by the relationship we share with trees.

Pentti Holappa, a Finnish writer, proclaimed, "If I were a mystic, I would join to a religious sect worshipping big trees as materializations of God." There is a religious sect that wove into their daily rituals a communion with invisible angelic forces and powers of the roots and branches of trees, in particular one tree – the tree of life. This group was known as the Essenes, whom I mentioned earlier in this chapter.

The Essenes were a mystical brotherhood that lived during the last two or three centuries, B.C. and the first century of the Christian era. They resided at Lake Mareotis in Egypt and the Dead Sea in Palestine. There is a belief that the brotherhood claims Enoch as their founder, and that the "communions" taught by the brotherhood were first given to Enoch by the angels. The Bible describes Enoch as a man who walked with God. Enoch was translated to heaven; that is, he did not die. "And Enoch walked with God; and he was not; for God took him." Genesis 5:24.

The Essenes lived their lives communing with all kingdoms of the earth. They honored all that God created. It is believed that they were the first group of people to condemn any form of slavery. Their lives were ones of simplicity. They would greet the new day before sunrise. They studied each morning and communed with nature. They performed daily labor as agriculturists and arboriculturists. They were vegetarians. They lived lives that were in excess of 120+ years.

In order to join the brotherhood, a three-year probation period was required, followed by three years of initiation work and then seven more years of service even before the new member was to be introduced to any of the inner sanctum teachings. Each neophyte was required to take a vow before the words of the communions were revealed. The first part of the sevenfold vow reveals an alignment with the Tree of Life:

"I want to and will do my best to live like the Tree of Life, planted by the Great Masters of our Brotherhood, with my Heavenly Father who planted the Eternal Garden of the Universe and gave me my spirit; with my Earthly Mother who planted the Great Garden of the Earth and gave me my body; with my brothers who are working in the Garden of our Brotherhood."

As I mentioned earlier, Dr. Edmond Bordeaux Szekely translated and published the ancient Essene teachings. All of his publications are available from the International Biogenic Society which describes itself on its website as follows: International Biogenic Society "is a nonsectarian, nonpolitical, scientific, educational association of Individual Associate Members and Associate Teachers, for the teaching of the various aspects of Biogenic Living as well as the many all-sided practical applications of the ancient Essene Teachings in our daily lives in the twentieth century." The Society was founded in Paris in 1928 by the Nobel prize-winning author Remain Rolland and the philosopher Edmond Bordeaux Szekely, Ph.D. The IBS evolved out of Dr. Szekely's research on ancient civilizations and religions, and in particular on the Essene brotherhood of first century A.D. Judaea. Early in his education, Dr. Szekely earned the privilege of studying ancient manuscripts at the Archives of the Vatican, under the direction of Msgr. Mercati. His research began with the study of the venerable Saint Francis, which led him to the writings of Saint Benedict and the manuscripts that he had preserved that dated back to the fourth century A.D. These manuscripts were Saint Jerome's translations of first-century biblical codices, which included the Hebrew writings of the Essene Brotherhood.

During the middle of the fourth century A.D., Saint Jerome spent twenty years traveling in the Holy Land deciphering fragments of ancient first-century A.D. manuscripts. During this time he gathered letters from an ancient brotherhood of the desert known as the Essenes, and began translating these fragments from Hebrew into Latin. Having gained a reputation as a scholar of first-century Hebrew manuscripts, he was commissioned by Pope Damasus I (St. Damasus), who founded the Papal

Library, to revise the New Testament, using the newly translated first-century letters. These new translations included a number of "Apocryphal Documents" which were preserved at the Vatican, and were recently rediscovered and translated by Dr. Sezekely. These writings explained a formula for living that the Essenes practiced, which Dr. Sezekely calls "Biogenic Living." In 1928 Dr. Sezekely translated "The Essene Gospel of Peace" into modern languages, and today over ten million readers have absorbed its message. Moreover, the International Biogenic Society is now represented around the world, instructing people in "The Essene Way." You can obtain information about the organization by writing the International Biogenic Society/ Box 849/Nelson, B.C. Canada V1L 6A5.

In Genesis we learn of the Tree of Knowledge, which is guarded by angels. The Essenes call this tree the Tree of Life and it represents fourteen positive invisible forces and sources of nature. The Tree has seven roots which connect with the earth and seven branches which connect with heaven. The Essenes believed that the balance in one's life is maintained by communion daily with the angelic forces that are guardians to the fourteen forces. They believed that by aligning oneself to these forces, you are putting yourself in harmonic balance with God. Communion with the forces is an alignment with wisdom, energy, and harmony. Through the Tree of Life, the Essenes recognized that we are inspired to live our lives linked with heaven and earth, just as trees are linked with roots and branches to earth and sky.

In The Teachings of the Essenes from Enoch to the Dead Sea Scrolls Szekely includes the following from the "Thanksgiving Psalms" of the Dead Seal Scrolls VI (iii, 1936).

I am grateful, Heavenly Father,
For Thou hast raised me to an eternal height
And I walk in the wonders of the plain.
"Thou gavest me guidance to reach Thine eternal company
from the depths of the earth.
Thou has purified my body
To join the army of the angels of the earth
And my spirit to reach
And congregation of the heavenly angels.
"Thou gavest man eternity
to praise at dawn and dusk
Thy works and wonders
In joyful song."

The morning communions were as follows: Saturday – Earthly Mother; Sunday – Angel of Earth; Monday – Angel of Life; Tuesday – Angel of Joy;

Wednesday – Angel of Sun; Thursday – Angel of Water; Friday – Angel of Air. The noon communions were focused upon and dedicated to seven aspects of peace: Saturday – Kingdom of the Heavenly Father; Sunday – Kingdom of the Earthly Mother; Monday – Culture; Tuesday – Humanity and Social Peace; Wednesday – Family (Feeling Body); Thursday – Mind (Thinking Body) and Friday - Body (Acting Body). The weekly evening communions were: Saturday – Angel of Eternal Life; Sunday – Angel of Creative Work; Monday – Angel of Peace; Tuesday – Angel of Power; Wednesday – Angel of Love; Thursday – Angel of Wisdom; Friday – Heavenly Father.

Prior to speaking the daily communions, the Essenes would prayerfully contemplate the angel or force with which they would be going to commune. Through communion the brotherhood members were able to become one with the forces flowing in, through and around them. The Essenes were definitely "earthangels4peace" as is mirrored through the sevenfold noontime peace rituals. The Sevenfold Peace practices were performed daily by the Essenes to create peace in all of their lifes' expressions. They believed the change for peace begins within us.

In Szekely's words: "The Essene considered that man lives in the midst of a field of forces, both terrestrial and planetary, and that his individual evolution progresses to the degree in which he cooperates with these forces. But there are other forces of a superior order with which it is even more important that he is in harmony. These are the spiritual currents in the cosmic ocean of cosmic consciousness. These higher current do not mingle with the terrestrial and planetary currents. Man by his own efforts, his own will, has to ascend to this cosmic ocean of universal life. Then and then only can he realize his oneness with the Law (God)."

Szekely's translations revealed that the "teachings which Moses brought forth at Mount Sinai were practiced fifteen hundreds years later by the Essene Brotheroods in Palestine and Egypt." These teachings brought Moses to the conclusion "that if man is to reach God, he must first become master of all the forces which are manifestations of God, of the Law." He wanted to make his people "strong with the Law," which is the meaning of the word Israel. And he wanted to create a system of life which would make it possible for them to conquer the angels (forces and powers serving as connecting links between man and God) as their forefather, Jacob, had done.

In his research Szekely reveals that Moses wanted his followers to recognize they are in contact with angels every second of their lives and that perfect health, happiness and harmony are possible by consciously contacting these forces and powers continuously. This information was on the two stone tablets that Moses first brought down from Mt. Sinai. He destroyed the wisdom when he realized that the people were not ready for the teachings. However, the wisdom was not lost. Moses taught the knowledge orally to those who were ready to commune with the angels. This information was preserved by the Essene community and brought into modern-day consciousness by Dr. Szekely.

From The Essence Gospel of Peace, Book Three: Lost Scrolls of the Essene Brotherhood comes an inspirational writing about living the Essene Way by communing with the trees. The words of the first paragraph of The Trees of the Earthly Mother are as follows:

Go toward the high growing Trees,
And before one of them
Which is beautiful, high growing and mighty,
Say thou these words:
Hail be unto Thee!
O Good living Tree,
Made by the Creator

In honor of the trees of the earth – the ancient record keepers – be guided by the tree angels to explore trees as symbolic messengers of God's wisdom. Our ancestors recognized trees as elders and "wise ones." Throughout Northern Europe and the Middle East there are trees that are called "wish trees," or "prayer trees" because people make requests to God by attaching their written requests to the branches of the trees.

Trees teach us to ground ourselves and the importance of being rooted with the Mother Earth. They mirror to us a skyward stretch toward heaven and inspire us to reach for the stars. In short, trees are special and wonderful friends. Make time for them in your life.

Let yourself be guided to a tree that can bless you as your "wisdom tree" or "wish tree". It can be a tree that you learn about through study. Consider researching the roots and branches of the tree of life in the Essene teachings, some of which I've shared in this chapter. Delve deeply into the wisdom of Jewish mysticism revealed in the Kaballah. Acquaint yourself with the bodhi tree at Bodh Gaya in India, the tree under which the Buddha attained supreme enlightenment. Or, it can be a tree in your own backyard; a tree where you sit with your back against its trunk and feel yourself spiritually supported by God. Meditate, pray, sing, or journal beneath your wisdom tree. As Joseph Campbell so aptly said: "God is the experience of looking at a tree and saying, Ah!"

Chapter 7

QUILT ANGELS

While fulfilling the Star of David energy grid assignment with the angels, I was inspired to drive on Route 66 across the United States, because it is the Mother Road of our country. As I shared in DUI Angels, I drove through Sayre, Oklahoma. When I was Sayre, I started thinking to myself, "Why is the name of this small town familiar to me?" I remembered that twenty years prior, while vacationing in New Orleans, Louisiana, I had purchased an antique quilt from a Women's Exchange. The quilt was a friendship quilt; women who stitched the quilt together had embroidered their signatures on the quilt. The quilt had been made in the 1930's by a group of women who belonged to the Methodist Church in Sayre, Oklahoma. It was sewn as part of a fund raising effort in support of a new church project. The quilt had either been sold or raffled off and through the years made its way to New Orleans, Louisiana where it had a divine appointment with me. When I purchased the quilt, I even ordered from the telephone company a Sayre, Oklahoma phone directory and tried tracking down families who may be related to the women who embroidered their signatures on the quilt. After a number of unsuccessful phone calls to Sayre, I lost interest in the idea.

While in Sayre I found that Methodist Church and absolutely thrilled the church office staff when I told them what I had in my possession. I realized that all those years I had simply been the guardian of the quilt and that another mini-angel assignment was to gift the quilt to the church, which I did upon returning home to Upperco. It was such joy for me to be able to help reunite the quilt, which contained the energy and love of past members of the Sayre Methodist Church, with the present congregation. Interestingly, I believe that 20 years earlier, when I had the "sensing" that I needed to find people who were connected to the ladies who had sewn the quilt, I was simply picking up the angelic inspirational vibration that in God's time, I would be returning this quilt to where it first was "birthed".

When I first began serving God together with the angels, I was inspired to contact a woman who made art quilts and commission her to make a quilt for me. Her name is Meryl Ann Butler. She is a truly amazing woman. Years ago, prior to the fall of communism, Meryl would teach American school children how to make a quilt. Once the quilt was completed, she would then go with the quilt to Russia. She would gift the quilt from the American children to the Russian children. Meryl would then teach the Russian elementary school children how to make a quilt to gift to the Americans. She did this numerous times. I believe that communism fell stitch by stitch because of people like Meryl and the children she taught to make quilts in the name of peace.

Meryl created for me a beautiful pink quilt adorned with a glorious purple angel. She hand-painted the face and so many people have seen the face of the Blessed Mother when looking at the quilt. The quilt has traveled around the world with me. It has served as an altar cloth; a banner; and more importantly it has wrapped people as I sang and played my harp for them. The quilt is similar to the angels' mission in that it delivers a message from God. The quilt reminds us that God's love wraps us, warms us, envelops us, covers us, and protects us.

When I teach classes, I love to pass the quilt around and let people place it across their laps, wrap it around their shoulders, or simply examine the artistry up close. I was given the assignment to commission Meryl to create this quilt as it carries an important message in my service. When we get caught up in all the seriousness of life, we forget that we are God's babies. We forget that we all need to be held and need to be reassured that we are loved. There's no magic in the angel quilt. God's love is waiting to wrap you up and envelop you if you simply follow the words: "Be still and know I am God."

A simple exercise to do to recognize that you're God's baby begins by first finding time when you won't be disturbed. Unplug the phone. Then curl up in your bed or favorite chair with your favorite quilt or blanket. Imagine yourself being held by God. If you want to add to the experience with song, I recommend buying the CD "The Best of Country Sings the Best of Disney." One of the songs on this CD is "Baby Mine" sung by Allison

Krauss. I truly believe Allison Krauss has the voice of an angel. This song is from the Disney movie "Dumbo". Perhaps you remember the scene where Dumbo's mom has been locked up by the villains. Dumbo wants to be held by his mother; after all, he just's a little baby elephant. His mother stretches her trunk through the bars of the prison and rocks him while singing, "Baby Mine". I have used this exercise in workshops. I have participants pair up and take turns. One person takes the part of the mother – the one who does the holding and rocking - and one person, the baby. I encourage everyone to really get into the role playing. The "babies" are to surrender and let themselves be loved as the holy children of God they are; the "mommies" are to whisper sweet blessings into the ears of the person they are loving, rocking, holding next to them. Of course, there are giggles and laughter when everyone pushes through the awkwardness of the exercises, but then the room becomes God's nursery and everyone is giving and receiving love.

Have you ever noticed how babies enjoy themselves? They lie on their backs with their feet up in the air and absolutely delight in seeing their toes. Additionally, when a baby discovers her voice, all of a sudden, out of the blue, the child will let out a scream and be absolutely thrilled at hearing themselves. I do admit that usually the people around them aren't as happy as the baby is; however, I am always amazed by how uninhibited babies are. We sometimes forget how precious we are.

Because the first commission assignment I was given by the angels was the making of a quilt for my service, I was introduced to the world of women expressing themselves artistically through the creation of quilts.

I did not come from a line of quilt makers. None of the women who came before me made quilts, at least not my mother, or grandmother or great-grandmother.

I was always kept abundantly warm with bedspreads and blankets, but no handmade quilts.

One of my first introductions to family quilts came during my first marriage. My "ex's" grandmother was exceptional at quilt making. She had gifted each of her grandchildren a special quilt she made just for them. My "ex" had a quilt, which he had had since childhood, depicting fanciful chickens. I adored the quilt. Because we divorced, we divided all of our belongings and each of us took items that had originated with our respective families. I can to this day remember holding the quilt that was called "Chicken People" and wondering if he would notice if I took it. It's in situations like these that the angel of good conscience appears on my shoulder and says two words: "Right conduct." Of course, I knew that the quilt had been sewn in love for him and it was "rightfully" his heirloom, not mine.

Not too long ago, a historical society in the county next to ours had a special evening when they brought out and displayed antique quilts that had been donated to the society but had never been shown to the public before. Many of these quilts had wonderful stories of the women who had made them. I didn't want the night to end because each quilt was a treasure to behold and I felt so blessed to be able to witness them.

Whether quilts are exhibited by a historical society, or quilts are displayed at shows and exhibits, you will find people known as "white glove angels" and the role they play is very important. White glove angels are the only ones allowed to touch the quilts. Our hands have natural oils on them. Actual human hand contact will result in the possible breakdown of the fibers in the quilt as well as staining. Without the white glove angels, the quilts would not be kept in pristine condition for future generations to enjoy, too.

Robert Shaw in "Quilts: a Living Tradition" wrote: "For a substantial part of this country's history, quilts were virtually the only means of personal and artistic expression readily available to the average woman." I guess that's one of the reasons that quilts speak to my soul. There's a creative voice that speaks to me whenever I stop and admire a quilt.

Angel Heights is about an hour and a half away from Lancaster, Pennsylvania where a large community of Amish lives. Some years ago I stayed at a bed and breakfast owned by an Amish family. Every bed in every bedroom was covered with a beautiful hand-stitched quilt. Chuck and I love taking day trips to Lancaster where the Amish women's quilt handiwork is offered for sale in Amish markets.

I was given a difficult lesson to learn when it comes to recognizing that quilters feel differently than most of us about how quilts that are tattered and worn should be treated. I was a speaker for an ARE Conference at Mt. St. Mary's College in Emmitsburg, Maryland. The same weekend ARE was holding their Mid-Atlantic Conference, a quilters conference was on campus, too. One day at lunchtime I was in line next to a lady who I knew was attending the quilting conference because of her badge. I started a conversation with her by telling her about my love for quilts. I added that I especially loved teddy bears made of old quilts. That was the wrong thing to say to this woman. The expression on her face changed to a look that clearly indicated she saw me as a threat to the integrity of quilters around the world. She proceeded to give me a thorough lecture and tongue-lashing on how old quilts should always be preserved as quilts and never be made into anything as frivolous as teddy bears. I was extremely grateful she wasn't armed with her quilting needle.

One of my favorite quilts was made by Ruth Lee, who lived from 1893-1965. The quilt is called Angel Quilt. The quilt was based on the last words of her five-year-old son. He was dying of scarlet fever, and said, "Momma, see the pretty white angel?" Ruth had a dream later about it and based the quilt on the dream. The quilt depicts an angel in a flower garden of roses. There is a pink rosebush which represents Ruth's family. There is one rose bud missing on the bush, which the angel has picked.

Ruth loved to write poetry, too. Her poem, "Originality" speaks volumes about the opportunities we have in life to make something unique and original - "something that is of God and me."

Originality
Before my race is run,
Before the setting of my sun,
I pray that I may leave behind,
Something that is truly mine
A plain whereon no man hath trod,
Unmistakeably from the hand of God.
And all who may chance to see
This something that is of God and me,
May see His face in every line,
And I know His hand is guiding mine.
And into every subtle phase,
I weave a prayer, a song of praise.
-Ruth Adams Lee

When I look at Ruth's quilt, and see the rose bud that has been "picked" by the angel, I think of the message from another poem: Little Angels.

When God calls little Angels to dwell with Him above,
We mortals sometime question the wisdom of his love,
For no heartache compares with the death of one small child,
Who does so much to make our world seem wonderful and mild.
Perhaps God tires of calling the aged to his fold.
So he picks a rose bud, before it can grow old.
God knows how much we need them, and so He takes but a few,
To make the land of Heaven more beautiful to view.
Believing this is difficult, still somehow we must try.
The saddest work mankind knows, will always be 'goodbye'.
So when a little child departs, we who are left behind must realize,
God loves children & ANGELS are hard to find.
-Author Unknown

I always keep a look out for quilt exhibitions and shows. Quilts are truly works of art as well as historical records. If you have attended quilt shows recently, you will understand when I say that quilts are masterpieces of art.

While attending the Quilt Odyssey 2003 held in Gettysburg, Pennsylvania, I learned about The American Quilt Study Group. This group originated in Mill Valley, California at Sally Garoutte's kitchen table. The group's mission is to preserve quilt heritage. Membership is comprised of traditional and contemporary quilt artists, quilt enthusiasts, historians, researchers, collectors, dealers, folklorists, authors, museum curators, quilt appraisers and students of all related disciplines.

In contemplating my life's passions, researching would be at the top of the list. My girlfriend, Sharon Shreve, calls me Research Angel of the 21st Century. I love it when the angels give me clues to my current mission, and I then do research and learn more about an unknown topic.

The American Quilt Study Group publishes "Uncoverings", an annual journal of research papers that are presented at the group's annual seminar. Additionally the group has a newsletter, "Blanket Statements", published four times a year, which contains at least one research article per issue.

Sally Garoutte expressed her feelings about the importance of historical research: "Historical research never ends. We come to an understanding of our history only through small steps continually taken. Each research paper is a small step and each one is a challenge for someone else to go a little further. This enterprise of quilt history is a continuing process…There is much yet to uncover." I totally agree with her words for they apply to everything in life: "There is much yet to uncover."

I have been inspired to learn more about quilt history, especially the quilts that I have been drawn to such as friendship quilts and crazy quilts. Friendship quilts were sometimes gifted between friends as a way to "stay connected" in eras before telephones and Internet connections. I can imagine a woman living somewhere in the pioneer West, holding her friendship quilt – with the signatures of good friends living back East. –reminding her of their love for her.

In Better Homes and Gardens' Friendship Quilting, there are two quotes featured in describing "Friendship Quilts: Pieces of the Heart." One by Carolyn Edwards and one by Eliza Calvert Hall. In explaining how friendship quilts preserve a tradition of women quilting together a "circle of friendship" over the quilting frame, a tradition that has been on-going for centuries, Carolyn Edward said, "Within those stitches you will see and feel the special love and bond that is shared by a group of gals who quilt together." The love shared is stitched into the quilt as well as the energy of words spoken by all hearts of the group members: Remember my story? Years later, a stranger can purchase the quilt and still feel the joy of the fellowship of those who made the quilt together. Eliza Calvert Hall remarked in 1898, "Some folks has albums to put pictures in, some folks has a book and writes down the things that happen...but these quilts is my albums and diaries. I just spread out my quilts and it's like going back 50 or 60 years and living my life over again."

Crazy quilts were first created following the 1876 Philadelphia Centennial Exposition. At this event, the Japanese pavilion showcased asymmetrical art. Women who attended the expo wanted to create this same look in the quilts they made and this new fad continued in the early 1900's. Because it was a new fad, the name "crazy" described the new "craze" in quilting. Additionally, the many different shapes found on the quilt gave a "crazy" or wild appearance, which was quite unique for the prim and proper Victorians.

In my exploration of quilt shows I have come across a new rage in quilting that began in the 1990's that has stirred an excitement similar to the crazy quilt craze of the 1890's. The quilt pattern that caused the excitement is known as the "Dear Jane Quilt". The unique pattern was originally designed by Jane A. Blakely Sickle, who made the first quilt in Shaftsburg, Vermont in 1863. It consists of 225 geometric designs. The quilt gained notoriety through Brenda Manges Papadakis' book Dear Jane: the Two Hundred Twenty-five Patterns from the 1863 Jane A Sickle Quilt.

Brenda saw a photo of Jane Stickle's 1863 quilt in Donna Bister's and Richard Cleveland's book, Plain and Fancy. Up until seeing the Dear Jane Quilt, Brenda felt she had seen every old quilt block design known to woman. When she scanned the photograph she realized that the majority of the designs were new to her. She became emotionally involved with the blocks and also with Jane's story. Brenda researched Jane's life, even going as far as traveling to Jane's burial site.

Dear Jane, the Jane Sickle's quilt, is of course the first "Dear Jane Quilt"; however, many little "Dear Jane" babies are being born by quilters in America and around the world. Brenda also has http://www.dearjane.com/ website where "janiacs" develop Internet friendships and the creation of Dear Jane Quilts.

I have also learned that the American women before us quilted in times of tragedy. Many women made "mourning quilts" in memory of family members who died in The Civil War. Interestingly, quilts became a similar form of healing after 9/11. Some made quilts to comfort those who experienced great loss; some made quilts as an expression of their patriotism; some made quilts in support of their own healing. An American

Quilt, Inc. is a grass-roots organization that responded to the terrorist attack of 9/11 by creating "An American Quilt" through which families and friends could express their grief and pay tribute to the memory of their loves ones through fabric/collage panels. In fact, all people affected were invited to participate to demonstrate America's resolve for the future. The Aids Memorial Quilt was a similar project that brought people together to create a quilt of healing, love and remembrance of all the precious people who died because of Aids.

Anne Johnson wrote an article entitled, "Soothing the Edges of Pain – how women use quilting to cope with tragic loss," and shared the following exquisite words:

"As it did for women generations before us, quilting is helping us concentrate on creation rather than destruction. The soft feel of washed cotton is soothing to our hands. As we sort out the cut shapes of fabric and organize how we will place them we also sort out our own fears and priorities. Quilting has given us a mindful space where we can begin to consider the overwhelming problems that we face." Anne's article as well as others can be found at www.historyofquilts.com - Patches from the Past - Scraps of History About Women and Their Quilts.

Just as angelic healing can be found in teddy bears, there's angelic healing that is stitched into quilts. The Angel Quilt Project, founded by James Farmer, is a group of stitchers dedicated to stitching center panels to be finished into quilts. Once the quilts are completed, they are donated to children's cancer clinics, burn centers, and hospitals all over the world. There's something very healing and comforting about having a quilt when you are ill. When my dad was dying and was moved from the hospital to a nursing/rehabilitation center, I brought a quilt from home to cover him on his bed. The minute I unfolded the quilt, and placed it on his bed, the energy of the room changed from "hospital" to "home".

Sandy Bonsib, an author of numerous quilting books including Americana Quilts and Quilting Your Memories, and who has appeared on Home and Garden TV's Simply Quilts coordinates Quilts for the Children, a group that makes quilts for children of battered women. In the past three years, the group has made more than 1,000 quilts.

In Maryland there is an organization called Speak, Inc., which makes Lifekeeper Memory Quilts. These quilts are made up of squares depicting the lives of loved one who died from suicide. The quilts mirror to the public a "picture of suicide". Speak, Inc. wants to educate the public on the incredible number of suicides that occur in America everyday. Lifekeeper Memory Quilts have been displayed on the steps of the Capitol in

Washington, D.C. as well as all over this great nation promoting the prevention of youth suicide through education.

My interest in quilts led me to discover Speak, Inc., which was founded by Lisa Hurka Covington. Her younger sister, Laura, was 28 years old when she shot herself on July 9, 1991. The letters in SPEAK stands for Suicide Prevention Education Awareness for Kids (http://www.speakforthem.org/) and this organization promotes the prevention of youth suicide and works to dispel the social stigma surrounding suicide and depression through a campaign of education and awareness at the community level. They provide literature, speakers and programs teaching stress management and coping skills to schools, religious organizations and youth groups. The logo of the group contains precious pictures of bright and shining faces of young people who all took their own lives. Speak has this quote at their website: "The faces on our logo all died of suicide. They wanted the pain to end, not their life. They entered a dark tunnel, unfortunately, not seeing the light at the end."

In connecting with SPEAK I learned the following statistics about youth suicide:

For every 2 homicides in the U.S. there are 3 suicides.

Every 1 hour and 53 minutes, we lose another young person under the age of 24 by suicide.

Most teen suicides are impulsive with little or no planning and 70% occur in the victim's home.

Suicide rates amongst youth ages 15-24 have increased more than 300% since the 1950's.

Facts about suicide:

Suicide is the ninth leading cause of death in the U.S., claiming approximately 30,000 lives each year.

The suicide rate is higher for the elderly than for any other age group.

Suicide is preventable. Most suicidal persons desperately want to live. They are just unable to see any alternative to their problem.

Most suicidal persons give definite warning signs of their suicidal intentions, but others are often unaware of the significance of these warnings, or unsure what to do about them.

Talking about suicide does not cause someone to be suicidal, not does it mean that someone is less likely to commit suicide.

Four times as many men kills themselves as do women, but three to four times as many women attempt suicide as do men.

Firearms are the most common method of suicide across all age, sex, and ethnic groups, and rates are increasing.

Suicide cuts across all ethnic, economic, social and age boundaries.

Surviving family members not only suffer the trauma of losing a loved one to suicide, but are themselves at a higher risk of suicide and emotional problems.

I have chosen to end this chapter with information about SPEAK because I believe just like quilts, God intends for us to "cover our lives" and keep ourselves safe and protected with wisdom and knowledge. I have served together with the angels in helping those who have lost children, and have found that the stigma that society places upon suicide adds an additional burden on the families. I truly believe we need to be talking about and looking for ways to help prevent suicide.

SPEAK offers warning signs to look for:

Giving away prized possessions

Poor school performance

Change in eating habits and sleep patterns

Feelings of worthlessness or guilt

Extreme personality changes

Family history of suicide

Anxiety or panic

Trouble concentrating

Previous suicide attempts

Aggressive, destructive, or defiant behavior

Neglect of personal appearance or hygiene

Increase in alcohol or drug consumption

Talking, writing or drawing about their own death

Withdrawing from family or friends

Personal Loss:

A break up of a relationship

Parents divorce

Death of a loved one

Rejection of a friend

Low grade or failure in a course

In Lisa Hurka Covington's words: "Every negative situation has something positive that one day will evolve."

Growing up in Maryland, my family would watch local Baltimore television stations and certain television anchors became almost like family members because they "came into our home" the same time every day.

One of those people is Susan White-Bowden. She was employed at WMAR-TV in Baltimore as a reporter, anchor, writing and producer and received numerous awards for her work. The awards didn't surprise me because Susan has such a "presence" about her and it radiated through all her reports. I simply remember the "presence" as a beautiful light energy. She glowed in everything she did.

I remember learning through the news that her husband had committed suicide; and then some time later hearing that her son committed suicide, too. My heart was so saddened for her and I remember saying a prayer for her. I didn't want her light to dim.

Years later I would be comforted when Mary Dansicker told me that Susan White-Bowden would be appearing at Joshua's Lighthouse Angels for a booksigning.

Susan has written two outstanding books: <u>Everything to Live For</u>, in which she shares the story of the suicides of her husband and son and <u>From a Healing Heart</u>, about her own recovery from the suicides. Her light continues to shine brilliantly as she strives to be a messenger to others – especially parents - to prevent suicides. She has appeared on Oprah, Donahue and Good Morning America and Maryland Public Television.

On MPT's Healthweek, Sharyl Attkisson asked Susan,"You have said before, if you knew then what you know now, you believe he would still be alive. Specifically, what would you have done differently?

Susan White-Bowden: Oh, I do. So many things. Oh, Sharly, so many things. I would have asked him, first of all, if he was so depressed that he was thinking about suicide. I would have mentioned the word "suicide." I would have released the pressure valve. It's okay! Give kids permission to talk about this unspeakable thing called suicide. It's a normal feeling.

Sharyl Attkisson: And then the next step, though, once a parent has broached that subject, if you're not the one that's capable of helping, or if he's not opening up to you, what do you do?

Susan White-Bowden: Get somebody else! Get somebody from outside, a counselor, a doctor, a minister, a priest, whoever! that they can open up to, because sometimes you're too emotionally tied to that child to have them feel comfortable in talking about these deep, deep, which can be deadly feelings."

Events happen in all our lives, some more tragic than others, that make us feel as if the fabric of our soul has been torn apart from feelings of grief, loss and sadness. Somehow the hand of God helps to guide us in stitching ourselves back together with a patch here and a patch there. For myself, when I come to my life's end and look back over my life experiences, I think I'm going to realize that my life was very much like a quilt. To get to the point of completion, a great deal of "patchwork" was involved.

Chapter 8

LAS VEGAS ANGELS

At one of the summertime spiritual conferences in which I taught a week-long class, I offered a course called, Camp Earth: Where Your Divine Parents Sent You for a Lifetime of Play. I gave out t-shirts with that inscription to the registrants. The focus of the class was to inspire people to put playfulness back into their lives. Materials for the class included angelic halos to wear and bottles of bubbles to blow. Sometimes we get too doggone serious for our own good. I have also found that I often am inspired by the angels to teach what I need to learn the most. One of the wisdoms Michael Landon left with us is found in the following words: "Whatever you want to do, do it now. There are only so many tomorrows." It's important to put play into our busy schedules.

In December, 1999 Chuck's son, Scott and his fiancé, Ann Marie, were married at a wedding chapel in Las Vegas. Chuck and I flew to Las Vegas to attend their wedding. I always thought that Las Vegas was simply a place for people who like to gamble. Just as we have divine appointments with people in our lives, God takes our datebook and makes appointments with places on the earth. Once we keep those appointments with destiny we are never the same again. Las Vegas and I were destined to meet in December, 1999 and fall madly in love. Las Vegas became one of my favorite playgrounds.

As I shared in Driving Under the Influence of Angels, the day we flew out to Las Vegas was the same day that the memorial service was held for

Sharon and John Shreve's daughter, Melissa. Because I officiated the memorial service, we didn't arrive at our hotel, The Luxor, until almost midnight on that Friday evening. As we flew into McCarran International Airport, I noticed a beam of light shooting straight up into outer space. There's something that happens to you when your taxi pulls up in front of a 30-story onyx-hued pyramid, complete with a 315,000-watt light beam at the top of the pyramid. This light beam can be seen from outer space. According to Luxor's public relations, it is "the most powerful beam on earth." If the pyramid and light beam aren't enough to amaze you, there's a 10-story sphinx, which is larger than the original one in Egypt, that acts as guardian to the Luxor. You'll find incredible replicas of the statues of Ramses inside; Egyptian décor everywhere; and people strolling through the hotel in Egyptian costumes. I think the first day I was there, I just walked around the place with my mouth hanging open in total awe of the décor. There's just no place like Las Vegas. It is in a category all by itself.

In one of the gift shops at Luxor you can purchase authentic Egyptian artifacts. There's a high-tech simulator trip you can take, called "In Search of the Obelisk," and an IMAX theater which features "Mysteries of Egypt." Luxor has recreated a full-scale replica of King Tut's Tomb and even brought in an Egyptologist to make certain they had reproduced it accurately. If you have any sensing that you had a past life in Egypt, treat yourself to a stay at the Luxor just for the sheer hoot of it. Las Vegas is just too much fun to be missed! There is an enchantment to be found in this city of lights.

We were only in Las Vegas for a short three-day weekend on my first visit, however, that brief encounter awakened me to the incredible "art energies" waiting to be experienced as well as the playfulness of the city. I love being able to tell people about all the wonders that I have discovered in Las Vegas with the angels of art.

If you need an infusion of playtime, head for Las Vegas. The architecture of the hotels' designs and wizardry of entertaining with their special effects alone will speak to your inner child. Romance and fairytales are conjured up when you see the hotel Excalibur with its hourly show featuring an eight-foot-high dragon that comes out from beneath the entrance causeway. The dragon shoots 20-foot fiery breath in the air. The world of King Arthur and knights and tournaments is alive and well at Excalibur.

You'll be singing "I love New York" when you experience hotel New York New York's 150-foot-tall replica of the Statue of Liberty, 300-foot-long Brooklyn Bridge and a Coney Island roller coaster. We were in Las Vegas shortly after 9/11, and the exterior of New York New York had been turned into a memorial honoring our fellow Americans who lost their lives in that tragedy. Chuck especially loves New York New York's corned beef deli sandwich, just as he enjoys the same when we are in the genuine New York City. The Vegas hotel has captured the essence of all the offerings to be found on the streets of New York.

Outside of The Mirage a volcano erupts every 15 minutes complete with steam and flames spreading across the boiling waters of the Mirage's lagoon. It is quite a spectacle! For those whose fantasies include living the life of the pirates of the Caribbean, Treasure Island is a swashbuckler's dream complete with outdoor hourly battles between pirates aboard the Hispaniola and the crew of the British Frigate HMS Britannica. The hotel Paris is complete with an amazing Eiffel Tower, a half-scale model of the original with an elevator that will take you to the top for a fabulous view of Las Vegas. Chuck and I love the romance of going inside the Paris hotel for a lunch of French bread sandwiches at their café, which has all the ambiance of Paris itself. They have even painted the ceiling a beautiful sky blue.

My favorite of all the outdoor presentations is Bellagio's dancing waters. One year at Christmas time, Chuck and I booked a room at the Bellagio with a view of the lake. The music heard outside by the public is piped into the room on a television channel. We were like a pair of kids with our noses pressed to the window, watching an unobstructed view of one of the most inspiring water ballets on earth choreographed to popular Christmas music. Even if you don't have a room at the Bellagio, enjoy the show from the sidewalk because it's the best and classiest free show in Vegas anytime of the year.

Belaggio boasts a lobby unlike any other in Las Vegas. The gorgeous glass-blown flower sculpture on the ceiling is a 2,000 square foot garden of glass flowers creator by Dale Chihuly. Over 100 public sites around the world feature Chihuly installations including the Mayo Clinic, the Gonda Building in Rochester, Minnesota and his works are part of over 200 museum collections including the St. Louis Art Museum in St. Louis, Missouri. I encourage you to acquaint yourself with Dale's glass masterpieces. He's a national treasure. His website is: www.chihuly.com.

Chihuly was awarded a Fulbright Fellowship in 1968 to work in Venice, Italy at the Venini factory. This experience greatly impacted his glass-blowing career. In 1971 Chihuly co-founded the Pilchuck Glass School in Washington and he has been revolutionary in the recognition of glass blowing as a fine art. He's a modern day master.

Every single flower "blooming" in the Bellagio ceiling is different. The sculpture is the largest of its kind in the world. It's dazzling and inspires people to look up!

Additionally there is a conservatory and botanical garden in which Bellagio changes the flowers and plants every few weeks to reflect the seasons. It takes a minimum of 150 people to orchestrate the "changing of the gard"-en. Even if we do not stay at the Bellaggio, we make it a point to stop in to see Dale's masterpiece ceiling, which always takes our breath away, and to see the floral display in the conservatory. We love the huge – and I mean HUGE – Christmas tree in the conservatory.

Bellagio has built a special theater for the Cirque du Soleil's production, "O". It features a 1.5 million gallon pool which can be reconfigured to accommodate the one-of-a-kind spectacular O, which represents the French word for water, "eau" pronounced "o". The theater was modeled after the famous Paris Opera. The theater is equipped with state-of-the-art sound and lighting systems. O is a work of art whose staging and acrobatics offer a mind-expanding experience. Frommer's guide book describes Cirque du Soleil shows for first time visitors (at either O at Bellagio or Mystere at Treasure Island) as shows for which you should be prepared "to have your brain turned inside out." After Chuck and I saw O, we felt as if our brains had been rewired.

Additionally Bellagio has a first class art gallery. Whenever I know I am going to Vegas, I always check out the exhibition at Bellagio. On one trip I viewed the private art collection of Hollywood actor, Steve Martin; another time I saw the exquisite Faberge eggs; another show featured an amazing collection that included the work of Picasso, Monet, and many others in the Who's Who of Art. The art museum was the vision of the man who built Bellagio, Steve Wynn. Steve is now building another hotel, which at the time I am writing this is to be called Le Reve. This is the name of an incredible Picasso painting which Steve owns. It means: the dream. Steve Wynn has a glorious art collection himself, which until Le Reve is open, can be seen on the strip at a building next to the Le Reve construction site. It's the Wynn Collection of Fine Art. I truly believe that Steve Wynn must have been inspired by the angels of art because he started the divine thought process of making sacred space inside Vegas hotels for art galleries.

Bellagio isn't the only hotel to wrap itself around fine art. The Venetian is another "must see" to believe experience in Vegas. The Venetian has a Grand Canal with gondolas, fresco reproductions adorned in 24 karat gold gracing the ceiling of its lobby, the restaurants of super star chef Wolfang Pick and Emeril Lagasse, and a Hermitage-Guggenheim art museum. This is the first permanent museum outside of Russia to house treasures from the Hermitage. I have longed to go back to Russia to visit St. Petersburg for the purpose of going to the Hermitage. I am grateful to The Venetian for bringing a taste of the Hermitage to America.

Las Vegas also has many wonderful art museums and cultural centers waiting to be explored including the West Sahara Library Fine Arts Museum and the Marjorie Barrick Museum, as well as the Las Vegas Natural History Museum. There's also The Arts Factory, located in the Gateway district of Vegas that features galleries as well. To give children hands-on experience, take them to the Lied Discovery Children's Museum, which offers lots of way to keep kids busy.

You can dine with fine art surrounding you at Mirage's Renoir where Renoir originals can be found as well as Bellagio's Picasso, which, of course, has Picasso originals to admire during dinner. And there's real live angels in Vegas. At Mandalay Bay's Aureole there's a wine angel who fetches your wine selection for you from a wine tower that houses thousands of bottles of wine.

You can go to Las Vegas, ride the trolley and spend your vacation exploring the unique architectural themes of the hotels and admiring the amazing interiors. Whenever we are in town, Chuck and I always head to the The Mirage because of the exquisite orchids that are part of the tropical oasis complete with waterfalls in their atrium near the lobby. Chuck and I both love orchids. We also enjoy attending orchid shows staged by the many orchid societies in Maryland.

Cutting edge entertainment is the norm in Las Vegas. The arts truly rock with shows such as the Blue Man Group, which is at the Luxor. The Blue Man Group is another show you have to experience to believe. We are here to allow ourselves to be wrapped up in art, and that literally happens at a Blue Man Group show.

At the end of the show we attended, the entire audience had covered itself successfully with crepe paper by passing streamers from the back of the theater forward, over and over again. I felt as if the theater was a blank canvas and we were making a unique group art creation together while at the same time being joyously buried in crepe paper.

In Vegas the arts rule. The great chefs can be found creating their culinary delights at restaurants that bear their name, the great masters can be found in the art museums, and great entertainers fill the theaters. Mr. Las Vegas himself, Wayne Newton, offers one of the most endearing shows I have ever experienced. He is an absolute sweetheart and kind-hearted man. At the performance we attended, he sang, entertained and somehow gave a kiss or handshake to the majority of the ladies in the audience. No wonder Bob Hope asked him to be the USO Ambassador for our troops once Bob's health prevented him from continuing in that role. Wayne has shared that even after coming back from the USO tours, he and his staff make phone calls to families of soldiers that he met and spoke to while on tour.

A talented troupe of Irish step dancers have been leaping and twirling in Vegas since July 1998 when "Lord of the Dance" first opened at New York New York. Broadway's "Mamma Mia" now has people dancing in the aisles at Mandalay Bay. The arts are a permanent fixture of Las Vegas just as much as the slot machines.

A Las Vegas "must do" for those who love the arts is Liberace's Museum. It is a treasure trove of his glittering costumes, dazzling jewels, spectacular pianos, exotic cars and his own collection of rare antiques. After touring his museum, I came away missing his presence and his phenomenal piano playing. Not too far from where I grew up was a theater-in-the round called Painters Mill Music Fair located in Owings Mills, Maryland. Liberace came yearly to perform inside the Music Fair "tent" and my parents would take my sister and me to his show. I wish I could see him perform "I'll be seeing you" one more time. At the museum, I loved catching a glimpse of Liberace's devotion to the saints. In one of the rooms of the museum there is a collage of images of St. Anthony that Gloria Vanderbilt made for Liberace. The collage was presented to Liberace on the Mike Douglas Show. Liberace had a great devotion to him, and even had a St. Anthony Shrine in his former Palm Springs, California home.

Other galaxies are waiting for you, too, in Vegas. If it's the spaceship Enterprise and crew that make your toes tap, then the Hilton Hotel's Star Trek: Experience complete with self-guided tour of Star Trek memorabilia and clips from the TV show is the ticket. During our visit, Chuck was photographed and his picture was super-imposed onto a body of one of the actual Star Trek TV show's crewmembers. The result is a picture that looks like Chuck was serving on board the Enterprise. It really is a fun picture. At a recent women's retreat that Ann Bell and I co-led, we hosted a Saturday evening activity in which everyone dressed up as their soul. The purpose of the activity was to consider what our souls look like. I loved the brilliant creativity of the ladies who attended. The costumes were all wonderful to behold, including Gloria Todd's golden goddess, and Ann Bell's stunning and radiating seven rays. My fashion creativity is a little more simplistic in expression. I wore a large black trash bag with holes cut out for my head and arms. Affixed to the front of me was a 3' foot pink plastic outer space alien; affixed to the back was a 3' foot green plastic alien. I wore a salad bowl on my head covered in aluminum foil complete with antennas. On my wrists were aluminum foil cuffs. I walked around the group showing Chuck's picture and asking if anyone has seen this space man as I was in love with him. The pink alien was my feminine self; the green, my masculine. I thought the attire was appropriate because I am convinced my soul is from another world and my life has been spent in the twilight zone more times than not.

Las Vegas is magical in so many ways, and it is fitting that it offers the opportunity to take in the shows of the world's greatest magicians. The masters of illusion can all be found here: Penn & Teller, Lance Burton and Magicians of the Century: Siegfriend & Roy. Each of the magic shows has its own identity. You cannot say that if you have seen one magic show in Vegas you have seen them all. It's just not true. The sights and sounds and illusions give everyone thrills and chills. Chuck and I are like two five-year-olds when it comes to magic shows, and sitting in the audience of these greats, we share one common thought the entire show, "How did he do that?"

The healing arts are not neglected in Las Vegas. All the Las Vegas hotels offer environments in which you can pamper yourself at their luxurious spas. You can treat yourself to a spa vacation in Vegas and never spend a nickel in a slot machine.

No city does lights the way Las Vegas does lights. The top of the list of light experiences in Las Vegas is the Fremont Street Experience that appears overhead in the evenings. The Freemont Street Experience is a five-block open-air pedestrian mall. Overhead is a 90-foot high steel-mesh canopy of 2.1 million lights. Four times nightly the light show, accompanied by music, provides a delightful Sky Show. At Christmastime the music and lights celebrate the season with snowmen, marching tin soldiers, and best of all, Santa and Rudolph. It delights all who are young at heart.

Additionally one Christmas past in Vegas we went to the very posh Four Seasons Hotel to see their adorable Teddy Bear Exhibit. That's right. One of the swankiest hotels in Vegas opened one of their Presidential Suites (President Clinton actually stayed in this suite) to the public for a holiday exhibit of Teddy Bears. When you toured the suite you saw room after room of teddy bears. The teddy bears were thoroughly enjoying their stay at the Four Seasons. One teddy bear was playing a grand piano while looking out over the city of Las Vegas, one was on a tread mill, one lounging in a bath tub, one reading a newspaper in bed. I used up a whole roll of film inside the suite and giggled my whole way through the tour. I thought to myself, Clinton should have played with teddy bears and he would have saved himself a world of trouble.

Mother Nature is an artisan in Las Vegas, too, with the beautiful landscapes of the desert, the lakes, and canyons. Chuck and I toured Red Rock Canyon and also Nevada's state park, Valley of Fire, where we explored the art of ancient Native American petroglyphs. And since Chuck is a retired IBM engineer, I have to mention the monumental engineering marvel always worth seeing – Hoover Dam.

I am certain you have the sense that when Chuck and I met in 1999, we were each waiting for the other because we are soul playmates. When we go on angelic adventures together the playfulness runs wild. We have spent vacations at Mandalay Bay in Vegas where after breakfast we head out to the "beach" area and spend the day holding hands as we float in inner tubes side by side around Mandalay Bay's "lazy river".

I have found that in networking with people whose life service is spiritually focused, Vegas is regarded as a sort of sin city because of the adult entertainment and gambling. You will find these things in Vegas; however, it is a vibrant city filled to the brim with a passionate art energy and opportunities to play with total abandonment.

On one of our Vegas play vacations, the angels made me aware of a new art venue to explore. I never would have known this place existed without the art angels' prompting. We were inspired to rent a car and drive north of Vegas to Beatty to experience the Goldwell Open Air Museum.

The Goldwell Open Air Museum began as a project of Belgian artist Albert Szukalski in 1984 with the installation of his major sculpture, "The Last Supper," which he created in cooperation with several Beatty residents. In subsequent years, six additional pieces were added to the site by three other Belgian artists, Fred Bervoets, Doctor Hugo, and Dre Peters, who like Szukalski, were major figures in the European art world with extensive exhibition records. A fifth artist, David Spicer, a Beatty contractor, also contributed an original sculpture in 1992. Many people have discovered the outdoor museum making their way to the Nevada ghost town of Rholite. The outdoor sculptures are quite large, colossal in fact. In addition to the "Last Supper," it's inspiring to see a 25-foot high pink woman made of cinder blocks entitled "Lady Desert;" and a magnificent carved winged woman who is reaching for the sun from high atop a wooden pillar entitled "Icara". All have the beauty of the upper Mojave Desert as the backdrop.

Finally, it was in Las Vegas that I learned the magical word SARMOTI. If in saying the word out loud, it conjures up the same vibration as "abracadabra" or "alakazam" you are exactly right. It's a magical word that is an acronym for the world's greatest magicians – Siegfried and Roy. The word SARMOTI stands for Siegfried and Roy, Masters of the Impossible. From Siegfried and Roy I have learned that this word is not just about them, it's about everyone who believes the impossible is possible. What a truly angelic message! Siegfried and Roy have shared in their shows, "to rise above what seems impossible, one must first believe."

One of the visions these two great magical beings have believed possible and have energized with time, money and heart conviction is that children of the future will never ask: "What happened to the animals?" When it comes to modern-day saints, I truly believe the animals of the earth refer to them as St. Siegfried and St. Roy.

Siegfried and Roy have dedicated their lives to preserving the Royal White Tigers. This dedication was born from a dream Roy kept having back in the 1980's. In the dream he was viewing white tigers without any stripes at all. God was introducing Roy to his heart's service here on earth: to save the world's magnificent white tigers and magical white lions for future generations.

Siegfried and Roy have created an open-air white tiger habitat in Las Vegas that gives visitors a chance – and it's absolutely free - to be a part of their monumental conservation effort. The facility offers the tigers a spectacular living arrangement and a sense of security, while allowing the public to unobtrusively observe these great creatures.

Shirley MacLaine told Roy he was a tiger in a previous life. If you have ever seen a video of Roy with the tigers, you'll be convinced as I am, he's part tiger in this life. In an interview in Esquire Magazine Roy shared this thought: "Name your pets after qualities you desire. Among my white lions are Pride, Joy, Passion, Destiny and Vision. They have all slept in my bed. When they shed, their lessons rub off on me."

In the book, <u>Siegfried & Roy's Gift for the Ages</u>, you will find a photograph of the two magical men holding four white tiger babies in their arms. Beneath the photograph are the words: Rarer Than A Rembrandt.

I am a big fan of Siegfriend & Roy, not only because of their brilliance as master magicians, but also their commitment to raising global awareness of our roles in preserving the animal kingdom by including the message in their performances. Gandhi was once asked if he had a message to share. He replied, "My life is the message." This is true for Siegfried and Roy. Their lives are the message that if you truly believe in saving the animals of the earth, and you support that belief with every fiber of your being, the impossible becomes possible.

It was the Government of South Africa in 1994 that asked Siegfried and Roy to work their magic, after seeing the success this dynamic duo had achieved on behalf of the Royal White Tiger, to help save the Magical White Lion of Timbavati, which was literally disappearing from the face of the earth. Siegfried and Roy have since raised 19 white lions.

Additionally Siegfied and Roy have a Secret Garden and Dolphin Habitat in Vegas at The Mirage that gives the public the opportunity to discover dolphins, white tigers, white lions and a four-ton elephant, too, in an exotic jungle setting. In Maya Angelou's word: "There is no secret in this garden. Its beauty belongs to the world and to futures now unknown."

I am not one who has ever left her heart in San Francisco; however, sometimes when I am getting way too serious for my own good, my inner child opens the Sunday Travel Section of The Baltimore Sun and shows me the discounted fares for flights to Las Vegas.

Chapter 9

HEALING ANGELS

There are many ways the angels bring God's healing to our lives. One of these is by acting as heavenly switchboard operators and supporting communication between us and our loved ones in heaven. In DUI of Angels I wrote about Reverend Reed Brown and Reverend Rachael Salley, two gifted mediums, whom God has blessed with the ability to receive messages from spirit from our loved ones. Both of these individuals have provided healing and comfort to people who long to hear from loved ones in heaven. Reed and Rachael are a pair of healing angels.

This past year Mary Dansicker hosted at her store Joshua's Lighthouse Angels Reverend Hoyt Robinette, who is also a very talented medium. At Mary's store, for several days he gave private readings and held two evening message circles. I signed Chuck and myself up for the message circle. All who attended sat in a circle. Reverend Hoyt Robinette put in a small light-tight basket a lot of markers, pencils, crayons and other writing utensils. He then had someone in the group open a package of blank index cards, inspect them to confirm to all of us that they were blank and put them in the basket, too. The basket was closed and placed in the center of the circle where it was left undisturbed for about an hour. Then Hoyt covered his eyes with masking tape, and covered the tape with a blindfold. Earlier in the evening each of us had filled out a billet, a small sheet of paper on which we wrote the names of people in spirit we would love to hear from. Additionally there was space to ask a question that we would like spirit to answer for us. The billets are folded and there is no way, even if he could see through the tape and blindfold, that Hoyt would be able to read the folded up billets. Hoyt held each billet in the palm of his hand and from the energy of the handwriting somehow drew into his sphere of consciousness loved ones in heaven who are connected to the person who wrote names and a question on the billet. He gave every one in the room messages from loved ones in heaven. When he finished with the messages, he opened the basket in the center of the room and there was a card for each person in the circle in the basket. There was one index card that read: Jayne Feldman and another index card that read Charles Feldman. No one in the group had signed their names to the cards; the index cards were totally blank when put inside the basket. One side of the card had a beautiful picture that appeared almost photographic in image. The pictures were of scenes in nature and also included faces of people. The other side bore signatures from those who are with us in spirit. It's called precipitation and is a form of spiritual phenomena. All the pictures were different; all the signatures were different.

On my billet I had asked to hear from my dad, and my dear friend, Charlie Cole and Padre Pio. I wrote the following question, "What is it that God wants me to be doing in service?" When Hoyt held my folded billet in his hand and was communicating with my loved ones in spirit, he said, "There is someone here named Robert Howard, who says he is your father." He then proceeded to give me personal messages from Dad. Hoyt then added that Charlie Cole was here in spirit. Hoyt found this interesting as Hoyt has an uncle whose name is also Charles Cole. He then said there was a priest here as well and he said the priest's name was "Padre." Hoyt started writing in the air and then remarked, "You are to be writing, writing, writing. God wants you to be writing. There is wisdom you are to be sharing through your writing."

Chuck had written on his billet that he wanted to hear from his dad, who died when he was eight years old; from his mother, who died a year ago; and his sister, who had died about ten years ago. Chuck's question was for his father. Chuck wanted to know why his dad had to leave him so early in Chuck's life. When Chuck and I first met Chuck had shared with me that he was very angry over his dad dying, which resulted in Chuck not having father/son experiences in childhood. He was envious of other little boys who had dads with whom they could go camping and fishing. Because of Chuck's sadness over his dad's sudden death, Chuck had blocked out all memories of his childhood prior to his eighth year.

Hoyt was an angel of healing to Chuck that evening. Hoyt shared that Albert Korman was here in spirit. Chuck's mother remarried, and Chuck's step-father adopted him, changing his name to Feldman. Charles Korman was Chuck's name at birth. Albert explained that there are things that happen in our lives in which there is no choice offered. He emphasized to Chuck that there wasn't a choice of staying or not staying. From the message it became very clear that Albert was greatly saddened that he had to leave Chuck, his mother and younger sister. He died at his appointed time to leave the earth. Albert didn't want to dwell on his death but rather went on to explain that he had been by Chuck's side all of Chuck's life, watching over him, supporting him and he would continue to do so until he and Chuck are reunited in heaven. Chuck's mom, Mildred, then stepped in and said, "You can tell him you love him, Albert!" Which Albert proceeded to do. Chuck's sister, Anita, also came through with messages of love. Later that evening Chuck was beaming when he said to me, "After 61 years, I got to talk to my dad."

On my personal index card Charlie Cole had signed his name. The month prior to the experience with Hoyt, I had been talking to Chuck about Charlie and what a blessing he was in my life and how I wished the two of them had been able to meet each other. Charlie's grave is in the same cemetery as my dad's, so I visit with each of them there at least once a week. In addition to Charlie's signing my card, there was the signature of an H. Gordon Burroughs. I had no idea who that individual was, but I love a mystery, especially clues that are dropped from heaven. In researching the name I found that Burroughs was an author, too and wrote Becoming A Spiritualist, and Meditations, Reflections, and Spiritual Philosophy. I was able to track down a copy of Becoming A Spiritualist and found that Burroughs and I are two peas in a pod. He wrote about the beliefs of spiritualists: "We believe that Jesus placed his hand upon the blind and that they saw. We believe that he returned from the dead and that he appeared to those whom he loved. And he made a promise: 'Verily, verily, I say unto you, he that believeth on me, the works that I do shall he do also, and greater works than these shall he do." I, too, believe that we are here to do great works that exemplify Christ's service and glorify God. Burroughs stated, "Know that our purpose in being here is to learn, to accomplish, and to experience." I am very grateful that Hoyt introduced H. Gordon Burroughs to me that evening in Reisterstown.

I teach a Thursday evening spiritual enhancement class entitled "Pathway of Love," and a woman by the name of Carol Sanzone attended one of my classes. We were very blessed to have her join our group as she told us of her book The Journey: a Journey of Love, of Light and of Spirit, which she co-authored with her husband, Joe, who died at 49 years old. Fr. Joe Breighner wrote the forward to this book and his words are so eloquent that I feel inspired to share them with you here:

"This may be the most important book you will ever read. It is the journal of a dying man, and the woman who stayed by his side. It is, at its heart, a love story – the love of husband and wife; the love of a father and children; the love of extended family and friends.

It is the story of an "average Joe" who didn't think his life had much meaning or significance. Joe was not a member of any clergy, nor was he a psychologist or philosopher. He was a working man of 49 who was forced to face the reality of death much too early. It is a story of faith. On another level, this is the story of everyone. At some point, most of us will be involved in the dying process. We can identify with Joe in our own dying. At other times, we can identify with Carol in the role of caring for a dying loved one. This book offers comfort, hope, encouragement in both roles. This book could profitably be read by anyone at any stage of life who wants to wake up to living fully again. After reading this book, it's impossible to ever again take for granted such seemingly mundane things as eating a meal, going for a walk, riding in a care, doing a job, seeing a friend or loved one. Things most of us take for granted are suddenly seen as unique and precious gifts. Joe has been gracious enough to give each of us a window to his own dying. Through that window we can see the magnificence of life that far surpasses its tragedy, and we even get a peek at eternity where life and love are stronger than death!"

Joe was truly an earth angel. He reached out to others in his final journey. He was courageous enough to take the last precious moments of his last two months of life here on earth and share honestly and openly his fears and hopes and shattered dreams through the journal he kept, which became a legacy of love and a source of hope to all who read that God is always there; and life is eternal.

The evening Carol joined our group she told a story of her experience with Joe, following his death, through the heavenly switchboard angels. Before Joe died, Carol and Joe watched John Edwards' "Crossing Over" television program. They talked of their longing to stay in touch with each other following Joe's death. One evening on the program, a woman shared how someone in heaven made contact by flushing the toilet. Carol and Joe rolled with laughter. This sparked their conversation on how Joe would make initial contact. Joe suggested that he would turn on the water faucet. Carol at first hesitated in agreeing to the idea because they lived in an older home, and the faucets weren't easy for humans to turn on, much less someone doing it with finer light energy. Joe insisted, he would turn on the water so Carol would know that his love for her was still flowing. Carol shared this agreement with no one.

The day after Joe's funeral, Carol was sitting in the living room with her daughter and daughter's fiancé. They were talking about missing Joe and sharing special memories to comfort each other. Carol's daughter then said, "Mom, the water in the bathroom is running!" Carol jumped up and with tears streaming down her face ran into the bathroom to see the faucet turned on full force and water flowing. Joe and the heavenly switchboard angels had turned on the waterworks. In moments like these I can only imagine the angels saying something similar to what NASA's Houston Control Center expresses, "Heaven, we've made contact!" I know the joy is both heavenside and earthside. If you would like to order a copy of this book, simply call Mary Dansicker at Joshua's Lighthouse Angels at 410.517.0200.

Another joy-filled story occurred in the lives of Mary Dansicker and her son, Skeets. Skeets is serving our country as a Marine, and was home one weekend to visit with his folks. Mary had gone to the video store to get some videos for the family to watch while they had Chinese carryout for dinner. Mary asked Skeets to look through the video titles and see which one he wanted to watch. He picked the title: "A Rumor of Angels." This movie is based on a book entitled, Thy Son Liveth – Messages from a Solider to his Mother. Skeets and Mary knew nothing about the movie except it had "angel" in the title. After watching the movie, they both felt that Joshua in heaven had had a hand in the video selection because messages through a lighthouse were an important part of the story, also an important part of Joshua's communication with his family After the two of them watched the movie, Mary sent me an e-mail telling me about their "dinner and movie experience," and how at the end they saw in the credits the listing of the book with the powerful title: "Thy Son Liveth." As I read Mary's e-mail, the angels whispered to me, "Track down the book for Mary." I immediately went to Barnes and Noble's online site for out of print books and purchased a copy as a gift for Mary and Skeets. Just as I finished my AOL service told me I had mail. I clicked to my mailbox and found Mary writing me an "after thought" from her earlier e-mail. She was asking if I could help her find the book. I wrote her that her angel team was one step ahead of her and the book was on its way to her.

I have shared the last paragraph of the book in many of my lectures. The words are powerful in their mirroring to us the young soldier's experience after dying:

"We have now reached a river of unsurpassed beauty. I have always felt, and I am now more impressed than ever with the feeling now, that a river is more spiritual than any other expression of physical nature. It may be that this is our port of egress. It is. We have been commanded to halt. One desire seems to animate us all: that is to run down and swim in this shining stream.

We have thrown away our outer garments and are plunging in. Good-by for now. I am running down to the water as I used to run down to the old mill-stream, tingling with joy…."

The book was written anonymously by a mother whose American solider was killed in France in World War I. Prior to his death, her son had qualified for wireless communication service in the army. The mother was also able to use the wireless. Following his death she began receiving wireless messages from her son in spirit assuring her he was really alive, and eager to comfort her. "There is no death. Life goes on without hindrance or handicap. The one thing that troubles the men who come here is the fact that the ones who love them are in agony…They believe in the immortality of the soul. But the proof of their belief scares them." I love the image of death being the opportunity to cast off our outer garments and run down to the river…tingling with joy.

The mother wanted to author the book anonymously so that the book could be a message to all mothers who have lost sons in wars. Since first being introduced to the inspiring movie, "A Rumor of Angels" by Joshua Dansicker and the heavenly video angels, as well as the glorious book behind the movie, I have gifted many copies of Thy Son Liveth to comfort those mourning the loss of their child.

Chuck and I visit New York City often. We simply take the Amtrak train from Baltimore's Penn Station to New York City's Penn Station and spend the day in New York. On one of our visits we went to St. Paul's Chapel's exhibit "Out of the Dust – a Year of Ministry at Ground Zero." As you probably are aware, St. Paul's Chapel is where the workers at Ground Zero ate, slept and cried. It was the healing headquarters for massage therapists, podiatrists, chiropractors, counselors and volunteers who offered healing for all the worn-out bodies of the people who worked 'round the clock at Ground Zero. In the brochure about the exhibit was this quote, "St. Paul's will always be in mind, heaven's outpost." I loved the image. It inspired me to strive to make a heavenly outpost wherever I am called to service. Just as the volunteers at St. Paul's Chapel taught us by their unselfish service and compassion, in the midst of tragedy, God's angels always appear to deliver God's healing. As Chuck and I walked through the exhibit together, we paused and read the words of Police Officer Michael Browne, Shield 588, "I watched you take care of us in a way that was so pure. Now I will no longer see you on an everyday basis. You have been a comfort to a lot of guys. I work downtown and out of this terribly tragedy I have a faith in people I didn't have before September 11th. Because of you I watched and saw an angel."

Think about the times in your life when you first experienced a tragedy. And then out of the dust and the rubble you saw an angel.

I am someone who serves as a spiritual director to my clients. I assist them with moving through transitions and growing spiritually closer to God. My private consultations are known as Angelic Attunements. The experience is a ceremony that honors the life of the individual that has requested the session. Healing is radiated through my voice, whether I give a session held in person or over the telephone. All sessions are recorded so that the individual can continue to receive blessings from the messages on the tape as well as the energies of the experience. In Commune With the Angels, I wrote about Angelic Attunements and include a guided healing meditation and steps for serving with the angels of healing.

I have been given by the angels an initiation ceremony for blessing and energizing those who wish to serve God with the angelic attunement energy. If you wish to receive this blessing. I encourage you to tape record the following in your own voice. Then prepare yourself for your initiation by simply lying down or sitting in a comfortable position. Make certain that your arms, legs and body are extended in a relaxed position.

As you allow yourself to feel relaxed, attune to all the wonderful rhythms of your body. Feel your heart pumping. Feel as your heartbeats, that you are in sync with the larger heart beating in all life.

Feel your breath as you exhale peacefully. Attune your breath to the breath of heaven. You are one with the heartbeat and breath of God. As you attune to the oneness, and blend with the divine source of all life, feel yourself surrounded by a circle of angels.

Golden radiant beings of light surround you with their arms and hands outstretched towards you, palms facing you. They are God's angels of healing and they are blessing you with light for you have answered God's call to be of service to others. As you listen to the words of the initiation, feel God's healing love flowing through every cell of your body. Feel yourself becoming a vessel of God's healing as the words envelop you with the presence of God.

SERA KHOMAH/SERA KHOMAH/SERA KHOMAH
(Blessing of Love of God/Wisdom of Eternal Soul)

ZION ZOHAR ZION ZOHAR ZION ZOHAR
(Blessing of God's Knowledge upon all my thoughts)

YOD HEY VOD HEY VOD HEY VOD HEY YOD HEY VOD HEY
(Calling in the Light of God into my bodies –
physical/mental/emotional/spiritual)
MOZA (MOO-ZAA)/MOZA/MOZA

(MOZA is a Hebrew word which relates to everything that goes forth from Source – the issuing forth of the waters of life, thoughts of Truth; active faith; the outer and the inner; one Source of ALL)

SERA KHOMAH/SERA KHOMAH/SERA KHOMAH

(Visualize: Formation of Downward Thrusting Triangle)
MELCHIZEDEK – God's Great Initiator
METATRON – The Angel of God's Enveloping Presence
MICHAEL – Angel Who Serves as Protector
MELCHIZEDEK/METATRON/MICHAEL
MELCHIZEDEK/METATRON/MICHAEL
MELCHIZEDEK/METATRON/MICHAEL
MOZA/MOZA/MOZA
(The Power of the upward-thrusting triangle that takes us off the cross of space and time)
(MOSES – MOI-SHE
JESUS – YE-SHU-AH
ELIJAH – ELI-AH-HOO)
MOISHE/YESHUA/ELIAHU
MOISHE/YESHUA/ELIAHU
MOISHE/YESHUA/ELIAHU
MOZA/MOZA/MOZA
SHALOM/SHALOM/SHALOM
SHALOM/SHALOM/SHALOM
THE SPIRAL OF GOLDEN/WHITE LIGHT ENFOLDS YOU WITH DIVINE LOVE/DIVINE WISDOM/DIVINE LIGHT/DIVINE PROTECTION/DIVINE POWER
YOU ARE *MOZA*
(Heb: going forth; origin; source; rising; fountain; springhead)

I have included an explanation of the God-force energies that bless you and your service during this initiation experience. The following information was obtained from the Metaphysical Bible Dictionary published by the Unity School of Christianity in Unity Village, Missouri.

"MELCHIZEDEK – The divine will established in humanity/divine righteousness/divine justice/divine peace. Represents divine consciousness/ establishes and maintains right doing, right use of will, profound peace. Melchizedek is priest of God Most High, serving with light that transcends all light; King of Salem; King of Peace.

METATRON – The head of "World of Creation," called also the body of the shekinah. Shekinah means "abiding place of God." Metatron gave Moses all the shapes of the tabernacle; he blesses; anoints all who offer themselves as a holy tabernacle in which God's light burns eternally. Metatron is also known in the Talmud as Angel of the Universe. The Zohar says the angels of Ezekiel's chariot vision are in the midst of a wheel and that this wheel is Metatron.

ARCHANGEL MICHAEL – One who is like the expanding power of God. His name in Hebrew means "he who is like God." Represents divine inspiration; realization of the all-conquering power of God, the perfect state of being. Michael serves in the heavenly temple/tabernacle of Metatron and is the most powerful of the archangels.

MOSES – Name means drawing out; drawing forth; water-saved. Represents humanity's development in consciousness of divine law; to draw out from negativity new growth and awareness. Moses represents moral law; disciplining the thoughts; the process from within outward; drawing out of ourselves the inner wisdom center of God; leading with new ideas safely through the wilderness of our undisciplined mind. Moses represents evolutionary force of new ideas that lifts us out of a sense of bondage, moving forward to Canaan. Note: Canaan is the name of the invisible substance that surrounds and interpenetrates all form of which it is the mother. In Hebrew it means: "realized nothingness."

ELIJAH – My God Jehovah. Represents the spiritual "I AM". Elijah started out with the roar of a whirlwind and ended with the whisper of the "still small voice." Represents the effect of the law; in the transfiguration experience – the association of Elijah and Moses represented cause and effect. The presence of Moses and Elijah represents the two processes through which the purification demonstrated by Jesus is achieved. First, the mosaic or evolutionary process of nature through which there is a steady upward trend of all things. Second, they are spiritual discerners of truth to make conditions change rapidly on the mental plane. We are told that Elijah must first come and restore all things. The mind must first be set right through spiritual understanding.

JESUS – YESHUA OR JOSHUA – Deliverance through Jehovah; whose help Jehovah is; safety; salvation; deliverer. Jesus went up into a mountain to pray, and was there transfigured. Prayer always brings about an exalted or rapid radiation of mental energy, and when it is accompanied by faith (Peter), love (John), and judgment (James) there is a lifting up of the soul that electrifies the body; the raiment (the aura surrounding the body) shines with glistening whiteness."

The angels have taught me the healing in laughter and inspired me to lighten up my life by laughing at myself. In February, 2003 the news media was encouraging Americans to be prepared for a possible terrorist attack by stocking up on plastic and duct tape. I am certain that you probably didn't panic and succumb to this outrageous suggestion; however, a few weeks earlier my dad had died and I was quite frankly, not a well woman. My rational husband could not console me with this wisdom about the worthlessness of duct tape in such an emergency. We had to go out and stock up on plastic and duct tape. It was so out of character for me, but due to the grief I was out of my divine mind and was grasping for things that could in some way bring a sense of peace into my world. I'm laughing at myself as I share this story with you because of my foolishness.

As I mentioned, rational thinking couldn't sway me until the morning of Thursday, February 13th, 2003 when I opened The Baltimore Sun and read Kevin Cowherd's weekly column. I have contacted The Sun and have been given permission to share with you this column in its entirety. I honor Kevin for being a healing angel. With laughter he healed the fear that had a grip on me and was causing my insane thinking.

Fighting fears with plastic and duct tape.

By Kevin Cowherd

The Baltimore Sun

Let me begin by saying I'm as concerned about this newest terrorist alert as the next person, unless the next person happens to live in New York or Washington, where the level of concern is a good deal higher.

But...*duct tape*?

And plastic sheeting?

For a chemical or biological attack?

If that's what the government recommends to seal off a "safe room" in a house, all I can say is, good luck.

Me, I'd keep that bio-hazard suit pressed and handy, just in case.

In the first place, have you ever *watched* the average person duct-tape anything?

It's not a pretty sight. The average person can barely duct-tape the pedal on a kid's Big Wheels, never mind expertly seal off windows and doors.

Invariably, the sticky side ends up all wadded and bunched and unevenly aligned – assuming you can even tear it off the roll.

And that's when people are *calm*!

Can you imagine trying to seal a room when air raid sirens are wailing and people are screaming and your TV is blaring news of a terrorist attack?

People would be so jittery, they'd be lucky not to tape their hands together.

There is also another little matter to consider when trying to turn a room into your own personal biosphere.

If you do manage to make the room airtight, what exactly would you breathe?

Wouldn't things get a little, um, close after a while? As in close enough for everyone in the room to keel over?

What good does it do to create a secure environment if everyone's gasping for breath before the first cloud of nerve gas even arrives?

Still, during a quick check of various stores near me yesterday, duct tape and plastic sheeting were flying off the shelves.

At Office Depot, where I went because someone told me customers were buying five and six rolls at a clip, the duct tape was sold out by early afternoon.

(Office Depot, isn't that a strange place to visit in preparation for a terrorist attack? How does the mental checklist go there? 'Let's see…printer cartridges? Check. Sticky pads. Check. Two-inch duct tape to seal windows and doors in the event of a lethal contaminant released into the atmosphere? Check.')

At the Cockeysville Home Depot, they had two pallets of duct tape parked at either end of the main aisle.

The store always does a steady business in batteries and flashlights, assistant manager Elaine Gavin said, and those weren't moving any faster than normal.

But duct tape and plastic sheeting were selling as if al-Quida operatives were coming up York Road.

'To be honest, it's been mostly seniors buying those items,' Gavin said.

As we strolled back to the plastic sheeting section, which had been picked over like the $10 sweater table at Hecht's, I asked Gavin if she thought duct tape and plastic would actually save someone in the event of a biological or chemical attack.

Gavin smiled. It was the kind of smile the teacher gives the dopey kid who says two and two equals five.

'If it's gonna happen,' she said of an attack, waving at the sheeting, 'this isn't gonna do anything for you.'

Amen, sister.

Instead of fooling around with plastic sheeting and duct tape if a toxic cloud were to appear anywhere near them, I think most people would be reaching for the car keys.

And dialing the reservations desk at a Holiday Inn in, say Montana.

Gavin went on to say that she was 47 years old and that what we were seeing now was just a new twist on an old fear: annihilation at the hands of another international lunatic.

'Back in the 50's, we had the (atomic) bomb scare issue,' she said. 'And what did everyone do? They built bomb shelters.'

Back then, I told her, they held drills in my elementary school where a whistle sounded and all the kids ducked under their desks and covered up, as if Soviet ICBMs had suddenly been spotted in the skies over the jungle-gym and swings.

Now people of my age look back at that and laugh. Because the Russkies must have had pretty lousy A-bombs if you could save yourself by diving under a tiny wooden desk.

Luckily, we never had to use those bomb shelters.

You hope the same holds true for duct tape and plastic sheets."

- Reprinted with permission of The Baltimore Sun

The best part is that Chuck and I have used the duct tape and plastic. The plastic was used in gardening projects; duct tape in home repairs.

Sometimes it's up to us to make the fun happen not only in our lives but in the lives of others too. Sometimes we need to be the "fun meister".

My girlfriend, Mary Dansicker, owner of Joshua's Lighthouse Angels and Girlfriends, is starting a new chapter of the Red Hat Society. The Red Hat Society is based on the poem "Warning" by Jenny Joseph which begins with: "When I am an old woman I shall wear purple with a red hat which doesn't go and doesn't suit me."

Mary recently wrote about the chapter of The Red Hat Society that she is forming in her store newsletter: "We will get together once a month to laugh, catch up and of course…wear red hats and purple dresses! Lord knows we need and deserve and owe this to ourselves."

Perhaps you'll be the founder a The Red Hat Society chapter in your community. The only rules are these: Members must wear a red hat and purple outfit if they are 50 years of age or older. Members under the age of 50 may wear a pink hat and lavender outfit. You can find more info at www.redhatsociety.com. We named ourselves "The Scarlet O'Hatters".

Some years ago I was contacted by the producer of the television program "Connie Chung: Eye to Eye." The producer was putting together a show about people who believed in angels and wanted to know if they could film me teaching one of my classes. I indicated I was going to be at Kutztown University for a week-long Life Spectrums Conference and encouraged them to get approval from the conference organizers for their filming my workshop. Approval was given and the cameras started rolling.

During the week I was teaching two classes. One class was Monday through Friday, two hours each morning, where conference registrants who were staying on campus the entire week, signed up for a week-long "Commune With the Angels" workshop experience. On Thursday afternoon of the same week I was teaching a "sampler" class entitled "Angelic Healing," which was offered to people who were coming to the conference for one day only; the Angelic Healing class was two hours in length. The TV crew wanted to film that class, too. My week-long class was held in a normal-sized college classroom and created an intimate, cozy environment for the angelic experience. The location of the Angelic Healing workshop was to have been in the same classroom until the conference organizers made a change in plans; I would later realize the change was made by God.

Thursday evening Deepak Chopra was a special guest speaker for the evening program. Deepak Chopra speaks to packed houses and because of the huge turnout expected, he would be speaking in the large Kutztown University auditorium on campus. Because the conference organizers wanted to be of assistance to the Connie Chung show people and at the same time get ready for Deepak Chopra's arrival, they moved my Angelic Healing workshop into the auditorium, too, so they had a handle on both activities. I like to tease that on that afternoon I was the lead-in act for Deepak Chopra.

When I was told of the change, I said to the angels, "How strange!" because my angelic healing service and angelic attunement initiations are usually done in intimate retreat settings with small groups, i.e. with a group of 12 at The Spiritual Center in Windsor, New York. I had fully expected to have about 12 people gather in a small college classroom; instead the class was going to be held in a very large auditorium.

Earlier in the week, I was walking back to my dorm room and conversing with the angels about the demonstration I do as part of the angelic healing class. I always ask for a volunteer who will receive the healing. I said a prayer that God would put in front of me the person that God wanted to receive the healing. Just then, as I turned a corner of a campus building, a young man almost collided with me. He had been looking for me. He said he had heard that I was doing an angelic healing demonstration, and if I needed a volunteer, could he volunteer. I told him, YES! and informed him to be at the auditorium on Thursday afternoon.

When the time came for the class, I entered the auditorium to find about 30 people on hand for the experience. I hope you can imagine 30 people spaced out all over the auditorium. I asked everyone to move up and fill the seats in the first two rows. My seminar is part teaching and part demonstration. Following my lecture, I sat a chair in front of the class members and called up on the young man who had volunteered to receive the healing.

Even though I had served with the angels of healing numerous times before, and had said the initiation words I shared with you earlier in this chapter, nothing had ever happened like what happened that afternoon.

As I rested my hands on the young's man's shoulders and began my honoring of God through prayer and invocation, with my inner sight I saw hundreds of people from spirit walking down the aisles coming toward me and this young man. They walked down the aisle, to the center of the auditorium where the young man was seated and I was standing behind him. They were literally pushing me aside. They came because of him, not me. I heard them say, "Let me touch him. Let me bless him. Let me thank him. Let me heal him." I leaned over the shoulder of the man and whispered, "Who are all these people in spirit?" He obviously was feeling the love energy directed towards him, because tears were streaming down his face. I figured the best thing I could do was to continue doing what God had taught me to do, hands-on healing. And so I went through the entire healing demonstration, the whole time assisted by hundreds of people in spirit. I've heard of group hugs; this was a group healing.

When I had completed my service, I praised God and stepped to the front of the young man. I asked him, "If you feel you want to, can you tell us who all those people in spirit were?"

He shared with us that he had been so moved by all the lives that had been lost to AIDS. He was saddened when he heard that some people had died alone. Some people didn't have anyone who remembered them or cared about them. And so this dear precious man had created his own healing project of obtaining all the names on the AIDS Memorial Quilt. Using this list he had made a ritual of reading a number of names every day and saying to those people in spirit: "I love you and care about you. I bless you. I remember you. I honor your life." Because of this incredible service of caring and compassion, all those he had loved, blessed, remembered, cared about and honored came to Kutztown University's auditorium and gave love and healing to him.

It was so perfect that we were moved to the auditorium. I feel had we been in a normal classroom the windows would have been blown out by the energy. Oftentimes when people come through from spirit, glass will shatter because of the movement of their energy. Perhaps after someone you loved died, a picture fell off your wall and the glass shattered. That's a sign of a visitation by your loved one. Can you imagine the impact of the energy of hundreds of people from spirit visiting this young man in a small college classroom? As always, God knows best.

Everyone who witnessed the experience was blessed. People that were not previously clairvoyant were literally blown wide open and were seeing angels all around the young man. People received healings just sitting in the audience. And I was in total awe of the energy of love everlasting that transcends all dimensions and even death. One of my girlfriends had driven up from Baltimore that afternoon to participate in the class. After the class we talked about the happenings of the afternoon, and she remarked, "God knows how to work a room." I loved her remark; in fact, God knows how to work our lives if we just get out of the way!

Chapter 10

FENG SHUI ANGELS

In DUI Angels I devoted a small chapter to the introduction of Angelic Feng Shui, angelic inspirations to make your home heaven on earth. I do not pretend to be nor do I promote myself as a feng shui master who has studied the techniques of this ancient healing art of bringing well being to any environment. I encourage you to seek out in your community professional feng shui practioners because they will bring to your home or office an expertise that follows the rules of various schools of feng shui, i.e. The Form School, Traditional Chinese Compass School Feng Shui, and Black Hat Sect (BHS) Feng Shui.

I am simply someone whose life has been blessed by being of service together with the angels in helping people make their home a bungalow of blessings. From my experiences, I have gathered practical ways to make an angelic attunement in your home, to align the energies in support of you and your family members physically, mentally, emotionally and spiritually.

It is important to regard your living environment as heavenly real estate and consider the space inside your home as divine. All space is sacred, even where the dust bunnies are living.

Acknowledge the angelic guardians of your home and property. Thank them daily for watching over you, your family and your home. You can visualize specific angels, such as Michael the archangel of God's protection, watching over your home. If you are someone who likes tangible re-enforcement, consider purchasing two angel statues for placement by your front door. Later in this chapter, I will share information on the choirs of angels and archangels that watch over the energy sector or portals in your home. The front door of your home is blessed with the energies of the seraphim. Seraphim are more identified with dragons than any other members of the angelic hierarchy. It didn't surprise me that a feng shui treatment for home protection is the placement of dragons or lions in the front of the home. The statues represent an invisible energy of protection that is guarding the occupants of the house.

We refer to our home as our "household." It's important to take that word seriously and ask yourself this question, "What does my house hold?" It is a mirroring to us of the energies that our souls hold as well. Chances are if there's a lot of clutter in your home, your soul is feeling the cramped energy as well. You can ask my husband, Chuck, and he will confirm that I am someone who always takes out the garbage. I encourage you not to let trash, waste or garbage build up inside your home. This is important because our trash – until it is moved out – is in a "holding pattern," waiting to be recycled or disposed. If you allow it to build up, it creates a "holding pattern" vortex of energy inside your home.

Take time to truly sense the soul energy of your home. Your own soul, your home's soul energy, the surrounding environment's soul, the earth soul, and "soul on and soul on" all overlap and share growing room together.

Sense the center or heart of your home and honor it by placing something that mirrors to you the passionate energy of your heart. Walk through your house to get a sensing of the place that feels like the "heart of the home". At that spot place something that mirrors "heart" energy to you, such as a picture of your family. You want to support your own happy heart by having a "happy heart" inside the "body of your home."

Just as God assigned the angels to watch over you, you are guardian, keeper and caretaker of all you possess. Love your belongings abundantly. Treat everything you have as precious and take good care of your belongings.

If you have a fountain in your home, which is a wonderful feng shui treatment, whenever you walk by it or tune into the sound, acknowledge that your life is flowing with God's goodness in all that you do. Let the belongings of your home be more than objects. Let them be messengers of all the goodness in your life.

Walk through your home imagining a feng shui angel by your side. You may even want to honor this angel by offering a gift of love in the form of a name that you bestow on this angel. I call my feng shui angel: DEB. D – E –

B stands for Divine Eternal Bliss. My feng shui angel inspires me with ways to attune the energy of our home to divine eternal bliss.

Dedicate a meditation to communing with your feng shui angel and ask for help in lifting up the energies of your home. In researching feng shui I learned that it was first known as "Kan Yu." I know this may sound a little corny, however, as you walk through your home with the feng shui angel or angels by your side, hear them whisper this question: "Can you see your home as a holy sanctuary of peace?" Feng shui angels help us to see divinity in everything within our home.

D. H. Lawrence described angels as "potent sensual entitites," and I agree because the feng shui angels help you sense the energies of the divine wind of blessings that can blow through your house and the divine rivers of energies of goodness that can flow. A wonderful way to infuse your environment with uplifting blessings is through sensual treatments, i.e. soothing sounds such as flowing fountains, enticing smells such as aromatherapy candles, and calming music.

Sometimes we have to re-learn our home. Goethe said, "We see only what we know." If you haven't given yourself the chance to really know your home, then you don't see it. Walk through your house observing all the shapes. How many items are circles? How many items are square or boxes? How many items are triangles?

Walk through your house and observe all the colors. How many things do you have that are dominant in the color blue? In red? Go through all the colors of the rainbow. Create a rainbow connection with your home.

Walk through your house and observe textures. Do you have a lot of items that are metals? Do you have a lot that are wood? Become conscious of the choices you have made and are living with every day.

Give the walls of your home a voice. Sit down and imagine the walls have ears. What have they heard? Let them tell you. Now there's really not a voice inside the walls that's going to talk to you, but there is an accumulation of the energy from the voices of the people within the house. Give yourself a chance to listen to the energy vibrations. You may find yourself being inspired to do some smudging because there's a residue of energy from an argument in the past. If you sit down in a room, and the first thing you think of are angry words that were spoken in the room, that's a definite indication that there's still some energy lingering that needs to be cleared.

Sit in a particular room and commune with the feng shui angels. Open yourself to a word that conveys the energies of the room. What is the soul statement of the room, that is, what statement does the room make about what's important to your soul? Is it a word or soul statement that you are content with? If not, start by making minor changes to the room. Move one item to a different place in the room. Notice what happens to the energy of the room.

Henry Miller shared that "The aim of life is to live, and to live means to be aware, joyously, drunkenly, serenely, divinely aware." Approach your house with awareness. Make a conscious effort to see your home with a new awareness that everything in your home is a fulfillment of an inner wish or desire. Walk around your home and stop in a room and explore all the belongings in that room. What wish and desire do the items fulfill?

We all experience loss in our lives. There are ways in our home that we support ourselves by letting something be born in the midst of loss. Think about a loss you have experienced and then think of something in your home that is a blessing that mirrors to you what was born as a result of the loss.

We are here on earth to transmute conflict; for example, if life gives you lemons you make lemonade. Think of a space inside your home that has conflict energy waiting to be transmuted. It could be bills on a desk; it could be a hall closet; it could be a pile of old newspapers. Let peace on earth begin by healing conflict in one room at a time. Wash, dust, clear, and smudge negative energies away. Be a peacemaker in your own home.

Enjoy all your belongings. Share everything you have with the feng shui angels. Have show and tell. In the show and tell experience, you may find items over which you pause and wonder, "Why am I keeping this?!" Or you may find an item that causes you to rejoice, "Wow! I forgot I had this!" Take time to really look at what you have. It's a great exercise of gratefulness.

Take stock of all your possessions. Before you go out and buy something new, ask yourself if you are making the most of what you already have. Have you ever paused to reflect on a time in your life when you didn't have as much materially, yet in your memories you seemed a lot happier? When that happens, perhaps it is our inner "God-voice" reminding us to be content with all the blessings we have in our life in the now. A good question to ask is "What would be enough?" Take time to treasure the things in your life that are priceless. We sometimes buy things out of guilt or boredom. That energy comes right home with us in the bag. Perhaps that gives meaning to the statement, "You got more than you bargained for."

When you have things you are saving for later, such as fabric that you bought on sale for a future dressmaking project, take time to at least savor what they represent to you. When you move things around, it allows you to do this. It allows you to remind yourself, "Oh yes! I have this fabric ready to make a wonderful new dress and one day I will use it!" This memory jog will be helpful when you are in a fabric store and are feeling pulled to buy additional fabric that is enticing you.

Look at home improvement as soul improvement. Divine order starts with bringing order into your own private sanctuary, your home. A show that is now airing on the Bravo channel is "A Queer Eye for the Straight Guy" and it features five talented gay men who are invited by a straight guy to literally come into his life and help him get his act together. I've been amused by the program in that the "straight" guys featured certainly don't have "straightening up at home" genes that were dominant genes. The five men bring to each week's assignment "makeover" energies in the areas of fashion, grooming, food and wine, culture, and interior decorating. One evening one of the "Fab Five", as they are known, said to the homeowner, after surveying the interior of the home that was the epitome of total chaos, "Have you ever just stopped and asked yourself, 'What the heck happened here?'"

The way you organize things or collect and gather them in your home conveys your own personal integrity. Oftentimes when we are not supporting ourselves outwardly, this feeling has already been expressed inwardly in our treatment of things in our home. You will find feng shui masters agree that a messy living environment blocks the flow of chi. The energy force of the universe is known as chi. You may have heard it called other names such as prana or spirit.

The reason I love this program is even in the midst of the very frank humor about the project, the Fab Five are able to go in and cleanup, cleanout, and give the man a "recitation experience" in his living environment. In most of the cases there is literally no breathing room and I am quite certain that what goes on in our home impacts what goes on in the rest of our lives. At the end of the program you witness a man who is feeling good about himself, his looks, his home and his life. By removing the clutter in the man's life, cleaning up, and tidying up, the chi is able to flow unencumbered and the space radiates an energy of being "brand new". The individual feels "brand new," too.

I've already shared the importance of find the heart of your home. Additionally, every room needs a "heart space". It is a simply a place that is all about love. Once you establish the heart space, perhaps by simple recognition, it becomes a vortex of love. It's a space that welcomes the angels to come into your life and celebrate with you your divine identity. I feel every room needs to have a heart place that you can recognize as the heart of the room and everything else will align to that space and energy. A "loving" space that then radiates out to the rest of the room. Simply stand in any room of your home and ask yourself, "What is the heart space in this room?" Once you determine the heart space, honor it in some small way if possible, i.e. with a special picture or flowers.

The total space of your home, every inch of it, is a safe haven to give you peace and sanctuary from the outside world. If you feel you need more peace in your life, take a look at your home and start there by giving your home an infusion of peace. One way to do this is to call on the fairy kingdom for support.

I am a big fan of the fairy kingdom and I encourage you to consider allowing their precious energy into your home. One way to do this is to work with the way the elemental energy is expressed in your home. Observe the elemental energy of your home and how these energies have expression in your home. By nurturing the elemental and fairy kingdom, you nurture yourself. Fairies are magical beings. When you invite them into your home, you are giving your magical self an invitation to come out and play.

In "A Midsummer Night's Dream," William Shakespeare wrote a house blessing that is given by the elf and fairy sprite:

"Through the house give glimmering light
By the dead and drowsy fire;
Every elf and fairy sprite
Hop as light as bird from brier;
And this ditty, after me,
Sing and dance it trippingly.
First rehearse your song by rote,
To each word a warbling note;
Hand in hand, with fairy grace
Will we sing and bless this place."

I love Shakespeare's poem and use it often to bless our home because I want our home to be a place of peace for humans, animals, angels and fairies.

Just as I encouraged readers of Commune With the Angels to believe in angels, I also encourage you to open your heart to the fairies.

"Believe in the Fairies
Who make dreams come true,
Believe in the wonder,
The stars and the moon.
Believe in the magic,
From Fairies above.
They dance on the flowers,
And sing songs of love.
And if you just believe,
And always stay true,

The Fairies will be there,
To watch over you!"
-Anon

Many cultures believe in household fairies. In Ireland a "bean sidhe" is a fairy housekeeper or fairy godmother. Her name means "woman of the house." She is a guardian to the children of the household as well as the pets and supports the woman of the household. She helps with the chores around the house. The Scottish believe in brownies, fairies with brown skin and brown clothes, who come out at night to help with housework. Because of the brownies' helpfulness, thank you gifts of food are often left for them.

The fairies live in a parallel world to ours. Their world is within our world, in a different dimension, vibration and frequency to ours, which makes it more difficult for us to see them when we focus on our human reality.

When you invite fairies into your home, it's important to be willing to make an effort to create a fairyland atmosphere for them. One way to do this is to have things in your home that make the fairies feel welcomed and "at home" in your environment. Fire spirit or "Sparkies" energy is supported with candles, lamps, lights, triangles, fireplaces, sun images, and red colors. Earth "Gnome"energy is supported with terracotta and clay pots, bricks, stone, squares, and the colors yellow, orange and brown. Woodland and tree fairy energy is supported with indoor trees, plants, wooden furniture, decks, green colors. Etheric or air "Bubbles" fairy energies are supported with round shapes, domes, kitchenware, coins, clocks and colors that are silver. Water baby or "Gillies" fairy energy is supported with fountains, ponds, fish tanks, mirrors, glass and blue colors. One thing that all fairies cannot resist is a rainbow; in fact, a rainbow is such a special place for the fairy energy it can even turn you into a fairy. Marion St. John Webb's poem "At the End of the Rainbow" gives the particulars:

If you want to be a fairy
You should simply look around
For when you reach a rainbow's end –
You will see, waiting to be found,
A pair of gleaming fairy wings
Sparkling on the ground.
So put them on, then count up to ten –
Smile, and you're a fairy then!
Some people shake their heads.
'No, not wings,' we're told.
Lying at the rainbow's end
You'll find a pot of gold!'

The people who believe in this
Are not like us, they're too old.
But we believe in fairy things,
And we shall find those sparkling wings.

We have in our home a special light that when turned on will cast a huge rainbow on a wall or ceiling. We love turning off the lights and turning on the rainbow, because when we do this we feel a "rainbow connection" with the fairies in our home. Additionally, I have fairy houses, made from tree stumps and other materials from nature, throughout our house in case the fairies want to sleepover.

This past year has been a hard one emotionally for me because of my dad's death and my mother having to be placed in an assisted living home because of advanced Alzheimer's disease. My mother, who once had an incredibly brilliant mind, no longer remembers her children. In a sense, I have lost both of my parents. I lost Dad physically when he went to heaven; I lost Mom mentally to Alzheimer's. This has been a tough adjustment in my life because I have always been extremely close to my parents. That closeness has been one of my life's greatest joys. My mother and I loved to do things together, such as going on shopping excursions, out for lunches, visiting local craft fairs. One day I said a prayer to God asking for His help in dealing with my sadness in the loss of my mom's memory; the loss of the fun times we shared together. Shortly after saying the prayer I felt inspired to look through a collection of Mom's recipes. There amongst the handwritten collection of recipes was a faded newspaper clipping. My mom had written at the top: "Want to try." The title of the article was: "Plan A Fairy Tale Evening," and offered the creative idea of acquainting children to the magic of fairy tales and even included a recipe for a Snow White/Rose Red dessert. Plan a fairy tale evening in your home and awaken your own inner connection to the essences of the natural world, the fairies.

I recently read an Associated Press article by Gregg Aamot entitled –Elf in tree enchants children – and grownups. Kids leave letters for Mr. Little Guy behind 6-inch door. Mr. Little Guy has "enchanted Twin Citians ever since the 6-inch wooden door appeared eight years ago, just off a walking path around poplar Lake Harriet." There is a local man named "Thom" whose wife spotted the tree opening and thought it would make a wonderful home for an elf and his family. The man said "he never meant his little house to attract so many youngsters – it was just a secret place for him and his family, at first."

Mr. Little Guy receives 1,500 notes a year and Thom answers every single one of them himself. In his replies he lets children know "...Mr. Little Guy is just a guy that's in their corner...It's all about being affirmative.

Every letter finishes with 'I believe in you.'" Perhaps there's a tree with an opening in your neighborhood that simply needs a tiny door to invite the wee people to come and take up residence in your community.

If it ever seems like you are in a spiral of negative communication, i.e. bad news coming from everywhere, re-think the ways you are "receiving" information into your home. Switch on the answering machine rather than picking up the phone when it rings; don't read your computer e-mail as regularly as before; cut back on newspapers. Look for ways to take control of "receiving" messages. It is a statement that you are making by choice that you will not allow yourself to be flooded by negative messages.

After Chuck and I were first married, we had to come to an understanding about each other's communication needs and the outside world. Chuck is someone who, whenever the phone would ring, would pick it up, answer the call and if it was for me, hand the phone to me fully expecting that I should be ready to talk to whoever was on the other end of the line. Chuck is someone who can be accessible to the world at a minute's notice. He is very gifted at being able to do two things at one time; in fact, he's happiest when he has lots of "balls in the air". He has an energy that can start a project, stop in the middle, and get back to it later. I am someone who wants to start something and stay with it to completion. When I am on one train track of focus, I do not like being "side-tracked," and I have found for myself that phone calls can be a distraction or side-tracking energy for me. It has been interesting, however, when the angels say to me, "Take that call." When I pick up the phone and say hello, the person on the other hand usually says to me, "Jayne, I am amazed I got you," and it is always a situation where I needed to be there in that moment. For my own peace of mind, I have to be selective as to how I receive communications that come into our home. I learned this lesson from Edgar Cayce's life. Cayce would go into a trance and be able to give to the people who came to see him for help, answers and solutions to their concerns. However, he couldn't say no. He didn't give himself healing space and as a result his physical body was impacted and he died from simply not taking good care of himself.

Leave open space in your home for the invisible to be made visible. Leave open space for the fairies to play. Leave room for the angels to dance. Leave room for whatever and whomever you want to come visit. Remember as a child you left milk and cookies for Santa. It's a great angelic feng shui technique to honor spirit by leaving offerings.

Honor your ancestors with a shrine. In my research of religions and cultures, I have greatly admired the way in which shrines are created and dedicated to family members and those who provide spiritual guidance. A shrine is an outward expression of your thanksgiving to God for the presence of these precious souls who have gone on and your openness to their continued support and blessings.

Pay attention to what you see outside your windows. If there is anything that you see outside of any window in your home that "stirs you up," either change the view on the outside if you are able to do it, i.e. a bush with dead branches needs to be trimmed, or do something about it from the inside of the house, i.e. place something near the window that balances the negative energies outside. It's also very healing to open the windows. When you open windows and let in fresh air you are letting in new energy. Even in the wintertime, I love opening windows for a few moments to let the air inside of the house receive an infusion of fresh outdoor air. Air quality is important, too. Smudge to clear the air of any impurities. Consider an air purifier for your home.

Before beginning any new project that requires that you flow with new ideas or new visions, walk through your home with the feng shui angels and eliminate any cramped spaces. Remember to create wing space for wingspan.

Seek balance. Just as I recommended supporting yourself with elemental energy to amplify peace in your life, too much of one particular element is an imbalance, so pay attention when there's too much of one element in your home, i.e. too much wood. Balance it with another element.

Flowing water means flowing energy. If you need contemplation time and time to connect with the still small voice within, consider the support of "still water". You've heard the saying, "Still waters run deep." The energy of still waters allows you the gift of deep contemplation within yourself.

If you are feeling depressed, wake up in the morning at daybreak. Create a circle of candles on the floor and sit smack dab in the middle. People often equate campfires with nighttime; however, I have found that if you want to juice your fire spirit, do it with the support of the new dawn. Remember, however, that just as an abundance of fire energy gets you "fired up," too much can cause you to fire up emotions with others.

A simple healing you can manifest inside your home is to leave your shoes at the door. Taking your shoes off allows for a very intimate exchange between your feet and the floors of your home. You are able to "get in touch" with the foundation of your home and feel grounded and supported by the earth beneath you.

Cracked items weaken your energy and your energy field. Chipped items can create a "chip on the shoulder" experience, and broken items can cause wounds that are not fully healed to open.

As we learn in Genesis, when God was creating the heavens and the earth, God said, "Let there be light." This is a good rule to follow when creating new energy in your home. Let the sunlight into your home through clean windows. Have a place – whether inside or outside of your house – where you can go to sit in the sun. Helen Keller said, "Keep your face to the sunshine and you cannot see the shadow."

Dick Clark calls music the soundtrack of your life. What are you playing as your life's soundtrack? Think about your life energy as songs you love. Make a CD or cassette with songs that reflect messages or feelings about who you are and what's important to you. Music and songs that you love speak to your soul profoundly. I'm sure you've had the experience of hearing a song for the first time, and having it touch your mind, heart and spirit in a very powerful way, so much so you cannot wait till you hear it again and again. Enrich your life and your home with music that lifts your spirit.

When spring cleaning, or in fact cleaning in any season, playing Benedictine chants will clear and bless your home's energy.

Bells are wonderful feng shui treatments. Ring a ding ding! Bells clear space of negativity.

Place in a prominent space in your home a JOY JOURNAL. Keep it out in view where you can easily see it. This helps you remind yourself to record all the joys in your life, and also reminds you that yours is a joyous life.

People shower rose petals on a bride's path. Take rose essence and bless your walkway as a blessing to all who come up your path. Remember, all of us are in a mystical marriage with the divine. God is the beloved.

Here's an easy angelic feng shui treatment. Buy a new broom…and yes, sweep every room clean. It works with moving energy, not to mention dirt. To clear out negative energy, put the Hallelujah Chorus on a loop-to-loop recorder and feel the energies of the house lifted up to heaven and totally transmuted into light.

Chime in abundant energy by hanging chimes so when your doors open the chimes ring. If you want abundance to "flower" or some aspect of your life to blossom, hang a painting of blossoming flowers where you can see it or place a vase of beautiful flowers in a prominent spot. Whenever you walk by the painting or vase, connect with the consciousness that your outer world mirrors to you that your love life is blossoming; your career is flowering and flourishing.

If there is something you want to do as a new hobby, dedicate space in your home for all the materials. The way to make a dream start taking shape is to start making it tangible. Bring the dream into reality by having the tools or supplies you need to do it.

Rearrange your furniture every now and then. Do it if for no other reason than to clean thoroughly the floor underneath the furniture.

Always have plenty of lighting around your doorway. The angels have inspired me that when you make it easy for people to find a door, it in turn makes it easy for you to find the doors you need to find in your life. If you want something new to come to you, make certain the entranceway to your house is uncluttered, in other words, clear the pathway.

Once I decided to place a beautiful banner over my front door for people to see when they drove up. The only problem was it totally covered up the doorknocker. Immediately, my service as a spiritual consultant, which was flowing nicely, totally stopped. No one was calling me for appointments. I tried to figure out what I was doing differently and was inspired by the angels to do a walk through the house. As soon as I opened the front door, I intuitively knew what I had done to myself. I removed the banner and at that very moment the phone rang.

Avoid anything intense and over-bearing in your home, i.e. harsh, intense lighting. The earth is intense enough. Let your home be soothing to your soul.

Determine your animal totem in feng shui, which is the totem for the year you were born. Have this totem in your home. It is a messenger of universal consciousness.

What's cooking in your life? The word "kitchen" derives from the Latin word which means to cook. Even if you don't like to cook, support the energy of cooking up a delicious life by having a joyful, clean kitchen. This is an area in which I had to really do a healing. I have no cooking genes. I have never enjoyed cooking. As I shared in Commune with the Angels, my girlfriends tease and say, "If Jayne made it, it means she made it from the store (where she bought it) to her car." Close friends fully expected to come in my home one day and find the kitchen was turned into a new library.

The angels helped me realize that by not allowing space in my home for a kitchen that is alive and well, I was shutting down ways in which I am fed and nurtured. I was impacting my own "wellness" energy. Cooking is done in order to feed and nourish our bodies. I tried buying cooking magazines, thinking that would inspire me. Celeste McDonald and I went to Taste of Home cooking classes. Celeste is a fabulous cook. She gained more inspiration; I gained nothing.

I gave a great deal of thought to how I could heal this blockage in my life. When I got out of my own way, and opened myself to inviting into my home a master who would help me heal kitchen karma, he instantly appeared. His name is: the Pillsbury Doughboy. His message: "Nothing says loving like something from the oven." I decorated our kitchen with a

Pillsbury Doughboy theme. In fact, there is a pass-through between the kitchen and our dining room. On that pass-through stands a 3' Pillsbury Doughboy. Whenever I go into the kitchen, I feel his giggly energy enveloping me and I have been inspired to fill our refrigerator with nourishing foods and plan healthy menus. I have no aspiration for being someone who lives to cook. I doubt that I will ever love cooking. The healing is that I no longer hate it. That's a BIG healing.

I truly believe that the angels gave me a sign that I had transmuted my kitchen karma. Shortly after transforming my kitchen into a Pillsbury Doughboy shrine, I found on EBAY original doughboy art by the creator Mart Nodell. The Pillsbury Doughboy became another messenger of the healing of art, in all forms. Interestingly, there were numerous prints of the doughboy offered for sale. One print showed the doughboy teamed up with The Green Lantern, a cartoon action character also created by Mart. When I saw this print, I got up from my computer and walked into Chuck's office. I said, "I bet I know a cartoon action figure that you loved as a boy?" He was intrigued and said, "Ok, who is it?" I said: "The Green Lantern." His expression changed to one of total awe for my intuitive abilities and he said, "That's absolutely right. That's amazing! How did you know that?!" I said, "Because the same man who created the Green Lantern created the Pillsbury Doughboy." We have on the side of our refrigerator, held up with Pillsbury Doughboy magnets, a print of the Doughboy and Green Lantern together. God gave us the angels to help guide us in discovering our true selves.

Additionally, make sure the refrigerator and pantry in your home are well stocked. This practice speaks volumes to our inner sensitivity of having enough. You are mirroring to yourself and those in the household the message of never having to worry about a shortage of food. In Chinese households, the rice jar is never allowed to be empty. Once the bottom of the jar can be seen, it is filled with rice because rice represents such a key part of family meals.

Crystals are great to use for feng shui treatments; however, recognize that they have an amplifying quality. Make certain before bringing any crystals into your home, you clear the crystals by washing them in sea salts and also clear your home of anything no longer useful or positive. People often ask me which crystals have the best energy for alignment to the angelic kingdom. One of the best I have found is celestite and its celestial blue color. Celestite has a heavenly vibration.

I believe King Arthur was very hip when it came to feng shui. He had the vision of the Round Table. Round tables promote togetherness. I mentioned earlier the importance of a walk-through in your home to see what shapes are predominant. You can utilize shapes to help bring forth "the shape of things to come." Sacred geometry works. Shapes support what you want to come to you. If you want wholeness, bring out the circles and the round bowls to decorate your house. If you want stability, call up the energy of squares. Squares mirror to us a cubic energy – very much like the salt cubes. There's no coincidence that dependable people are referred to being "the salt of the earth."

If you want direction, have objects that reflect a triangular energy. Rectangles are messengers of expansion. Waves are healing messengers of flexibility and adaptability. Banners are a wonderful treatment for healing inflexibility. They "wave" and allow you to show your colors to the world. For forward direct movement, use straight lines.

As I've shared in my writing, I have studied spiritual astrology. I help clients align themselves to the will of God for their life through their astrological birth map and solar return maps for each new year.

Thomas Merton wrote, "We cannot be happy if we expect to live all the time at the highest peak of intensity. Happiness is not a matter of intensity, but of balance and order." I encourage you to think about your life as a balanced astrological wheel. There are 12 rooms to the "house of you." Twelve is the number of completion.

Each room is equally important and needs to be given attention and kept in order. You need to make time for each room. To open the windows in the room. Let fresh air inside the room. Experience the room's energy. I have outlined the twelve rooms, which are aligned to the twelve houses of the zodiac wheel. Think about which room most needs a visit from you.

Room 1 – Your personality/persona/ego/self awareness/self-discovery /identity

Room 2 – Your personal resources/money/property/possessions/values

Room 3 – Your lower mind/thinking mind/expressing yourself/learning/ communicating

Room 4 – Your emotions/feelings/inner sense of security/home and hearth/family/ancestors/benefactors

Room 5 – Your creativity/playfulness/inner child/children/enthusiasm for life/romance

Room 6 – Your health/body/well-being/self improvement/habits/ patterns

Room 7 – Your relationships with others/husbands/wives/significant others

Room 8 – Your desires/passions/sexuality/sharing/life/death/changes

Room 9 – Your higher mind/enlightenment/travel/quests/awareness of the big picture/cosmos/learning about other cultures/religions

Room 10 – Your career/your work/contribution to society/your higher calling/the mastery you have come to express on earth

Room 11 – Your hopes/wishes/dreams/groups you are involved with/friends/clubs

Room 12 – Your secrets/your search for unity and divinity/your transcendence/the unknown/the mysterious you

If you want to energize prosperity in your life, have a Prosperity Pot by the door of your home. Always have a coin in your pocket to put in your Prosperity Pot. When you hear the sound of the coin falling into the pot, affirm that you are hearing abundance in your life loud and clear.

Any pockets with holes? Mend them immediately. Anything where energy is leaking, heal it. With regard to your wardrobe, get real about your clothes. If they don't fit, pass them on. If you keep clothing of multiple sizes in your closet, it is a confusing energy that conveys your weight is in flux. Only keep the size you are wearing, and if you are in a weight reduction program, keep a size that is your goal. Release the rest.

Have a blessing basket of little gifts that you have ready to give to friends when they come to your home to visit. We are here on earth to be blessings to others.

Make a photo album of people who are family members by heart as well as by birth. Cherish the common traits you find in others. Have a camera with film in your home, and ask visitors if you can take their picture for your photo album in order to cherish the visit in the future.

Have a place in your home where you gather goodness for others. A place for a bag of canned goods that is ready to be given to a canned good drive.

Staying connected with people is important. Keep a telephone directory of people you want to stay in touch with; have on hand cards for people you want to honor; have a place in your home, i.e. a "parlor", for visiting with friends. Try to surprise someone once a month with an act of love that will come to them unexpected. Send it from your home. You are establishing the energy of your home as being a place where blessings originate and then travel out into the world.

Make room in your life for simple joys. For example, if a simple joy is hot chocolate on a chilly morning, have a mug, hot chocolate and marshmallows on the shelf in your cupboard. We always have first aid ready, for when we have a physical boo-boo. It's important for us to have a "first joy" kit, too. Have a humor medicine cabinet, too. It's where you keep things that make you happy, i.e. videos that make you laugh. Keep a comic relief photo album. Only funny pictures are allowed.

When you want to start something new, support yourself by listening to a new radio station, eating something new, learning about something new, watching a new TV show. For any new season, or any new adventure, support yourself by uncluttering. Give newness a chance by giving it breathing room. Clutter is a variant of the word "clotter," which means to clot. Our home is an extension of our body. This is one reason clutter has to go. To everything there is a season, so allow seasons to change in your house, too.

If you are someone who decorates the refrigerator door with pictures, change it every so often with new pictures of your loved ones. We "freeze" people in time on our refrigerators. I do believe that pictures we place on our refrigerators are wonderful in that they mirror to us the love of friends and family that feeds our soul as well, in addition to what's behind the refrigerator doors that feeds our bodies. I once saw the following message on a church bulletin board: If God had a refrigerator, your picture would be on it.

Have a fiesta in your home. Celebrate! You don't have to go out to dress up. Decorate your home for whatever is special to you. Let your house sparkle with the enjoyment of various activities. When your house sparkles with joy, so does your soul.

When we sometimes misplace items in our home, we generate a frustration energy which floats around the house like a cloud of negativity. Next time you cannot find an item, look at the situation with a whimsical attitude, "Ok, I get it! This is a game of hide and seek!" Let your playful inner child do the looking. Decommission the frustrated adult.

And of course, don't forget to call upon St. Anthony. Make problems fun games that are like puzzles to be solved.

If you feel your spark plugs are "missing," tackle one thing that you have been putting off doing. Connect with completion. That helps our inner spark plugs be charged with energy.

It may sound corny, but get a key. Place the key on your altar. Call it your happiness key. Meditate holding the key in your hand so that you mirror to yourself that you truly do hold the key to happiness in your own hands.

Ok, life isn't always a bowl of cherries. When you have problems with others, dedicate a space in your home to "common ground". Energize it with pages that you write, and pictures that you find of things you hold in common with them. Energize the likeness rather than the differences.

My dad grew roses most of his life. He's tending roses in heaven now. In honor of him, I remind you to buy yourself a bouquet of roses and then be sure to stop and smell them.

While writing this chapter, I received Sean David Morton's Delphi Associates Newsletter. Included in the issue was an article on "Cleaning House," and Morton mentions the importance plants play in absorbing and transmuting negative energy as well as creating oxygen for us to breathe. I was delighted when I read that his personal favorite plant is the Peace Lily. He states, "For most indoor environments, the Peace Lily is, in my opinion, the best plant for ease of care, effective removal of toxins (such as formaldehyde, benzene, acetone and alcohols), and the ability to tolerate shifting indoor environments. Its name contains the word Peace (something that I'm all for :)."

Since my email address is earthangel4peace@aol.com; and my website is www.earthangel4peace.com, peace is something that I am all for, too. I have found that a Peace Lily is a wonderful housewarming gift because it tolerates low lights and the dry conditions found in most home environments. It's great knowing the gift you are giving will make the home healthier, which will be a blessing for the family that you care about. NASA even did a study on "sick building" syndrome. Peace lilies were rated among the top ten air cleaning plants for interiors.

Make places in your home where you can nap or sleep comfortably. Have places in your home that invite your soul to take a much-deserved rest. Just as care of your belongings is important, personal feng shui is important, too. Take good care of yourself by having an ample supply of whatever grooming products you need.

Doormats make an important statement. They are a message you are sending to the outer world as to what you are inviting into your home. The "welcome" mat evolved from the words "will come". People saw it as making their house open to, or welcoming in, the will of God. The front door is the part of your house that faces the world. Make it a happy face with a beautiful wreath or lovely door decoration, and remember – don't cover up the doorknocker.

Get your camera out. Take pictures of your home while walking with the feng shui angels. Look at the pictures carefully. You'll be amazed at the new perspective you get from a photograph.

Put little white feathers throughout your house to remind you to keep your heart as light as a feather. Breathe enchantment into your home by opening your heart to doing something light-hearted and fun at least once every week in your home.

Einstein was once asked, "What the most important question in life?" He responded, "Is the Universe a friendly place or not?" Your home is your mini-Universe. Make it a friendly place. I mentioned earlier the program, "A Queer Eye for A Straight Guy" where the Fab Five did life makeovers. In one show, one of the Fab Five asked where did their friends sit when they came to visit. The individual replied that his friends never came because there was no place for them to sit, and yet the person really wanted to have people over to visit. "Clear it" and they will come.

St. Brigit was a messenger of keeping the home fires burning, symbolic of always keeping the inner light burning bright. The hearth energy is truly connected to heart energy. The hearth in a home was the place of warmth, fire and light. Many homes do not have a hearth, yet you can create the energy in other ways. Be a fire tender to your soul's light. Light a candle for a short time every day. Used colored candles for supportive energy of what you desire. Burn green for healing and growth. Burn red for passion. Burn pink for love and nurturance. You can identify what is important to you and support yourself with warmth, fire and light. Make certain you have things in your environment that kindle those energies.

Objects in your home that are meant to shine, keep them shining. If they are meant to sparkle, keep them sparkling. Keep hallways open and clear. Just remember the angels are coming through and wing space is definitely needed to come down the hall.

Love every inch of your house. Make time to admire the beauty of your home. Have an astrology chart cast for the date you bought your home, or you can use the settlement time as the time of birth, because it's the date and time you took over guardianship and stewardship.

Objects that convey symbolic messages can also help shift energy in your home. If you want more love, have more images of hearts around your home. The hearts become messages of your desire to see more love in your life and this starts by your seeing the hearts throughout your home.

Life consists of doors of opportunity opening to us. Make certain the doors in your house open freely.

Buy a wand at a children's store. Consider the wand as a spiritual tool that supports your ability to direct energies in your home. Point the wand to the front door of your home and say a word that conveys a powerful energy of manifestation to you. It can be something magical like Abracadabra or even a word you create. Visualize yourself magnetizing the door with an energy that draws wealth and abundance to you.

If there is something that is a mystery to you, a problem you haven't yet solved, get a mystery novel out of the library or off the shelf of your book collection and put it on your altar. It will energize you with the belief that you are a good sleuth and can solve the mystery.

If you want to support your spirituality, and open more fully to God, buy sunflowers and keep them in a vase on your altar. Sunflowers are messengers of keeping our faces fully open to God's light and love.

In the ancient feng shui teachings wisdom is given on nine energy sectors in each room and overall for the entire home. I have taken the basic nine sectors and integrated the energy of the archangels, angels, and choirs of angels.

Stand facing inward to the room in a doorway in your home. For example, if you select the living room, stand in the doorway with your face looking into the room. No matter where the door placement is, whether in the center of the room, or left or right, imagine that the room has nine equal size sectors. Three sectors make up the left side of the room; three the center of the room; and three sectors are the right side of the room.

Back left sector	Center back	Back right sector
Uriel	Zadkiel	Blessed Mother
Abundance/Wealth	Fame	Love/Relationships
Sixth Choir of Angels	Seventh Choir of Angels	Fifth Choir of Angels
Powers	Principalities	Virtues

Left middle	Center middle	Right middle
Gabriel	Raphael	Chamuel
Family	Health	Playfulness/Inner child
Four Choir of Angels	Ninth Choir of Angels	Third Choir of Angels
Dominions	Guardian Angel	Thrones

Left front	Center front	Right front
Jophiel	Michael	Aquaiel
Self Knowledge	Adventures -	Benefactors
Wisdom	Coming to you Eighth	Choir of Angels
Second Choir of Angels	First Choir of Angels	Archangels
Cherubim	Seraphim	

Center front:
Archangel Michael/First Choir of Angels/Seraphim
Life path/journeys/adventures/face to the world
What we have come to do in the world. The adventure of our life; our mission.
The seraphim bless this sector with vibration of love just as in their service to God they glorify God with the vibration, "Holy, holy, holy. Holy is the Lord of Hosts, the whole earth is full of His Glory." This sector is where the outer and inner meet.
Make it a happy encounter. Enhance it with images of your life's adventure.

Left front:
Archangel Jophiel/Second Choir of Angels/Cherubim/Wisdomkeepers
Respect of time given here on earth/ inner wisdom, truth and understanding
Kerub translates to knowledge. Subtle vibration from cherubim is one of knowledge and wisdom. Enhance this sector with books, quotations, and a consciousness of wisdom.

Right front:
Archangel Aquaiel/Eighth Choir of Angels/Archangels/
Benefactors/invisible blessings made visible
Magnificent archangels/helpful people/benefactors/mentors/aid from spirit world
Archangels are messengers of divine decrees for our life. Enhance sector with saints, angels, pictures of people who are blessings to you.

Center middle:
Archangel Raphael/Ninth Choir of Angels/Guardian Angel
Health/well-being/stewardship ourphysical/mental/emotional/spiritual bodies
Listening to the physician within for holistic healing guidance. Being a guardian to what God has given you. Energize with green plants, i.e. peace lily, objects that mirror well-being to you.

Center left:
Archangel Gabriel/Fourth Choir of Angels/Dominions
Family/heritage/all my relations/ lineage and legacy of love
Learning about yourself from the family or tribe. The energy of the dominions as regulators of duty and responsibilities in our lives. Enhance with family heirlooms, pictures.

Center right:
Archangel Chamuel/Third Choir of Angels/Thrones
Inner Child/playfulness/wonder/awe/curiosity
The energy of the thrones expresses God's Will as constantly flowing waves of creativity. Enhance with playful things, childhood joys – toys, dolls, teddy bears.

Center back:
Archangel Zadkiel/Seventh Choir of Angels/Principalities
Fame/external recognition/where you shine/being seen/freedom to be you without obstacles/Enhance with pictures of people you admire. You can also

energize with power animal images. Expressions of freedom are powerful in this sector, too.

Left back:
Archangel Uriel/Sixth Choir of Angels/Powers
Wealth/riches/abundance/
Powers energize the sector with energies that balance and reconcile extremes. All wealth/riches/abundances can be used for goodness' sake or evil.
Enhance with items that reflect abundance, wealth, prosperity to you.

Right back:
Blessed Mother/Divine Mother/Fifth Choir of Angels/Relationships/Virtues
Intimate relationships/commitment energy/allowing romance and love into your life/feeling connected to divine love/mystical marriage with divine/beloved vibration
Enhance with hearts, artwork portraying great love

You can use the above angelic support for energizing sectors in a room or over the entire house. Approach the task of healing your home with exuberance and enthusiasm. Henry Wadsworth Longfellow wrote, "Enthusiasm begets enthusiasm." William Blake wrote: "Exuberance is beauty." Let your enthusiasm for your home soar to new heights. Let your exuberance open you to all that is beautiful in your "home sweet home," which mirrors all that is beautiful in you. Aligning your home to heaven is a wonderful way to praise God and also to exalt your spirit. In the wise words of Dorothy from Kansas, "There's no place like home."

Chapter 11

ARCHANGEL MICHAEL

In my earthly service I have worked very closely with Archangel Michael. I have been given angelic assignments which have been fulfilled with the energy and support of Michael. Michael is a divine messenger of God's protection in our lives. Everyone can call upon Archangel Michael and his energy will be with you instantly. Michael commands legions of angels who radiate energies of God's protection of humanity. He ranks as the greatest angel in Islam, Judaism and Christianity. His name in Hebrew means, "Who is as God." The Dead Sea Scrolls call Michael the Prince of Light.

Michael is one of the archangels that have been the subject of many paintings. He is usually represented as a winged messenger of God with unsheathed sword either doing battle with Satan or slaying a dragon.

Henry Wadsworth Longfellow described Michael in his poem "The Golden Legend" as the spirit of the planet Mercury. Yeats referred to him as the "leader of God's host" in his poem "The Rose of Peace." Pope Pius XII declared Michael patron saint of policemen in 1950.

Archangel Michael is a powerful warrior angel. I sometimes refer to him as the "kick butt" archangel. Sean David Morton, a gifted intuitive and Managing Trustee of the Prophecy Research Institute, calls him the "bouncer angel". In Sean's words, "It's his (Michael's) job and pleasure to help you in situations where 'evil' lurks about. Archangel Michael does not mess around and will get right to helping you. And don't worry about taking him off of more important things or think that you're taking him away from people who need his help more than you. There is no time and space within the realms that Archangel Michael operates. He can be with everyone instantaneously."

I have had situations where people have confided to me horrific demonic encounters in their life. I immediately tell them to enlist the protection of Archangel Michael. It never ceases to amaze me that people will sometimes reply, "But isn't he busy?" You better hope not! Archangel Michael is always available to fight evil. God has delegated Michael in charge of fighting evil.

There is belief that it was Michael who stayed the hand of Abraham from slaying Isaac in sacrifice. He radiates to us God's ideals and virtues of divine power, strength, and courage. Ephesians 6:10-11 inspires us to "...be strong in the Lord and in the power of His might. Put on the whole armor of God, that you may be able to stand against the wiles of the devil." I believe that in calling upon the support of Archangel Michael, we are putting on the whole armor of God. Michael radiates energies of God's protection. Shortly after 9/11, Archangel Michael inspired me to call my dear friend Molly Sheehan and to ask what flower essence she had produced in connection with Archangel Michael. She shared with me that she had just completed an essence called "Golden Armor" which was charged with Michael's protection. Golden Armor contains Echinops, Eryngium, Abutilon, White Yarrow, French Marigold, St. John's Word, Elderberry, Goldenrod, Titan, Thistle, Leopard's Bane, and Wild Abutilon. Molly shared the following about Golden Armor, "The Angels have never been as adamant about us working with a remedy as this one – reminding us quite insistently that we need to take it every day and give it to the animals every day. I think it is to help us with harmonious mutation as well as to help us buffer ourselves from the electromagnetic noises of our world and everything else bombarding us. As with everything from spirit, it is so much more than the sum of its parts!" Needless to say, I ordered a bottle and shared the information with all the HA HA members immediately. You can order a bottle from yourself by contacting Green Home Farm Flower Essences' website: www.greenhopeessences.com or writing them at Green Hope Farm/PO Box 125/Meriden, NH 03770. Their telephone number is 603-469-3662.

Edgar Cayce described Michael as "the lord or guard of the change that comes in every soul that seeks the Way..." Cayce even received a message from Michael during a trance transmission about the Association for Research and Enlightenment's purpose to serve:

"Hark! There comes the voice of one who would speak to those gathered here.

I am Michael, Lord of the Way! Bend thy head, o ye children of men! Give heed unto the way as is set before you in that sermon the mount, in that on yon hill this enlightenment may come along men! For even as the voice of the one who stood beside the sea and called all men unto the way, that those that would harken might know there was again a staff in David, and the rod of Jesse has not failed: for in Zion thy names are written, and in service will come truth." (Reading 254-42)

Michael is a teacher as well. With his mighty sword he teaches us to cut through challenges and encumbrances that prevent us from embracing God's truth and wisdom for our lives. You may have perhaps experienced Michael's presence in your life with his sapphire blue flaming sword in a meditation or dream. You can invoke Michael and his sword to assist you in cutting through energies that bind you in any way. Additionally, sometimes we wrap ourselves around the axle with our thinking. Michael can help cut through the confusion to align us to God's infinite mind and consciousness.

Michael has served God in bringing order out of chaos. He will assist you whenever you have a feeling there is discordant energy around you, if you have a sensing that in some way you are being vibrationally attacked. I use the following decree when I get an uneasy feeling about the energy around me:

Michael's light descend, descend, descend
Michael's light defend, defend, defend
Michael's light expand, expand, expand
Michael's light command, command, command
Michael's light I am; I am; I am.

When I say that decree I visualize that Archangel Michael's light enters my body from the top of my head straight down to my toes. Michael's light is in me. The light that is in me then immediately defends me from anything attempting to attack my energy field. Michael's light doesn't stop there. It expands and pushes the negativity totally out of my environment. Michael then commands the energy to "be gone!" I rest in the peace and assurance that Michael and I are one. When you call upon Michael, you are aligning yourself to God's infinite power and there's no power greater than God's.

One day the angels gave me the following clue to research. I was to research the real story behind the movie "The Exorcist." I have to be truthful, I still get scared when I think about that movie. I remember I saw the movie with my first husband when we were visiting friends in Cape Cod. After seeing the movie, I was so frightened by the images that I woke my husband up in the middle of the night and made him walk down the hall with me so I could use the hall bathroom. Knowing what I know now, I would have let him sleep and called upon Archangel Michael.

All I knew about the story of The Exorcist was what I had seen on the movie screen. In researching I found out that Exorcist producer William Peter Blatty based his novel on an article he read as a 20-year-old English Literature major at Georgetown University. The article appeared in the August 20, 1949 Washington Post: Bill Brinkley, reporter, "Priest Frees Mt. Ranier Boy Reported Held in Devil's Grip." This article stayed in Blatty's mind to the point where it became the basis for his best-selling book The Exorcist. In fact, not only did Blatty write The Exorcist, he also wrote If There Were Demons, Then Perhaps There Were Angels in which he tells his story of learning of demonic possession through the newspaper article and how that article led to the incredible novel and movie. I love the title because you can rest assured that where there are demons up to no good, you will also find an abundance of God's angels ready, willing and able to "kick butt" and Archangel Michael is leading God's angels.

I was thrilled to learn that a diary had been kept by one of the attending priests involved in the exorcism of the young boy, Robbie Mannheim. In reading the diary I was amazed by the diligence, perseverance and dedication of the exorcism team. I recommend that you read Thomas B. Allen's Possessed, which includes the actual diary text. In the diary, Robbie is referred to as "R".

On Holy Saturday, April 16, 1949 the diary reads as follows: "On Holy Saturday, Brother Rector bought a small colorful statue of St. Michael the Archangel. The statue was placed in R's room. It should be remarked here that one of the most effective prayers of the exorcism was that dedicated to St. Michael."

On Easter Monday the priests attempted to give communion to R and had the boy say, "I wish to receive you" – an expression of receiving Christ. The diary records that "the devil laughed and said: 'That isn't enough. He has to say one more word, one little word, I mean one BIG word. He'll never say it...He'll never say that word. I am always in him. He will never say that word." Can you imagine the frustration of these precious priests being taunted by the devil and this riddle of a word that must be spoken by R?

Yet the priests never give up. They do what they know how to do; they continue to perform exorcism rites over and over. In researching this story, I was inspired by that message. We are asked to do our part; do what we know how to do; keep the faith; never give up; and let God be God.

The priests had been trained by the church to perform exorcisms. That is what their training had prepared them to do. I had the opportunity to hear

Rudolph Giuliani speak at a success motivation conference. He shared the message of the importance of relentless preparation. He indicated that no one in New York City had prepared for what happened on 9/11 because no one could imagine such a horrific happening; however, they had prepared for everything else, and so they responded quickly utilizing all the skills developed in their preparedness training, and trusted that God would take care of the rest. This is exactly what happened with the priests and Robbie. The priests kept focused on what they had been trained to do, and God took care of the rest.

Then at 10:45 pm on Monday, April 18th, "the most striking event of the evening occurred. R was in a seizure, but lay calm. In clear, commanding tones, and with dignity, a voice broke into the prayers. The following is an accurate quotation:

'Satan! Satan! I am Saint Michael, and I command you, Satan, and the other evil spirits to leave the body in the name of Dominus, immediately – NOW! NOW! N O W!'

Then there came the most violent contortions of the entire period of exorcism, that is since March 16....after seven or eight minutes of violence R, in a tone of complete relief said, "He's gone!"

R described that he had seen a brilliant white light and "in that light stood a beautiful man, with flowing wavy hair that blew in that breeze. He wore a white robe that fitted close to his body. The material gave the impression of scales. Only the upper half of the body of this man was visible to R. In his right hand he held up a wavy and fiery sword in front of him. With his left hand he pointed down to a pit or cave.

R said he saw the devil standing in the cave...First the devil fought the angel and was laughing diabolically. Then the angel smiled at R and spoke, but R heard only the one word 'Dominus'. As the angel spoke, the devil and about ten of his helpers ran back into the fire of the cave or pit. As the devils disappeared into the pit R felt a pulling or tugging in the region of his stomach. He felt a snapping, and then felt relaxed completely."

Dominus means "Lord" and Michael was commanding Satan to leave in the name of Christ, who was the true Lord and master of the body of this young man. Additionally, in watching the DVD "In the Grip of Evil" I learned that not only did Archangel Michael appear in body to the young boy, but as the boy saw Archangel Michael, priests in the parish church of the young boy (a separate location because the exorcism was taking place in a St. Louis hospital ward) also saw Michael appear before the altar.

If you ever have a situation in your life wherein you feel you are doing battle with an evil force or presence, call upon Archangel Michael and use the words that Michael used in rescuing Robbie Mannheim. First use the above decree to invoke the energies of Archangel Michael into your body. Once you sense oneness with God's power and might, then say the words: Satan! Satan! I am Saint Michael, and I command you, Satan, and the other evil spirits to leave my body in the name of DOMINUS, immediately, NOW! NOW! N O W!

You can use this command to remove evil spirits in your home as well. Please know that I was asked by Archangel Michael to include the above in this book. I am certain Michael is inspiring me to do this so that you are prepared. Use it when you need it.

Michael inspires us to be courageous and change our lives for the better. We can be positive in our own life and yet we are influenced by people around us who bring us down with their negativity. Michael hands us his sword to use in cutting ourselves free of people, places and things that negatively impact our thoughts and attitudes.

Personal development seminar leader Jim Rohn encourages us to "...constantly ask ourselves these questions: Who am I around? What are they doing to me? What have they got me reading? What have they got me saying? Where do they have me going? What do they have me thinking? And most important, what do they have me becoming? Then ask ourselves the big question: is that OK?" If it isn't, ask Michael to borrow his sword and cut yourself free of these people.

As I was working on this chapter of blessings from Archangel Michael, Chuck and I had the opportunity to go to Ann Bell's home and have our auras photographed by Mildred Acevedo of The Angel Walk Foundation, Inc. The photograph shows the color or colors of your full body and seven major charkas. I found it interesting that mine appeared as a sphere that was totally sapphire blue. I think Michael was participating in an angelic Kodak moment.

Another decree or call for help from Archangel Michael is as follows:

"Beloved Mighty I AM Presence, beloved Archangel Michael, and all the Ascended Masters, the Great Angelic Host, the Cosmic Beings, the Forces of the Elements, and the Entire Spirit of the Great White Brotherhood, I invoke the Tube of Light, a Wall of Blue Flame surrounding that Tube of Light, Triple Ring-Pass-Not, and a Wall of the Violet Fire of Divine Love, to be an Invincible Cosmic Atmosphere - over and around me - for *invincible, invulnerable,* and *indestructible* Protection from all misqualified energies and opposition coming from any and all sources - known or unknown.

I call to Archangel Michael for the Protection of all Sons and Daughters of God - all Lightbearers - so that they can fulfill their mission and destiny, and stand as "Pillars of Light" in the earth." – Ascended Master Research Center

I also call upon Archangel Michael when I am traveling because I am comforted in knowing his protection is with me. Here's a decree you can use before you head off to work in the morning or before starting your drive home:

Lord Michael before! Lord Michael behind!
Lord Michael to the right!
Lord Michael to the left!
Lord Michael above! Lord Michael below!
Lord Michael, Lord Michael wherever I go!
I AM one with Lord Michael's protection NOW!

I have found in my service that Michael is especially fond of Padre Pio. Years ago I was "called by spirit" to go to the North America Center for the Canonization of Padre Pio. At that time the center was literally located in a small barn in Barto, Pennsylvania. The volunteers were so wonderful to me, and even allowed me to hold a glove of Padre's – that was protected behind glass. I had been sent to the center on a mission to find out for myself what was delaying the canonization. As I considered the humility of this great man, I thought to myself, "Padre wouldn't have sent me here." Just as I was contemplating the origin of my divine orders, I looked overhead and saw a wonderful painting of Archangel Michael. Instantly I felt Michael's presence assuring me that it was God's will that Padre be canonized, Michael had called me to Barto, and I was to do my part in spreading the message of Padre's life of service to God to help move along the canonization energies.

As I shared earlier in this book, Padre was canonized on Father's Day, June 16, 2002. Archangel Michael called me to Italy following the canonization to visit Padre's church and home. In September, 2002 Chuck and I went to Italy. While in San Giovonni, I visited the crypt where Padre is buried. Because mass was being given in the church overhead, I was almost by myself in the crypt, something I never expected to happen. While kneeling near to his casket, I heard Padre give a blessing to all who either hear or read my words:

St. Padre Pio blesses you with roses that bloom in the daytime, and the rosettes (Hubble telescope images of rose formation) that bloom amongst the stars. Roses above you, roses around you. Roses are messengers of love. Feel yourself enveloped by God's love above you and around you. Padre gives you his love and offers you a bouquet of red roses and white lilies. May the red roses remind you to be givers of love here on earth; may the lilies remind us to know that Christ's resurrection isn't a happening that occurred 2,000 years ago. It is a spiritual experience that occurs every daybreak when we awaken and greet the new day with Christ in our heart. Together the roses and lilies are a message that every day you awaken reborn in the love of Christ, to live your day embodying the love of Christ and serve as a messenger of the love of Christ to others.

After leaving San Giovanni, our taxi driver Pepe drove us to Monte Gargano in the town of Monte Sant'Angelo, which is the most famous shrine in the world dedicated to Archangel Michael.

Archangel Michael himself consecrated this shrine so that its divine energies would bless all who answered the call to serve alongside him. On four occasions Michael appeared on the Monte. In fact, the grotto itself is the only place of worship not consecrated by human hands and over the centuries has received the title of "Celestial Basilica." You enter a Romanesque portal that frames bronze doors that open to the Celestial Basilica. This place was chosen by Archangel Michael and is a cavern made by nature itself in the calcareous rock. I couldn't believe my eyes when I first saw the Saint Michael grotto; in fact, it was an experience I call "joy sight." What I saw – both visible and invisible – was joy to my soul. It is said that when Saint Francis arrived at Monte Sant'Angelo to obtain angelic pardon, feeling himself to be unworthy to enter the grotto, he stopped in prayer and recollection at the entrance, kissed the ground and carved on a stone the sign of the cross in the form of "T" (tau), which in Biblical language is the symbol of salvation. I felt pure joy in every cell of my body to have been led by the light of Archangel Michael to this holy place where I was immersed in his energies of both tenderness and strength. In fact, while in the grotto I saw Michael holding a set of scales and receiving the inspiration from him to live life choosing to be tender in times that warrant tenderness as the response and strong when strength is needed.

In Michael's words given in one of the apparitions at Gargano, "I am the Archangel Michael and am always in the presence of God. The cave is sacred to me. I have chosen it; I myself am its watchful custodian…what is asked for here in prayer will be granted."

I encourage you to make the grotto a destination for a heart pilgrimage. Imagine yourself going there. Know that your heart has wings and can take you to Saint Michael's Shrine on the Gargano whenever you desire. Michael will give you a "virtual tour" of his grotto.

Michael's apparitions at this sacred site are an invitation to all of us to humble ourselves before God and feel God's grace showered upon us. Additionally, it is an invitation to accept Michael's personal love for each one of us.

Gargano is a "house of God, and a gate of heaven." Feel God's loving arms welcome you and enfold you as you make your heart pilgrimage. Know that pilgrims of the past have included Padre Pio, many kings, and many popes including John Paul II.

The guardians of Gargano are known as "Michaelites." I love that name and it inspired me with the following thought for my own: I want to be a member of the Holy Order of Michael Lights. I want to serve God together with the light of Archangel Michael – shining with God's power, protection and will energies.

I believe God has called all of us to serve. In 1 Peter 2:9 it states, "But you *are* a chosen generation, a royal priesthood, a holy nation. His own special people, that you may proclaim the praises of Him who called you out of darkness into His marvelous light." I believe our first calling of service is to pray. Start each day with prayer. As "a royal priesthood" we can pray for our nation, our leaders, our communities, our families and friends and for our own lives. Prayer gives you an opportunity to experience God's perspective to your problems. So often we look at our lives and problems from the human point of view. Prayer takes us closer to God and allows us to see and understand our challenges from a heavenly point of view, i.e. higher, clearer and even farther rather than what's right in our face. Praying also brings healing benefits to our lives. In short, it's healthy to pray daily. Whenever you pray, there's an immediate "sensing" that you are not alone in what you are facing. When you pray, you are turning to God for help and guidance or perhaps praying to give thanks and credit to where it's due – to God who provides everything in our lives.

Every morning and evening I join the angels in prayer for those who request prayer support and absentee healing. I am a big believer in the power of prayer. I have witnessed what prayer can do. Prayer works! On my altar I have a book called RAPHAEL'S GUEST BOOK. Raphael is the archangel whose name in Hebrew means: GOD HEALS. In that book I record the names of all people who have called me and asked for prayer support and to be included in absentee healing.

If you would like to be included, just contact me by either email: Jayne@earthangel4peace.com; phone: 1-866-peace2u; or write me at PO Box 95/Upperco, Maryland 21155. Give your name and indicate you are requesting prayer support and absentee healing. There is no charge whatsoever for this service. I am merely a vehicle for God's healing. I do not need to know what your need is. God knows that already. Once I receive your request for prayer support, by mail, email, or phone, I will include you for 21 days - morning and evening. I pray for you for 21 days because it is 3 weeks (the trinity number) times 7 (the sacred creation number) = 21 which is 2 + 1 = creating a 3 - the holy trinity blessing. I thank you for allowing me to be of service to you. I always feel so blessed when someone asks me for prayer support.

Additionally, I have joined the Presidential Prayer Team. You can, too. By joining The Presidential Prayer Team you can send encouragement to the President through prayer. The President will be notified of your involvement. There is no fee or obligation and your name will be kept confidential. You'll receive a free Presidential Prayer Team window decal in the mail and email updates on the specific prayer needs of the President and his Cabinet. To sign up, go to http://www.PresidentialPrayerTeam.org - It will only take a minute of your time. The Presidential Prayer Team is an independent, non-profit effort to rally concerned citizens to pray daily for the President. It is not associated with any party, political or government organization, or individual. Names and addresses of members will never be used for any other purpose or solicitation.

Chuck and I went to the outdoor theater at Wolf Trap in Vienna, Virginia and saw the musical The Civil War. One of the songs from that show, "Candle in the Window," is sung by the character, Lydia, a domestic servant in the White House. The lyrics of the song tell of Lydia's experience seeing President Lincoln every night on her way home from working at the White House. She describes him "a figure in a chair, always sitting there quiet as a prayer. Does he close his eyes? Weary with the weight of being suddenly so wise. Tired of the demons, he must sit up there and fight deep into the night. Praying that he's right?" Lydia goes on to express that when she gets home she falls on her knees and prays that he will keep the candle burning till he finds a way to heal the nation. The candle in the window reflects so much more than the light; it reflects the hopes and dreams of the nation. No matter what your political affiliation, I believe that once our president has been elected into office, he or she deserves our prayer support.

One of the assignments given to me by the angels is not only to offer prayer support to those who request it from me, but also be a "prayer guardian" to individuals who are leading with their light in various fields of research and service. The people that I am a prayer guardian to are individuals whom I believe in personally. Every day I include these people in my prayers and ask that God watch over them and help them in their life's work that is glorifying God here on earth. They do not know I am praying for them. I am not in any way interfering with their lives. I am simply being an earth angel to them and asking God to bless them and the good work they are fulfilling here for all of us. Consider becoming a prayer guardian, too. You simply pray every day for the individuals you believe in. Think about people in the fielding fields that inspire you, uplift you, and fill you with hope for our world: leaders in science, government, religion, the arts, medicine, etc. You are blessing them with your support and belief in them through saying prayers for them.

I once read a story where an individual came to visit President Lincoln at The White House. Following a few moments of polite conversation, the President asked how he could help the man, because everyone came asking for something. The individual replied, "Oh no, Mr. President. I don't want anything. I have simply come to tell you I believe in you!" I think one of the best ways we can show someone we believe in them is with prayer support.

Back in the late 1980's, I learned about Benjamin Solomon Carson, Sr., a man who had a childhood dream of becoming a physician. Growing up in a single parent home with dire poverty, poor grades, a pathological temper, and low self-esteem appeared to preclude the realization of that dream. But today, he is the Director of the Division of Pediatric Neurosurgery at The Johns Hopkins Medical Institutions, a position he has held since 1984 at the age of 33. He is a professor of neurosurgery, oncology, plastic surgery and pediatrics.

When Carson was ten years old, his classmates gave him the nickname "dummy," but he overcame the ridicule to become the youngest Chief of Pediatric Neurosurgery at Hopkins. Dr. Carson's philosophy is as follows, "It's not where you start from, it's where you're going that makes a difference."

In 1987, Dr. Carson gained world-wide recognition as the principal surgeon in the 22-hour separation of the Binder Siamese twins from Germany. In 1997, Dr. Carson was the primary surgeon in the team of South African and Zambian surgeons that separated type-2 vertical craniopagus twins (joined at the head) in a 28-hour operation.

Dr. Carson has received over 24 honorary doctorate degrees. He sits on the board of directors of numerous organizations, and was the keynote speaker at the 1997 President's National Prayer Breakfast.

He is president and co-founder of the Carson Scholars Fund, which recognizes young people of all backgrounds for exceptional academic and humanitarian accomplishments. He hopes this program will positively change the perception of high academic achievers among their peers across our nation.

He has authored three books: Gifted Hands, THINK BIG, and The Big Picture and over 90 neurosurgical publications. He believes strongly in God and in America and believes that we all can play a positive role in creating a better world.

In his own words: "Happiness doesn't result from what we get, but from what we give." For Dr. Carson one of his great heroes was Booker T.

Washington who taught himself to read even when it was illegal for slaves, and educated himself to the extent that he became an advisor to presidents. Another was Joseph from the Bible. "Even though bad things happened to him he never said, 'Poor me.' He worked hard and eventually triumphed. The fact is that bad things, difficult times happen in life. None of us is unique in experiencing them."

His mother, Sonya Carson was a guiding light in his life. "My mother worked with my brother Curtis and me, teaching us not to prejudge others – not to decide on their value before we knew them. She stressed treating everyone with kindness and giving every person a chance."

When interviewed by David Gergen, editor at large of U.S.News and World Report for Online Newshour, Dr. Carson shared his respect for the human brain as follows, "I've come to have great respect for the brain and its capabilities. You know the brain can process two million bits of information per second. It remembers everything you've ever seen, everything you've ever heard, and with brains like these, we really shouldn't be wandering around talking about what we can't do; we should be trying to create an atmosphere that helps our young people to realize that whatever they can imagine, they can achieve."

In this same interview, Dr. Carson again emphasized his mother's role in his life because even with all of her life's many hardships, she never considered herself a victim and wouldn't allow her children to regard themselves that way either. She always inspired her children to use their brain and would often quote a poem to them entitled, "Yourself to Blame." Additionally, she was a religious woman who prayed to God for guidance in raising her family. She came up with the idea of turning off the television and requiring that the boys read books and submit written book reports to her. From her guidance, Dr. Carson grew to love reading and he shared that even though his family had literally no money to do anything, through reading he could "go anywhere in the world, be anybody, do anything." As he read, he began to imagine and visualize himself in "intellectual capacities" and within the space of one and half years he went from the bottom of the class to the top. Carson's mother knew that education was the only way her sons were ever going to escape poverty and ridicule.

I recently was reading statements children had written at www.myhero.com and came across an entry by Tatianna Joyner from Baltimore, Maryland made on December 21, 2001:

"My hero is Dr. Ben Carson. When my cousin was about three, he was sitting on the steps playing with toys and got shot in the head. Usually when people get shot in their head they die, but Dr. Carson operated on him. Right now my cousin is 14 years old about to be 15 and nothing is wrong with him. He has no type of disabilities whatsoever, and it's all because of Ben Carson."

Dr. Carson has been a hero of mine for many years because of the incredible blessing he is to so many people. Recently I had the opportunity meet him in person and I was so excited that I walked right up to him and said, "Dr. Carson, I've been praying for you for years!" I don't think that came out exactly as I had intended. He is a very gracious individual and thanked me for my prayer support.

Archangel Michael's energy has inspired many artisans such as Michelango. In Commune With the Angels I shared the story of Michelangelo asking a member of his community if he could have a large stone on this individual's property for his sculpting. The individual told Michelangelo that he could indeed have the rock because it was simply a rock with no value. Michelangelo replied that there was an angel inside of the rock waiting to experience freedom.

While in Italy, I visited Florence's Galleria dell'Academia where there are several works by Michelangelo that appear not to have been completed. Michelangelo wanted to convey the message of how we are often like an angel inside a rock – waiting to experience freedom. The muscular figure struggling to free itself from the stone is symbolic of our own life's struggles to free ourselves from that which would hold our spirit captive.

Think about your personal life. Are there any things in your life that need to be chiseled away because they confine your freedom, your creativity, your life expression? Open to Archangel Michael's and Michelangelo's inspirations and think of what creative activities you want to energize and give freedom of expression to in the months ahead.

Michael gave this inspiration to me. "All that is asked of you is to remember…remember *the true*." Daily we forget "*the true*," and we have become spiritually unconscious to all that is within us. Michael calls to us to become conscious again, to remember…remember *the true*.

Michael calls us to remember when we perceived something beyond form, when we perceived something beyond our eyes, ears or even words. Remember when you recognized God in another being? When you allowed the sense of separateness to soften and the form you identify as yourself to disappear? When you were content with all that you had? In these moments you saw your life with God's eyes – with singleness of the sight of the Creator. There was no separateness.

When fear fills your awareness, focus on the assurance, support, love, safety and security God gives to us through Archangel Michael, protector angel. Michael is the energy of the messenger of "*the true*" intuitive knowledge which is singleness of God's power, light and love. When we see two – God and ourselves – we operate with a mental veil that is forgetfulness and prevents a direct flow of inspiration and awareness from that which is the single all – God. We trap ourselves with "my truth" vs. "your truth."

The next time you are in a quiet space meditating, ask yourself, "What is my truest quality?" If it comes as a feeling rather than words, simply open yourself to that feeling so you can really "get it." When you have a firm perception, intuitive or verbal, invent a way to express that quality of "*the true*" consciously at least once every day for a week or longer. Become conscious of "*the true*" of you.

The inside world within in us created the outside world around us. That which we are conscious of is reflected back to us from external experience. When fear fills our awareness, we draw towards us that which we fear.

Additionally while in Italy, Archangel Michael called me to visit Assisi. Shortly before his death, as St. Francis was on his way to Santa Maria degli Angeli from Assisi, he stopped halfway. Turning towards Assisi he blessed her with these words, "May you be blessed by God, holy city, for through you may souls will be saved and many servants of God will dwell in you and many of yours will be elected to the realm of eternal life." The field in which he stood is oftentimes filled with glorious sunflowers.

Archangel Michael and the angels bless you, your home and your home city, for you are in oneness with the spirit of St. Francis. You share with St. Francis a heart of love, a desire to exist as part of a civilization of peace, a continuous searching for closeness to God, a love of nature, a gift of dedication to serving God together with the angels and a desire for universal brotherhood.

Visualize yourself standing in a field of glorious sunflowers, just like the field where St. Francis once stood. The sunflowers remind us to always keep our faces turned towards God's light. Place your attention upon your home planet, your home country, your home city, your home community, and your own home. Hold the prayer in your heart: "May you be blessed by God." Hold in your heart this Biblical blessing from Numbers 6:24-15 for all kingdoms which reside on earth together: "May the Lord bless you and keep you. May he show his face to you and have mercy on you. May he turn his countenance toward you and give you peace."

There is one prayer that I use in addition to The Lord's Prayer in my prayer rituals. I call it the Prayer of Solomon. In 1 Kings 3:5-13, God comes to Solomon in a vision at night. God says to him, "Ask that which I should give you." Solomon honors God and gives thanks for all that God has already given to him and then asks, "Give therefore to thy servant an understanding heart to judge thy people and to discern between good and bad." God was so pleased with Solomon's request that God told Solomon he would receive not only what he asked for but also "both riches and honor, so that there shall not be any among the kings like you all your days."

I love to share with people Solomon's Prayer and encourage people to use it daily. "Oh, Lord my God, give to me, thy humble servant, (fill in your name), an understanding heart so that I am able today to discern between good and bad." I truly believe that no matter what challenge we may encounter in our lives, having an understanding heart is the answer in knowing what is good for us and what is bad. If we make good and wise choices for ourselves, based on an understanding heart given to us by God, everything else will somehow work itself out.

One of the ways I have found helpful in comforting myself in missing my dad's physical presence in my life is to attend the weekly Sunday morning service at the church of my childhood, Boring United Methodist Church in Boring, Maryland. It is a very small United Methodist Church with weekly attendance of about 21 people. My folks were faithful to God in so many ways, and regular Sunday church attendance was one of them. I have to honor my husband, Chuck, who joins me every Sunday morning when I go to church. When I sit in the wooden church pews, I am comforted when I look over my shoulder to the back pew, where Mom and Dad sat together for years. I am comforted by the familiar gospel songs we sing together and the uplifting and inspirational sermons of Rev. Rick Shamer. At the conclusion of the Sunday service the entire congregation forms a circle and joins hands to create a "vine of faith." My dear friend, Celeste, has shared with me that she, too, has returned to her childhood church as well and has been healed by the feeling of "coming home again". I remember once hearing Rev. Robert Schuller on The Hour of Power share that even though he encouraged the listening television audience to support his program with prayers and donations, it was important that everyone have a home church in their own community. He added that one day you are going to need someone to put his or her hand in yours and walk with you across a silent cemetery.

As I have shared, God gives us abundant signs and signals to let us know we are on the right path. One sweet experience for me occurred while I was writing this book. Chuck and I went to church at 9 a.m. one Sunday morning when the Old Testament Lesson was 1 Kings:3-14 – Solomon's prayer which as I have shared is a Jayne favorite; followed by the Epistle Lesson from Ephesians 6:10-20 – Paul's message encouraging us to "put on the whole armor of God," which is the protection radiated to us by Archangel Michael. The Hymn of Response for this particular service was:

"Be Thou My Vision," a hymn whose words I have included in this book for I truly believe if we see with our Father's eyes, we will see only love.

When I was a little girl attending Boring's Sunday School, I learned a special song. The words are, "Be careful little ears what you hear; oh be careful little ears what you hear. For the Father up above is looking down with love. Oh be careful little ears what you hear. Be careful little eyes what you see; oh he careful little eyes what you see. For the Father up above is looking down with love. Oh be careful little eyes what you see."

It is my prayer for you, that with the hearing of your ears, the sight of your eyes, the reach of your hands, the walk of your feet, the words of your mouth, the beat of your heart, the breath of your lungs, you only experience God's love.

I pray that this book brings you peace in knowing that God is loving and benevolent. God gives us an abundance of gifts daily. One gift that has been an incredible blessing in my life has been having angels by my side.

ANGELIC RESOURCE GUIDE

Within the pages of ANGELS BY MY SIDE I have mentioned the names of people and organizations that have been blessings in my life. I have listed here contact information for them in alphabetical order.

Americans for the Arts
Washington Office
1000 Vermont Avenue NW, 6th floor
Washington, DC 20005
Tel: 202-371-2830
Fax: 202-371-0424
New York Office
One East 53rd Street
New York, NY 10022
Tel: 212-223-2787
Fax: 212-980-4857
www.americansforthearts.org

Association of Research and Enlightenment
215 67th Street
Virginia Beach, VA 23451
Tel: 1-800-333-4499
www.edgarcayce.org

Ann Bell
3306 Milford Mill Road
Baltimore, MD 21207
410-922-8137
email: dbell13589@comcast.net

Boyds Bear Country
www.boydsbearcountry.com
located south of Gettysburg, PA
off of Bus. Rt. 15 at 75 Cunningham Road
717-630-2600

Rev. Reed Brown
Arlington Metaphysical Chapel
5618 Wilson Blvd.
Arlington, VA 22205-1303
Tel: 703-276-8738

John Begg
Caledonian Heritage Tours
11 Mavis Bank
Newburgh, Ellon
Aberdeenshire AB41 6Fb
Scotland
Tel/Fax: 01358 789513
www.caledonian-heritage-tours.co.uk/

Girlfriends
Mary Dansicker, Owner
311 Main Street
Reisterstown, MD 21136
Tel: 410-517-0200
Email: liteshop@covad.net

Rosemary Ellen Guiley
1290 Bay Dale Drive
Suite 311
Arnold, MD 21012
Email: REGuiley@aol.com

Jayne Howard Feldman
Angel Heights
PO Box 95
Upperco, MD 21155
Tel: 866-peace2u (732-2328)
Fax: 410-429-5425
Email: earthangel4peace@aol.com
Website: www.earthangel4peace.com

Green Hope Farm Flower Essences
POB 125
Meriden, NH 03770
Tel: 603-469-3662
Fax: 603-469-3790
Email: green.hope.farm@valley.net
Website: www.greenhopeessences.com

International Biogenic Society
Box 849
Nelson, B.C. Canada V1L6A5
Email:
seekersway.org/seekers_guide/international_biogenic_society_1_e.html

Joshua's Lighthouse Angels
Mary Dansicker, Owner
311 Main Street
Reisterstown, MD 21136
Tel: 410-517-0200
Email: liteshop@covad.net

Rachael Salley
1118 Cactus Cut Road
Middleburg, FL 32068
904-282-9612

Alan Seale
P. O. Box 709
Jeffersonville, NY 12748
Tel: 212-749-1817
www.mystic21.com

The Spiritual Center
712 New York Route 79
Windsor, NY 13865
Tel: 607-655-2264

Lucky Sweeny
Email: coachlucky@aol.com
805-884-1531
3905 State Street #7133
Santa Barbara, CA 93105

About the Author

Jayne Howard Feldman's lifetime involvement with the angels has given her the ability to provide readers with a rich set of angelic attuning techniques to help cope with many of life's most challenging experiences. She has shared her personal angelic encounters and sketched out for readers what she has learned about the angelic kingdom in her books, Commune with the Angels, Driving Under the Influence of Angels, and now her latest book, Angels By My Side.

Jayne had the privilege of being selected by Hugh Downs to write an essay, which was included in his collection of essays by "great Americans" in My America, in which she honors 9/11 firemen as angels on earth. Some of the contributors are George Bush, John Glenn, Barbara Walters, Donald Trump and 145 other great Americans.

Jayne is the founder of BE AN ANGEL DAY – celebrated annually on August 22nd. This is a global event promoting the message of being an angel and doing one small act of service for someone. Additionally she is the founder of INSPIRE YOUR HEART WITH THE ARTS DAY celebrated annually on January 31st; and TAKE YOUR TEDDY BEAR ON A PICNIC OR TO TEA DAY celebrated the first Saturday of August annually.

Jayne is an ordained interfaith minister, Reiki Master and, public speaker. Jayne maintains a private spiritual counseling and life enhancement practice and serves as a spiritual director for her clients. She is available for consultations by phone. She produces a monthly 90-minute inspirational tape for members of a subscription series known as the HA HA Group. "HA" stands for Human Angelus; people who strive to shine for God in their earthly service.

Every summer Jayne teams up with Sister Paula Matthew csj of The Spiritual Center in Windsor, New York in offering spiritual retreats at the center for approximately five weekends. She leads spiritual tours around the world. She has led "Inner Outings" to sacred sites in Bosnia, France, Turkey, Ireland, Scotland, The Netherlands and Germany. Jayne lives at Angel Heights in Upperco, Maryland with her husband, Charles and their three Jack Russell Terriers - Benny, Riot, and Jackie

Contact information: Rev. Jayne Howard Feldman/Angel Heights/PO Box 95/Upperco, MD 21155

Email: earthangel4peace@aol.com

Website: www.earthangel4peace.com

Additional books

These additional books written by Jayne Howard Feldman and products can be ordered from Jayne by using the order form at the bottom of this page.

$14.95

A fascinating book which shows how radiant beings, through their understanding of the Divine Plan, help guide both nature and the human kingdom. Here is detailed information on the amazing world of angels, which relates their unique messages to humanity and tells stories of their guidance and assistance. This book provides a chance for people everywhere to remove the boundaries from daily living and allow the energy, divine guidance, and love of the angels to lead to fulfillment in life.

$14.95

The inspirational stories included here show how a life guided by angels can be rewarding, full of synchronicity, and blessings. As Jayne travels, as she copes with and helps others cope with the deaths of loved ones, we see how God touches every aspect of our lives, using angels as His constant caregivers. No joy, no tragedy is unattended by these helpers in the Spirit.

$12.00

The Spirituals are a deck of 78 cards that by drawing a card daily will give you an Angelic message and blessing.

$12.00

This meditation tape features Meeting Your Guardian Angel on side one and Angelic Blessing Bath/Shower of love on side two. Each meditation is designed to soothe and inspire with music.

Order Form

Name: ______________________________________
Street: ______________________________________
City: ________________ State: _____ ZIP: __________

Products	Qty.	Price	Total
Commune with the Angels	____	$14.95	________
Driving Under the Influence of Angels	____	$14.95	________
Spiritual Card Deck	____	$12.00	________
Meditation Tape	____	$12.00	________
Shipping ($1.00 per. Item)	____		________
Md. residents please add 5% sales tax			________
Total:			________

Please Send To:
(Make checks payable to)

Jayne Howard Feldman, Angel Heights, P.O. Box 95, Upperco, MD 21155

Printed in the United States
21234LVS00003B/70-585